The Enchantment
of Writing

The Enchantment of Writing

Spiritual Healing and Delight Through the Written Word

JANICE GRAY KOLB

Blue Dolphin Publishing

Published by Blue Dolphin Publishing, Inc.
P.O. Box 8, Nevada City, CA 95959
Orders: 1-800-643-0765
Web: www.bluedolphinpublishing.com

ISBN: 1-57733-073-0

Library of Congress Cataloging-in-Publication Data

Kolb, Janice E. M.
    The enchantment of writing : spiritual healing and delight through the
    written word / Janice Gray Kolb.— 1st ed.
        p.   cm.
    ISBN 1-57733-073-0
        1. Kolb, Janice E. M.. 2. Spiritual journals—Authorship—Miscellanea.
    I. Title.

    BF1997.K65 A3 2000b
    808'.042—dc21

                                                                    00-040406

A portion of any profits realized by sales of this book will be used
to support various animal charities.

Cover design: Jeff Case

Printed in the United States of America

10   9   8   7   6   5   4   3   2   1

*Dedicated
to
my beloved
husband and soulmate*

Bob

and

*to my
beloved feline
soulmate*

Rochester

It is important
to honor our beginnings
to remember that we matter,
and that we have
a place in this world
that no one else has.

—Inspired by Native American Indians

'Tis the good reader that makes the good book;
in every book he finds passages which seem
to be confidences or asides
hidden from all else
and unmistakably meant for his ear;
the profit of books is according to
the sensibility of the reader;
the profoundest thought or passion
sleeps as in a mine,
until it is discovered by an
equal mind and heart.

—Emerson

Contents

Foreword

*A*S THE TWENTIETH CENTURY WAS ENDING, a great deal of effort was put into the question of who it was during the last hundred years that had the greatest influence on the course of human events. Those under consideration included hundreds of names like Franklin D. Roosevelt and Adolph Hitler. When the final choice was made, however, the choice was clear. Albert Einstein was far ahead of all others when the impact of his contributions to the human condition were considered. In 1915 he had published his thoughts on *"Relativity"* which were very radical, dealing with gravity and time and space. His life was essentially quiet—some lectures, some papers published, but no spectacular events, battles, of other things we generally associate with greatness. No, the reason he was able to influence the world in such a significant way was because he wrote it down. His thoughts, his theories, his wisdom—and his formula $E=mc^2$. He was often wrong in his evaluations of people and political events, but the things he wrote down were used by other people to make startling changes in the world. He influenced the development of the computer, nuclear power, space exploration, and thousands of other things, and will influence other events and inventions for the next thousand years. Why? Because he wrote things down. He was no giant charismatic personality. His genius would have gone largely undiscovered except for the fact that he took the time to record in writing his ideas and theories. Many of his thoughts and quotations are with us because others took the time to write down things they heard him say, like *"Imagination is more important than knowledge. Knowledge is limited. Imagination encircles the world."*

Where would Christianity, Judaism, or Buddhism be if ancient writers had not taken the time to write down events, thoughts, quotations, and the social impact these things had on their community and world. Would we have ever even heard of Jesus, Moses, or Buddha? The answer is, of course, "*no,*" unless God had somehow ordained that information be handed down to us through another source.

Every great invention since the world began has been the result of building upon the work of someone before. And how was that knowledge obtained? Through writing. The six basic machines include: the lever, pulley, wedge, screw, inclined plane, and wheel and axle. Once the use of these tools was discovered, future inventions were essentially applying the principles and combining these tools. And how were these basic principles brought into the next generation? By writing them down. Of course, many things were passed down through oral repetition, but knowledge transfer by language and tradition loses some element of its truth and eventually contains some inaccuracies and misinformation from the originating thought.

Our communication through language is the result of the very dynamic process of change. Our current English language is infinitely different than it was a few hundred years ago. It has evolved and modified. It has become infused with elements of other languages both modern and ancient. It exists in its present form because things were written down. It has become a tool of thinking—not just giving the objects of the world names.

In this book, the author has conveyed to you the meaningfulness of writing down your thoughts. She stresses the positive impact the simple act of writing down thoughts will have on the quality of your life—how it can convert your perception of life from one of mundane tolerance to excitement and positive contribution. Read these chapters carefully, and know that if you apply these thoughts to recording things in your own life, the effect could be magical. Thoughts are very fragile. They oft times flash across your brain—and then are lost forever. Write then down before this happens. The result will be a better *you*. A happier *you*. A more vital *you* who can contribute greatly to, not only the world, but to yourself.

—Robert A. Kolb, Jr.

Acknowledgments

All glory to
God
And to my Christ
and
I wish to thank my
Guardian Angel
and my special Angels
who are ever present.

I wish to express my extreme appreciation to Paul M. Clemens, Publisher for Blue Dolphin Publishing for believing in this book and to all his capable staff who helped in so many ways. I especially thank Chris Comins, Lisa Redfern, and Stephanie Rumsey for their fine work and their friendship.

I wish to thank Rochester for his constant love, presence, devotion, inspiration, and teachings throughout our life together. Because of him this book was written.

I am deeply grateful to my husband Bob for his love and support, for believing in me, and for our life together in New Hampshire. I am grateful too for the time he gave in endless hours typing this manuscript.

✏

May the words of this book—and the meditation of our hearts (the readers' and mine)—give glory to God—and love and gratitude to Blessed Mother Mary—who always intercedes.

✏

Introduction

"Writing is a spiritual act because it invites us to look beyond the surface of life, to attempt to capture the essence of love, grief, joy, fear, compassion, pride, forgiveness, nobility, wretchedness—in short, the whole gamut of human existence."
—HAL ZINA BENNETT
from "Write From the Heart"

WHAT I HAVE WRITTEN IN THIS BOOK are ordinary things about ordinary people including myself. They were written to mirror into your lives to show that your lives are important, that it is worthy to spend time capturing in writing circumstances that you lived through and experienced. To warn me to be careful when I left home my Mother often said to me in childhood and in adulthood, *"Just remember—there's only one you."* I say that now to you. Because that is a truth, it is up to each one of us to give our lives importance through remembering and writing. And the more we write the more we will remember. If we do not write about our lives it is doubtful anyone else will unless we are someone famous, and then perhaps another will write our biography. But since most of us are living in quiet ways, then it is up to each one of us to write about our own life. What a privilege it is to be alive, and though we may all go through trials and turmoils and in this may feel our lives are of little use, it is not true. *"There is only one you"*—and you are more precious than anything imaginable for you were created by God, and without you the world would not be the same. You matter! That is often hard to grasp

1

when we hit low points in our lives. I know for I have gone into despair just as you have and felt worthless. But I learned as a little child because of the circumstances in my life then, that writing is magic and enchanting and can lift the spirit so amazingly. As I grew older I realized writing can help bring healing, and I did not know that when I wrote and wrote as a young child that I was being helped and healed as well, far more than if I had never written or only written when I had to write in school. And I have continued to write all through my life because it is what I do, and how I help myself, and I could not live without writing. It is also how I express every emotion and capture all the joys and enchantments in my life to forever have to refer back to and relive. Someone has written; "*To write is to live twice*" and this is so. Actually it is to live many times!

This book is a group of eclectic writings to show the importance and the enchantment and delight in writing. The things included span my lifetime and follow an order, and because I pray before I write, I was led to include the things that I did. Often I was amazed myself at what I did include that I never intended to include and had not even thought of in years. Once you put a pen to paper it is often as if things write themselves and another force takes over if you are willing to put that pen on the paper. The book I planned to write has turned into something far different, including memories that I simply did not think I even had in my memory bank. And now I am sharing them with you! If we are willing this can happen again and again! But we must sit down and make time for it to happen with pen and paper. In the past I have written an entire book by sitting quietly with pen and paper and allowing it to be written *through* me. You will learn about that in these pages. A pen is like a magic carpet if we are open to be taken to enchanting places by placing it on paper.

Think of the sharings and chapters in this book as a path of lovely smooth rocks and stones leading you to a safe place of healing and delight. In childlike fashion, as many of the chapters in this book are written because it is as if my "*inner child*" wrote them, I have gone along this path as a small innocent one would. Some of the rocks I *walked* over slowly in order to write rather deeply. Some I have *hopped* on with one foot and those sharings are lightly covered. Many of the rocks on this path were *jumped* on and landed on squarely with both feet, and I truly went into the center and core of these subjects discussed. And then there are some topics and memories I have *skipped* over more buoyantly. But all have brought me to this place in my life now. The earthen places between the rocks are the places I did not write about, for already the book became longer than I planned because things appeared for me to share that I never intended. That is what happens when we write! Memories and happenings surface and are freed to live again to be reviewed anew and enjoyed or to bring healing, even if at first they come in the form of sadness or pain.

Perhaps you will look at a pen and paper in a new way after reading this book. Everyone can write. It is not for a chosen few. We were all meant to write our stories and expand our lives through our written words. It is the same as breathing! Never think only *some people* are meant to write for if you are not writing daily in some way, you are not allowing yourself to live fully. You are not breathing fully! You are denying parts of yourself to exist! Since I do not always breathe freely I *know* I must keep writing! Some areas of your life can only be reached through writing, and it is up to you to find them or let them find you by spending time each day putting pen to paper. And they *will* find you! So many found me in the writing of this book.

Begin by purchasing a journal or inexpensive note book that is pleasing to you to look at, for this is important. Or buy a plain spiral composition book and decorate the cover. All that matters is that it is attractive to you so that it will draw you to write in it. Journals are discussed in a later chapter. It is significant to have one that is pleasing to you or you will not use it. So take time in selecting one. Make it a special event and treat it as a sacred object. Then keep a pen with it that is to your liking and that works and will always be ready on demand. If you are just discovering writing or rediscovering it, it is best to have one notebook journal at first. It is like going home, a place to return to again and again and a place to contain all that will come forth from you and out of your pen and onto your paper. As you continue to write you may want more than one notebook for different reasons and interests in your life. You will be shown by the Angels what to do. But keep it simple in the beginning.

Perhaps to get your pen moving before reaching into Chapter 1, you may want to write down what you believe in. You may have never examined your beliefs in writing. I believe in God, in Jesus, that there are Angels with me always. I believe in love, and in the love shared with my husband and all my children, (and with my sons-in-law and daughter-in-law for they too are like my own) and the love shared with special friends. I believe that God can speak to us in any way He so chooses and I anticipate it, and too, the expectation of angels daily making themselves known. I believe in the precious love of my little cat Rochester and that we communicate this love and all else to each other. When you believe— it happens! I believe in the sanctity of life for all God's creatures as well as for humans. I believe in all of nature as other ways God speaks to us and is present to us for I have experienced Him in these ways. These are only some of the things I believe in. Oh yes, I believe in the sacred, in fun and laughter, in magic, and the more I write and pray I realize how precious life is and I experience it more fully here in nature by our lake in the woods.

After each chapter there is a short section entitled "*Reflect and Journal.*" You may not want to get involved in these sections at first especially if you have not written in some time. You may prefer to read the entire book first if that is more comfortable for you, and then return to reread more slowly and to enter into doing some of the things suggested in these sections that follow the chapters. Perhaps just reading these sections at first is enough but then return to use them so that you will begin to know the healing and delight of writing. However, do not let me deter you if you wish to begin writing immediately. It *is* best to write as you go along, for you are then in the "*Sacrament of the Moment*" of what you have just read and your responses will come out of that reading—out of that "*moment.*" This is important. That would be wonderful then to begin writing immediately and is what I had hoped would happen. You may still return to reread later and write more deeply.

When I was led to write this book on writing I was shown to use my own life and experiences as ways for you to look at your own. Perhaps in reading about the things in my life they will help you to recall things from your own past and even into your present life. If in sharing both the good and the bad with you it has caused you to reflect on your own life and to pick up pen and paper and begin to write, then this book will be like an Angel and will be accomplishing its mission.

I would just add one important thing. My little marmalade and white cat Rochester has been completely with me in the pages of three out of four of my last books. He is also with me in this book by his daily presence to me as I write, his love and constancy, his help and inspiration, and the joy he instills in me. But even though he may not be continually written about here as in the past—*he is in this book!* This book and any other I have written only came into being because his "*Angel being*" came into my life. Before God sent him to me I was sad and overcome by problems in my life that were very real. He is with me every day as I write and very especially this book. You will sense his presence even if his name is not mentioned in every chapter. Imagine him with me as I write. His paw prints are on each page and his love and presence are inspiring me and his thoughts and words, for we communicate deeply. It is not necessary that he is written about in every chapter of this particular book. He was there when they were written, every word, and his essence and spiritual presence are there. A lot of what I have written about took place before God sent Rochester to me but I cannot ever imagine life without him. He is all love, a precious soul, and I pay tribute to him now as always and to all the spiritual joy, love, companionship and writing he continually gives to me. He is my Angel.

This book was not written to be a memoir. It was written to be a book about writing. I have simply used my own life as an example of how writing should enter into every phase of our existence from early childhood on, and tried to show how deeply writing mattered in mine. Because I had a few unusual things happen along the way, as we all do, writing became my strength in these difficult and often bizarre situations. Because I always trusted God, He is my first strength and the One I believe led a very small girl to begin to write.

If your spiritual beliefs are not the Christian faith this will not affect what you read in these pages. The book is about healing, delight, and enchantment of writing, not religion, but for me spirituality permeates my life and sustains. Simply substitute your own belief system or way of life whenever I may have referred to mine.

May this book lead you along the path of *spiritual healing and delight through the written word*. May you truly discover *the enchantment of writing*. May God and His Angels bless you.

—Janice Gray Kolb

ORIGIN

I come from the stars.
I have sparkled and shone upon all.
I have sat in the curve of the moon
    and swung my legs.
I have bounced and played in the clouds—
And flown with the wind.
I fell to earth
And bloomed in the garden of life—
A fallen star
Given re-birth

July 15, 1997

CHAPTER ONE

The Turning Point

"Behold, I have graven thee upon the palms of my hands . . ."
—Isaiah 49:16, KJV

ON MARCH 20, 1986 I was waiting at a red light at the intersection of State Road and Lansdowne Avenue on my weekly drive to visit a very elderly woman in St. Francis Country House, a Home for the aged and infirmed in Darby, Pennsylvania. Sitting in my pale green Volare, my treasured old car that had belonged to my Dad before his death, I alertly anticipated the left turn I was about to make onto Lansdowne Avenue. As I waited there I was flanked by cars on both sides of me; on the right a car waiting to go ahead, and on the left, a car having just made a right turn off of Lansdowne Avenue onto State Road. It was coming along my left side followed by a stream of other cars making the same turn. My Volare and I were packed in. Suddenly, out of nowhere appeared a police car straight ahead of me across Lansdowne Avenue and headed down State Road with lights flashing and sirens screaming. It was incredible that this car should instantly be on the scene!

There was no room on either side of my vehicle yet the police car steamed ahead across Lansdowne Avenue speeding directly toward me. There was nothing I could do, nowhere I could go. In that moment I realized it was going to hit me head on! I closed my eyes and waited for the impact thinking I would die. I had no fear. None.

But it did not hit me! Only God could have intervened and protected me. Only He could have allowed the police car to pass me in some

7

supernatural way on my left where there was absolutely no passage! All I know is that when I opened my eyes I was still alive! The police car had been transported behind me and was driving off into the distance with the other cars, sirens still screaming. I turned my head to find another human being. The man in the car on my right just stared at me in awe. I felt his compassion and saw the alarm still in his eyes. He too had thought what I had thought for myself, that it was the end. I thanked God—and too all loved ones in Heaven who love me, for preventing this accident and saving me. Only God could have transported that speeding police car that had no place to go except into the front of my own car, to somewhere behind me, and with freedom to speed onward hurting no others. I could not comprehend it all as I continued driving to St. Francis House nor did I seem rattled or shaken. This is what amazed me, my calmness of spirit.

God had given me such complete peace before the incident as I waited to be crushed head on—and afterwards as I sat there whole. There had not been one moment of fear or panic.

I have thought about it over and over since then in amazement. It would seem He truly holds you in His Hand at moments such as these. Had this been my time to die I would have met death in peace and completely unafraid. I did not fear death before this happened but now have been shown that indeed—one *should not* fear. A new peace flowed through me following that incident because I sensed that insight had been given that I was spiritually ready to die. Though my interpretation may not have been correct, it comforted me greatly following this harrowing experience.

Reflect and Journal

✏ Think back on any life changing experience or turning point you may have had.

✏ Reflect upon the ways that it has since affected your life.

✏ Record that event in your journal and in free-flow writing release all that is within you concerning this and see where it takes you.

CHAPTER TWO

Feline Angel

"I was alone in my head without adult supervision."

—Renee Kizer

O N JUNE OF 1986 I sat in an old rocking chair and begged God to let me die. How ironic and ungrateful this might appear after God had intervened and miraculously rescued me from being crushed to death three months previous to this. But there were events in my life that were ongoing for years, and at times they flooded over me like giant ocean breakers only to subside to let me catch my breath in an attempt at normalcy. At this particular period I was floundering under the waves and had finally reached this point of despondency. I was crushed and did not have the emotional stamina to try to surface again. And so I sat in my old rocking chair and begged God to take me. This despair and utter helplessness had been filling me for weeks, and though I was strong in faith, somehow I could not surmount these waves of hopelessness.

A family situation had existed for years that could not be resolved no matter how it was approached, and it had indeed been deeply addressed by me in so many spiritual and prayerful forms. You will read later how I dramatically changed my Christian life and walk several years previous to these moments in this rocking chair, in order to help myself with this family situation. Again however, it was overwhelmingly enveloping me in new ways. I gave up, I did not want to live even through I was only mid-life. And too it was my father's birthday and I missed him and needed him. In the utter stillness these crucial moments eventually passed and

9

through tears I again forced myself to face life, the most painful of all things. God had been there and again intervened to bring me back.

Two weeks later on entering a small mall in Rochester, New Hampshire, as we headed north from our home in Pennsylvania to our lakeside cottage twenty-five miles from this mall, my youngest daughter Janna and my husband Bob and I saw a man and two children sitting on a round bench with a carton. A sign stated *"free kittens."* Our family, consisting of my husband and six children, had had many wonderful animals we loved, but never had we had a cat.

My husband refused to let a cat come into our home because he had personally never had a relationship with one. It was such a sadness to me along with these severe family problems, for I had had cats my entire childhood and teenage years until I married.

On this summer morning, without ever having seen the kittens in the carton, I knew in my spirit one had to be mine. With this *"knowing"* within and with undaunting persistence that seemed supernaturally charged, I relentlessly requested permission from my husband for one of these little ones, refusing to accept his repeated dissent and unwillingness to at last give a little cat a chance and to allow this joy in my life. With what could only be Divine Intervention he suddenly uttered the *"yes"* I had longed for for so many years. My heart danced for the first time in ages! By this time only one kitten remained in the box and that little kitten, I know, was set down on earth for me. God's gift of love that morning took the form of a tiny marmalade and white kitten approximately eight weeks old. I accepted that indescribable gift of love and in so doing have felt the Lord's love to me more powerfully every day. I believe with a certainty beyond comprehension that this beautiful creature is an Angel in the form of an animal.

It is written: *"Angels appear to make us want to live when we want to die"* (Unknown).

My Angel came to intervene in my life and I shall share further along more about our abiding love and what he has helped me to accomplish. Three months later in September of that same year I was able to go from Pennsylvania again to our cottage in New Hampshire to make a retreat. This was our summer place and I had never gone alone to the woods. Being a city girl this was a big step—even though I had stayed there year after year with my family. Rochester's companionship gave me courage to experience an unforgettable week of solitude with him; praying, learning, reading and writing and discovering the path of healing. Without him I would not have been in the woods.

It is written: *"Our perfect companions never have fewer than four feet"* (Colette).

But that is enough of our love story to share for the moment. We will come back to it. Many books have been written since my Angel was sent to me. Rochester was my inspiration to begin what I had always dreamed of doing—to write books. He also led me to meet head on the issues of Animal Rights and to speak out.

And since he has inspired me now to write this book about the path of writing through my life, I shall begin. And oh yes, Rochester (or Chester as he is known by also) won over Bob's heart within days and they have been incredible friends ever since. We three share a precious life together in a cottage in the woods on a lake.

Checking out the fizz in a soda

ADOPTION OF A LIFE CHANGE

So fresh from Heaven—God sent him down—
And right into the center of town—
Within a carton where he hid.
The man to others made a bid—
to give them kittens
"Free," said he.
In Spirit I knew
one was for me.

Nothing, nothing can equate
To this dear little feline mate.
He moved into my home and heart
Never are we two apart.
Little Muse
who keeps me writing,
All my days
gently high-lighting—

With pure love—faithful devotion,
Causing oceans of emotion.
Between us, ah—such understanding—
While my vision he's expanding—
of natural world
and all God's creatures.
Silently—one of His
finest teachers.

In appreciation and deep thanksgiving.
I cherish this furry exquisite being.

Dedicated to Rochester
in celebration of
the 6th anniversary of his
adoption in Rochester, New Hampshire
June 23, 1986

JGK
June 23, 1992
New Hampshire

This poem further attempts to express our joy in spending life together.

THE SILENT LANGUAGE OF LOVE

With marmalade tail wreathed 'round white paws
    (his claws—I have not known on me)
He lives by higher Holy laws—
    behavior tempered by inner decree—
To give companionship most fine;
    and I am blest that his is mine.

For when he curls upon my lap—
    in tenderness—to take his nap,
His sighs and purrs to me transfuse
    rich quality—from my dear Muse.

Only love does he dispense—
    we two communicate through gaze—
Eyes speaking tongue of loftier sense
    while sharing splendid silent days.

Dedicated to   JGK
Rochester   September 29, 1992
                              New Hampshire

*Checking out
the clean wash*

Reflect and Journal

⁐ Has an animal ever rescued you either spiritually or physically?

⁐ If you have never written about this incident and the wonderful animal, perhaps it is time to write about it in your journal so that it will be recorded for all time as is Rochester's and my life story.

Legacies
of Childhood

"It requires a tremendous leap of faith to imagine that your own childhood—punctuated with pain, loss, and hurt—may, in fact, be a gift. Certainly the unhappiness you felt was not, in itself, a blessing; but in response to that pain, you learned to cultivate a powerful intuition, a heightened sensitivity, and a passionate devotion to healing and love that burns deep within you. These are gifts that may be recognized, honored and cultivated."

—from *Legacy of the Heart: The Spiritual Advantages of a Painful Childhood* by Wayne Muller

CHAPTER THREE

Legacy of Neighborhood

"Enchantment is a spell that comes over us, an aura of fantasy and emotion that can settle on the heart and either disturb it or send it into rapture and reverie."
—Thomas Moore, *The Re-Enchantment of Everyday Life*

WRITING AND READING have always been essential in my existence. I cannot imagine life without them. Add too, the indispensable requisite of solitude. I did not desire solitude from the beginning for I was too young then to know its true worth but it came upon me uninvited. Once it arrived and the passing of time revealed that it was here to stay it became an unusual sort of companion. When it moved in with me as a small child I rather welcomed it because it seemed like some sort of entity or secret friend, and I was in need of such desperately. I was timid, shy and alone a great deal when in my home for I had no brothers or sisters. But in my solitude I began to dream and create, write and read, and I did not feel as lonely. Strangely, it was often comforting. My solitude was shared however, with one quiet little friend, my black angora cat, Mitzi. There had been two other dear cats before her but Mitzi entered my life at a very young age and she is the one who remained with me until I married. She belonged to my parents and to me but I treasured her company as if she was a little sister.

17

For reasons that you shall learn about in other chapters we spent a great deal of time in my childhood room. I did not realize it until I was much older, but this actually was my sacred space. Everyone needs their own sacred space and mine was lovely to me. It was just that I was in it too much and often for wrong reasons. But as I grew I learned creativity in the soli-

My cat, Mitzi (a black Persian)

tude of my room and I could console myself if I was upset through writing and reading, and the sweetness of Mitzi's presence. Let me take you back in time and share my room and world with you as it was then.

I have a bed and bureau and too, a vanity with a stool. A fine bookcase made by a neighbor named Jim as a gift to me is a special piece I appreciate. In times of aloneness, tearful or happy, I place my small vanity bench in front of one of the two windows in my room that are on either side of my bookcase. My view is of our back alley, a most unusual place. The alley is T-shaped, and our home is on a short block of nine two story brick row homes. We are the third home from the corner, and each home has a small back fenced in yard. Our yard has lovely grass my Dad cares for, and beautiful flowers that line the side fences that my Mother has planted and tends. Extending from the middle home of our block of nine, another alley exists creating the T. Two lines of many row homes are on this longer alley, their back ends facing each other. Because we are the third home from the corner and not the fifth, I can not see all the way down the longer alley the way those who live in the centered fifth home can. My view is only a third or less of that longer alley. These homes are much smaller than ours and have no yards with green grass. All is cement down that alley. Our small yard and the large alley are my places of play. From my window I view my small world. Through this alley the hucksters come with their vegetables and fruit, and the horse radish man who grinds it fresh as is needed while yelling "*horse radish*" all the while, the rag man, and others too enter this alley. And too, comes a very poor black man without any legs pushing himself by rotating the wheels of his low cart with his hands. He sings gospel songs and begs, and creates such emotions in me at this early age they cannot be written. I cry for him when alone, but fear him if he suddenly appears, for I have never known an amputee, yet this poor man is totally uninhibited. He seems not to mind the gawking of children and sings loudly and calls out to us. I always run home. My Mother puts coins in his cup attached to his cart.

In extreme contrast to this man whom I will think of often through the years and will pray for in these times of remembrance of him, is the small Merry-go-round that circles on the back of a truck. The driver parks it on Laveer Street near the entrance to our alley and it attracts all the neighborhood children. Though it is so very small, a ride on this amusement is a big treat on a summer's afternoon.

My friends and I play many outdoor games in the back alley and also have a strange place to meet for sharing and story telling. We sit upon a large gray wooden air raid box on Laveer Street, a box that houses equipment to be used at the time of an air raid drill, or horror of horrors, a real air raid. But I have written of the moments spent on this strange container in a later chapter and will leave this for now.

All of these things and more were part of my childhood and city neighborhood and helped to form me in many ways, some still surfacing only now in present years. In my previous book, *Journal of Love: Spiritual Communication with Animals Through Journal Writing,* I have written of the love I felt for the horse who drew the Harbison Milk Wagon on our street and the sadness always for his abuse by the milk man. These memories will always remain within me. It all seems like yesterday, where my life began and where I lived until I turned twenty-one years old and left.

This neighborhood and many of the things that happened were some of the first causes for me to begin to write for myself, aside from writing I had to do for school. I thought my world there was an amazing place with unusual people and incidents. Some memories are rich and lovely, but others strange and frightening. Writing about them as the truth I observed helped me, for there were many things I did not understand out there in that T-shaped alley, or on Third Street, or within my own home. Who can explain why I turned to writing as the means to help me understand? Only God. It was as if a magic spell had been cast over me that I took such delight in writing. I had been given the gift of "*the enchantment of writing!"* I also believe it helped me to survive emotionally for I had such an overwhelming desire to do it. I loved everything related to writing at a very young age. I believe too, knowing what I know now, that ,my special Guardian Angel and other Angels were there guarding and inspiring me along this path, for they knew it was a path of healing. I only knew that I loved to write and that it helped me. Even if I wrote about upsetting incidents in my young life and cried while doing it, or afterwards as I read what I wrote, there was still that special *"something"* that drew me to writing continuously. I realize now it was the *"enchant-ment—that spell that comes over us,"* and it was God-given to inspire and help a little shy girl through an unusual childhood, and was a permanent gift to be carried and used as she entered and travelled through an often unusual adulthood as well.

My home, 6231 N. Third St., Philadelphia, Pennsylvania

PETUNIAS

As a child I watched them grow—
Along the fence all in a row
In our small yard there in the city—
Sweet petunias—soft and pretty.

Years later—in woods and by a lake—
I planted them for beauty's sake
Near the water—and grassy knoll—
To pleasure eyes—to feed the soul.
They grew in earth surrounded by rocks,
With marigolds, snapdragons, phlox—
Lavender and white—blooms velvet and luminous
Were the enchantment for the numinous—
Within each one—within myself—
They were pure joy—a spiritual wealth.

I cried as frost just took each bloom—
But interiorly there shall be room
For them to grow—all winter long—
In sun and breeze with bright bird song—
For pastel petunias shall gently sway
In my heart's gardens every day.

Dedicated to   JGK
all lovely petunias
of my life

Reflect and Journal

➭ Reflect upon your first childhood neighborhood, seeing it in as much detail as possible.

➭ Record some memories of it now and as more come to you.

➭ Perhaps draw a simple diagram of your house or neighborhood—or both.

➭ Return to it in prayer and spirit as often as you wish.

CHAPTER FOUR

Legacy of Mystery

"Small children do not verbalize, they internalize."
—Yvonne Kaye

W HEN I WAS A LITTLE GIRL a picture was taken of me that has become a gift in my present life. It is a charming print about 3.5 by 5 inches that gives a first impression of having been taken in a photographer's studio. After further examination I considered also the possibility that it was taken in a booth. In the area in which I grew up, and into adulthood, these booths were usually in 5-and-10s such as Woolworths and Kresges, or other small department stores. For a very inexpensive amount of money one could step into these small enclosures concealed only be a curtain and have one's picture taken privately while people milled about outside. Often several went in at a time, and I own pictures produced in such booths of my husband, and our first two daughters as little children and myself, piled in together having fun. Long before that as a teenager I had gone into such booths with friends. Usually a strip of four connected pictures in different poses was the result—not a single larger picture as is this one of which I write. Yet for some faint reason I still consider the option that I could have been in a booth, for I remember another time my Mother taking me to one. Perhaps there are facts about the sizes of the photos that could result that I no longer remember or if there were backdrops with scenes. I under-stand booths like this still exist here and there today. I just have not seen any in years when once they were everywhere. Since there is no explanation written on the back I do not know anything about this picture. There is no date, no age, not even my name, which is always the case with all older photos I find. And certainly there is not a clue as to who took me to wherever this picture was taken. Such a shame.

I keep this picture with a gold oval matting around it in a little gold frame ever since I discovered it amongst some old papers about ten years ago. It is a precious photo to me and I think of this little girl as my *"inner child."* I often talk to her and comfort her and tell her lovely things. I tell her how wonderful she is and how pretty she is and how loved and cherished she is and that her life truly matters. But the mystery of it all is disturbing in a sense. I would like to know so much more about that little girl and too, about the specific day she had her picture taken and why.

I estimate this little girl to be about three years old. She has dark curly short hair parted in the middle and some of her hair falls in ringlets and dark cork screw curls about her forehead. A faint smile is at the corners of her lips and yet her eyes are sad and pensive.

She is wearing a dark coat with a large plaid collar. The collar is open and laid back to reveal a white sweater or blouse underneath the coat. All of this seems to be nothing unusual, but the rest most certainly is. To me—there is symbolism in this picture.

In her left arm she is holding a pink and white stuffed bunny and her little hand is cuddling the feet of the bunny in her palm. The bunny is about a foot high including its long ears. In the background are two beautiful windows—and not ordinary windows. This is what touches my heart. These windows are rounded at the top and the glass is divided into many sections but have no distinct patterns. A picture seems to be in the top curved glass portion of one of these windows but is not distinguishable. The windows have large sills beneath them but one window is longer than the other. Both seem to be the windows of a church yet there is no stained glass of various hues in them. Just the delicate divisions in the glass that seem almost spidery make them appear as church windows and create a Holy atmosphere. It is quite possible this picture could have been taken inside a church and not in a studio or booth—for my parents took me to church each Sunday.

Because this picture is ever so faintly tinted there is a pink hue emanating from portions of the divided glass. The windows sit back into the wall, framed by a thickness of the wall that could possibly be as wide as the generous sills. The child's body covers much and all of this detail concerning the windows can not be accurately told. The little girl is between the two windows but forward from them. Her little mouth has been tinted rosey and her right cheek has a pink blush of color. It seems that pink is the only color used on this otherwise sepia photograph, for the child's eyes are blue in reality but in this photo are light brown.

As to the left cheek and half of her eye, they are blotted out. A large portion of the photograph has fallen off and was in this condition when I found it. The corners of the picture also have missing pieces and only the underlying white paper is there. And so on this little girl's cheek is a large white area—fairly rounded but with a large point that extends up above the eye. This white blotch extends over into the area of her ear that is covered with curls. In other words, a portion of the little girl's face is missing! And that is the complete description of this photograph. I have searched it over many times to find any more mysteries within it. This pretty little girl just looks out at me and seems to want and need my love. She shyly stares out and penetrates my soul every time I even glance at her. But when I sit and deliberately stare back into her sad and lovely eyes, I am often in tears. How significant it is to me that my little child seems to be centered between two windows of a church for this empha-sizes the spiritual, and my spiritual interests and longings have always been at the center of my life. For as long as I can remember I have carried Jesus in my heart and look to Him for guidance and direction. How very meaningful I hold a stuffed bunny in my arm reminding me anew that at that very young age my love of animals, both stuffed and real, existed. That a bunny is in the picture with me shows this love I had for creatures. I know in my spirit it was no casual thing. I am certain it was most difficult for me to decide upon just one of my beloved animals to take with me that day. This love and compassion for animals only deepened within and is a constant part of my present life. The essence of this little girl is revealed in this old photograph and makes her legacies to me of spirituality and animal love more clearly given. I live them out daily. And the missing portion of her little face speaks to me as a personal message, for I am ever praying and yearning to learn about the missing portions of my childhood I cannot recall. It inspires me to never give up searching.

Therefore, at times when I feel drawn to do so, I dialogue with my little girl of the past prayerfully and write these dialogues down in my journals. Through writing, images and fragments of thoughts and memories have emerged and given me vague insights into this little girl's being. Using stream of consciousness writing is especially helpful in revealing submerged and stuck past memories. Once written down they can be prayed over and further disclosures may manifest both in the heart and mind and through further writing.

Yes, writing and its enchantment can cast a magic spell over the past and draw forth pictures, imagery, dreams and truths that we might never have had surface without putting our pen to paper. And unless we write them down they will escape somehow, no matter how sharp and brilliant we may think we are.

> *"I live, rejoice, grieve, and I am always struggling to become grown up, yet every day because something I do affects her, I hear that young girl within me. She who many years ago was I. Or who I thought I was."*
> —Liv Ullman from "Changing"

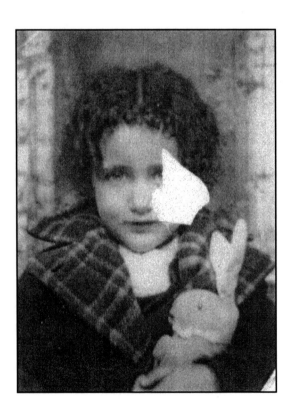

A VISIT WITH ME

I wish that I could go to be
With that little girl in me—
Returning then to her birthplace
I would greet her with embrace.
How good to see that little child—
Always shy and very mild.

Today I find her melancholy—
Arm wrapped 'round her little dolly.
But she brightens as we talk—
With doll in coach we take a walk.
Dark curly hair and olive skin—
Ah yes—this little one's my kin.

Now Daddy says we'll go to shore—
We can hear the ocean roar!
He gives us now such sweet attention
Holds our hands—no apprehension.
Jumping waves we feel the spray—
Oh—we are at the beach today!

Now we three build castles there—
In the sun and salty air.
Tiny bathing shoes on feet—
Protect her from the burning heat.
Striped umbrella keeps the glare—
From Mother in her folding chair.

Turning back my calendar—
I have been again with her—
Doing things she loved to do—
When she was small—before she grew.
I long to wrap her in a shield
Before life's blows against her wield.

But she'll be brave as she can be—
And trust in God—because she's me.

Dedicated to   JGK
little
Janice Elizabeth Gray

Reflect and Journal

✏ Find a picture of yourself in early childhood.

✏ Place it where you will see it daily; desk, bedside table, etc. One writer wrote how she clipped her treasured photo to her car visor and daily dialogued with her child. She then recorded what she felt and learned in her journal.

✏ Dialogue with the child in your picture.

✏ Reflect upon the things you hear your child telling you in quiet times and in prayer.

✏ Write all you receive into your journal.

CHAPTER FIVE

Legacy of Drawing

"Learn to meditate on paper. Drawing and writing are forms of meditation."
—Thomas Merton from "New Seeds of Contemplation"

WHEN I WAS A LITTLE GIRL I loved to draw. It was a pastime that kept me pleasantly amused for hours and entertained me in my times of solitude. I drew all sorts of things, animals, people, trees, and anything I saw in reality or that came to mind. Drawing was a means of self expression for me before I began to write and continues until this present day. To have pencils, crayons or colored pencils in hand was a joy. Because I was a child that lived in the city my scenes of nature were not as many as the scenes I drew of my neighborhood and things in it, and of my sweet cat Mitzi. But it was not just the mere drawing of anything that struck my mind and fancy—but that I developed this interest further. I often became a pretend "*art dealer*" for my pieces of work!

I have tried to recall again and again my pictures hanging up somewhere in our home where my Mother put them so we could appreciate them, but I cannot ever remember a display. Nor do I remember them ever being hung on the front of the refrigerator, a place now that is very popular for children's art work. I believe I would have retained the memory of my own drawings on display somewhere in our home if it had occurred, other than the ones I would stand around my own room on occasion on my bureau or bookcase. Yet memories often fade so I cannot claim their absence to be fact. It is lovely to remember, however, that my Mother always hung my own children's art work on her refrigerator and cherished these drawings by her grandchildren. And so—I devised a plan to show my own art. I became my own art dealer. I had a large sized heavy rust colored cardboard envelope, the type one can purchase in a stationery store. It had a flap that had a string on the end and I could tie the string around a heavy duty cardboard circle that was on the main portion of this envelope to secure its' closure. My Dad had given this envelope to me seeing my need for it, I believe—and oh the joy I had in using it!

I kept my collection of drawings in it and carried it around with me frequently feeling very important. Often I would just tote it around inside our home, other times I would take it out front and sit on our cement steps with it. On other occasions I would carry it along with me in the car if I went for a drive with my Dad or with both my parents. In the rust envelope I always had a fresh supply of blank paper too, and pencils. My pencils were normal lead pencils but also some were different colors. I always left my crayons in my bedroom to use there. There was not enough space for them in my heavy envelope with the string tie.

Inside the envelope I made dividers with pieces of cardboard and that way I could categorize my drawings. Hours of enjoyment came forth from this simple gift from my father, along with the contributions I had put into it. No matter where I might be with it—inside, out front, in the car—eventually my *"pretend art dealer self"* would emerge and I would quietly begin talking to my imaginary customers. Each was questioned as to what sort of picture they were interested in seeing, and then when they would answer I would draw out one of my prize pieces from that category. At times my customers were instantly pleased and wanted the first one they saw, and other times they asked to see more. Many of my customers appreciated my art so much they actually expanded their horizons to request to see my work in other categories. I would point out detail in each work and the reason for the existence of such a line and why each drawing came to be, and why such a color was chosen for a particular area. I was the finest art dealer in that end of Philadelphia and it was why I had so many clients. I paid attention to their choices and special inclinations and always had a new supply of art ready in these categories when they returned. They appreciated my work and the explanation of the background and energy and love that went into each drawing. Often I was asked to do a water color on special consignment which I always accepted, but water color was not my expertise nor my great interest. Such superior conversations I had with my customers because we shared the common interest of fine art.

And so a little girl passed many hours in the land of imagination and I remember those wonderful hours to this day. That period was not wasted for I was so interested in art my parents allowed me at a very young age to briefly go to a local art class in a store in our business district. I painted two small oil paintings during those sessions. One was a little girl trying on a very large hat that obviously belonged to her Mother. The other was a pretty little rural scene with two tiny white homes with red roofs, a small pond, a tree and a little dirt road. All the rest was grass and sky. This one hangs in a little maple frame here in my writing room and on the cardboard on the back in my Mother's handwriting is "*Painted by Janice—7 years old* ". It used to hang years ago and for many years over the radiator in the kitchen of our row home in Philadelphia. I cannot say if it was ever removed by my parents but I think not. I always recall it there. Since they seemed to treasure it, I too have always treasured it after their deaths. The painting of the child and the hat has not been seen in many years, forever lost.

This is a pencil sketch I made of my Dad when I was 14 and he was 43. I used to sketch and draw all the time, but unfortunately this is one of the few that have survived.

Later when I was in high school and became an art major in my last two years there, my Uncle Elmer, a dear generous man and a brother of my Mother's, sent me to a well known art institute in downtown Philadelphia. I went every Saturday morning for two years, travelling the buses and subway and walking the underground route. I do not think I would want to do that today in Philadelphia, but perhaps those underground areas of that former era are not even still in existence and all would be safe now. I was only a teenager then, sixteen and seventeen years old. During those years I did fine art work, for my teachers told me so. But there were two little characters I loved to draw just for fun ever since I was a little artist—and for some reason they amused my Dad also. One was a strange little man I created with long legs and knobby knees and big shoes, a man with head thrown back and a long nose in the air and mouth open wide with musical notes drawn in a cloud near his head indicating as is done with comic strip characters that the notes were coming from the large circle mouth on his face. I also enjoyed drawing Shmoos, the adorable, fat, white creatures that were popular in the "Lil Abner" syndicated comic strip by Al Capp in those years. I drew Shmoos everywhere, especially decorating letters and envelopes. Even as a grownup I still decorate my envelopes to this day—but now with Angels, animals, and little messages about animal rights, and brief spiritual messages from rubber stamps also. These latter were given to me by a beloved friend who entered Heaven in 1990. The little child in me is still alive and well, decorating envelopes just as I did when I was a small girl and a teenager.

My Mother felt a career in art was not suitable for a young girl at the time I graduated high school and so my great wish was denied and my life took another path. Looking back I can understand her thinking now in recent years, but I did not for a very long span. But the little artist and art dealer lives on—and the legacy she created for me is one of my profound pleasures. I have learned to see the simplest wildflower or weed or leaf as exquisitely beautiful and as a potential drawing. Often one becomes an actual sketch in my sketch book or on a page in my journal. Sketching and drawing have remained a part of my life to give simple enjoyment, all because of my solitary and artful imaginations of childhood. To me it has always been part of writing. I began by drawing when I could not yet write, and then just incorporated it into life. The art became less essential and the writing became overwhelmingly necessary. But they have the same root in my life, one just flowered into a larger and more fragrant bloom. I could not live without writing, therein lies the significant difference.

ANOTHER PRAYER FORM

I had not sketched for some time—now
More recently—somehow—
I have been drawn to pencil and pen
And blank paged journal once again—
To record what I am seeing—
To increase my sense of being.

My precious companion—faithful friend—
Now stretches leisurely end to end
Across the pages of my sketch book—
While most admittedly—I look
Upon that dear cat I adore
To simply capture—and underscore
More of his sweetness that I know—
To reveal the truest cameo.

Wildflowers also have their chance
As I stand and sketch and glance

Toward these lovelies—exquisite and meek—
To draw gentle beauty at its peak.
And rippling lake and rocks and grasses—
And the pine cone that surpasses—
In causing interest—all most unique—
Present as gifts their own mystique.

Yes, all that surrounds me is confirmation—
That to write and draw—is meditation.

Dedicated to   J.G.K.
Writing and Drawing
and to pens, pencils and paper

An added little legacy was given to me recently when seventeen
years after his death I found a little notebook that once belonged to my
Dad. Having seen the little notebook in my Dad's possession frequently
when he was living, I was overwhelmed to find it. I lovingly removed the
fat rubber band that encircled the small book and found many loose
papers folded and tucked within the pages covered in my father's neat
handwriting. But two small papers brought tears to my eyes. One I shall
keep to speak about elsewhere in this book, but the other I shall tell of
now. There before me on a neatly folded scrap was a drawing of the tall,
thin, knobby kneed man, head thrown
back with musical notes coming from
his big wide circle mouth! I had never
known that my Dad had a little "*art
dealer*" within him also! I
guess that is why he gave
his little girl that fine rust
cardboard envelope.

Reflect and Journal

➥ When is the last time you meditated on paper?

➥ Perhaps using a sheet of plain paper and a box of crayons, draw a picture that speaks of something from your childhood.

➥ Perhaps make a series of these pictures and prayerfully study them afterwards to see if you see anything within them that surprises you.

➥ Experience feeling like a child again.

➥ Perhaps display one of your drawings on your fridge—or even frame one!

➥ Now just write a few lines or as much as you wish in your journal about this experience.

CHAPTER SIX

Legacy of Writing

"I am grateful that I started writing at a very early age, before I realized what a daring thing it is to do, to set down words on paper—"
—Madeleine L'Engle from "Walking on Water"

WHEN I WAS A LITTLE GIRL I loved to write. Pencils and pens were a delight and paper my joy—and anything I could write onto that paper. My little friend Patricia and I used to play "*Detectives*" when we were quite young and this required having several special notebooks. By the hour we would discuss criminals we were in search of and write up descriptions of them and their last known whereabouts, and anything else that was helpful. We took this so seriously and carried our notebooks around with us. I can still see us sitting on her front cement steps on Laveer Street in the Olney section of Philadelphia, or on my steps on Third Street, earnestly writing and discussing our great work of being detectives. As I have explained earlier, our streets intersected and our back alleys combined in a T-shape. Sometimes we made up the people we were investigating, creating human beings that frightened even us—the great detectives! Other times we chose live ones at random that we would see on the street or in a newspaper or magazine and turned one or more into an imaginary "*most wanted.*" We truly enjoyed this game of creativity and imagination and the extensive writing involved in our notebooks.

As a child it was magic for me to see the all new displays of school supplies in the stores when September came and it was time to return to school. All those wonderful notebooks and writing implements! I particularly loved the black and white marbelized covers that were on some of the notebooks, and I do until this day. Now they also come in many other marbelized colors. I chose this type book for my creative writing (just as I do now) as well as for my school work.

When I was a little child I wrote stories and created so many happy ones in quiet times. I liked to try to write poems too, and thought this to be very special. I was rather alone in my strong feelings for poetry. Very few of my friends shared this interest. One of my sweet treasures of childhood was a small blue flowered volume of *A Child's Garden of Verses* by Robert Louis Stevenson and I carried it with me often. It is one of the dear books from my childhood I still own.

Writing letters was another joy. I wrote to many of my little friends that I would see regularly just to be able to share more with them than we were able to speak about when together. I especially wrote to friends who were sick and had to be absent from school, and they appreciated these letters and responded in fun and happiness. To write *"thank you"* notes was part of my upbringing that has always remained with me, and I am grateful for this teaching and I have passed it on to my own children. Writing these notes to relatives and friends for kindnesses and gifts received was always enjoyable. Two Aunts who lived at a distance often wrote to me and sent little books and spiritual bookmarkers with scripture verses on them. I would keep the little markers in my Bible and books.

Eventually I acquired penpals through programs at school, and through my Sunday School papers from my Methodist Church. These papers were given to us each Sunday at the end of our lessons and I kept all of mine in a notebook together. This was exciting to share news and thoughts in letters with a distant friend I would never meet and knew only through the exchange of writing and photos. Two interesting penpals of mine lived far away, one little girl in Mexico and the other in Manchester, England.

A very pleasing form of writing to me was the keeping of a diary. Oh, this was so exciting to me because it was secret. A diary was for my very own thoughts and dreams—to record my days. I had many diaries beginning with the little five year diaries that only allowed for five or six lines of writing space each day. Soon I outgrew this type and felt the need to write more. Discovered next was the one year diary, still small in size, but allowing the diarist a full page to write upon. Both these diaries, the five year and one year, had a tiny lock and key. Ah—this created an air of mystery to a child. As time passed I used larger diaries or school note books not used for school or homework, but to contain my private world. Not being confined to one tiny page allowed new freedom in my writing and this habit of using a diary became deeply implanted in my being at that young age.

Keeping a diary was like therapy, but I was not familiar with that word as a child nor would I have connected it to my own writing then— or at least I feel fairly certain I would not. Being an only child left me without a resident confidante as had most children I knew. Yes, I had a best friend and we shared our thoughts and feelings—but some difficult things in my young life I withheld and kept to myself. The diary became my friend for such intimate sharing. And even as I kept private diaries at the young age of nine or less—a little girl several years older than myself was also writing down her inmost thoughts to "*Kitty*"—the name she had given to her beloved diary. I was safe and secure physically from harm, but this child was hidden in an attic as protection from the Nazis who sought to kill all Jews. Anne Frank was this Jewish girl—but I never learned about her, her diary, or her death in a Nazi Prison Camp until I was an adult. I have read her diary numerous times, have given it to others and will return to it many more times in the future.

Often—even for a young child, there is a release in the written word—and often one is empowered by setting down one's thoughts and feelings and dreams onto a piece of paper. Seeing them outside of our hearts and minds and souls is freeing and strengthening. This often gives us courage to do what we have to do. And so I wrote in my diaries all through my childhood and "*growing up*" years. I am not finished "*growing up*"—and so I am still a journal keeper. The small child in me gave me this gift—this legacy—to write, and be a keeper of journals. Yes, and to be a writer of letters also.

HEART GIFT

A letter written is a gift—
To give another soul a lift.
To send in words a part of you.

Vulnerably etched out in full view.
It is a way of bringing healing
Through your own soul's self-revealing.
Kindred spirits recognize—
Unwritten love and gentle sighs.
A letter sets itself apart—
A paper joining heart to heart.
All excess clutter remains gone—
And friendship rises like new dawn.

JGK

Letters from the heart can enhance and lighten and brighten another's heart—and encouragement given can change a life. I had received such letters and my inner child wanted me to give as much as I could to others in this way.

Perhaps had I not written I would have become ill—for sadness, stress, and heartaches can affect us physically. In my process of growing up that is still in progress, I know I must write and release such traumas to the emotions to my journal, my silent friend—or I become ill and lose my breath. I have read only recently that each organ in Chinese medicine interconnects with an emotion. Sadness belongs to the lung. To speak to someone and not receive a response was part of the experience in my life and to which I had grown accustomed. Though I most surely would have preferred the sound of a voice, I was able to survive extremely long periods hearing no spoken words in my home. A diary was a most suitable and treasured friend.

TEAR

I am the tear
    that slips from the eye,
        rests softly on the cheek,
            a silent cry—
                only the heart can hear.
In a wisp of a streak
    I travel the face—
        the only traceable trace,

and in soundless sigh—
disappear.

JGK

I am grateful to the little, shy, curly haired girl who gave me the legacy and discipline of writing in so many forms—of the joy felt within of merely seeing pen, pencil or paper—and the excitement still of browsing on the school supplies aisle in any store. And above all I am grateful for being one who confided, and ever will confide—in the silent blank pages of a diary.

✏

I hear and I forget;
I see and I remember;
I write and I understand

—Chinese Proverb

Reflect and Journal

✏ If you have not written a letter or note to anyone in some time, write to someone on a nice piece of paper that you like. It can be any type paper that pleases you. It does not have to be fancy writing paper.

✏ Enter in your journal who you wrote to and how it made you feel.

✏ Write an entry into your journal as if you were a child or teenager using your non-dominant hand.

✏ In your dominant hand write your reaction to what came forth using your other hand. Try this experiment often to reach your *"inner child."*

CHAPTER SEVEN

Legacy of Fear

"But you cannot go on being silent. You have to go on.
You have to listen and be heard"

—Huub-Oosterhuis

*W*E WALK OUT MY FRONT DOOR *and down the several sets of cement steps, past the lawn still green in the colder weather and turn left when we reach the sidewalk. My friend is with me and we head for the corner Sweet Shoppe for a treat. She is continuing on home after our stop there. As we giggle and laugh in conversation on the one block stroll at dusk, I see the K bus stop at the corner right ahead at Third and Godfrey. Still in conversation I vaguely notice it again slowly leaving the corner. It is gone by the time we arrive there. Only a woman stands somewhat removed from the corner several feet away. She stands in an orange and black checkered coat and black hat, her back to us. I freeze within. My heart pounds, my mouth turns dry. Fear takes over.*

My friend seems to notice nothing unusual and we two, quickly checking for traffic, walk hurriedly across Godfrey Avenue to the corner Sweet Shoppe.

I become silent and let my friend talk on. We sit together on the stools at the counter and order vanilla cokes. She does not seem to notice I can hardly speak. I laugh at her funny words barely knowing what she is saying as we sip our drinks.

We part with enthusiastic good-byes as we each go our separate ways to our homes. In the almost darkness now I look across the street to see if there is anyone on the corner. There is not. I cross Godfrey Avenue and slowly walk up Third Street in fear. I reach my home in several minutes and see the lights now on in the windows. I have no choice but to go in. I am so afraid.

My Dad is in the living room and welcomes me with a smile and a kiss. On the dining room chair I see the orange and black checkered coat and the black hat upon it. I know she is home and upstairs. I sit down with my Dad in the quiet until we figure out what we will do.

When I was a little girl I had fears. I had fears of many sorts and I cannot explain how each one began but I can only believe that some came from my Mother. She was an unusual woman in many ways—appearing very strong at times, therefore being fearful did not seem to suit her personality. She was loving, capable, creative, and sometimes aggressive—yet these fears that were known to me inhibited her life. I am sure there were others that she never let me detect.

She had a generous and giving heart and nature, always reaching out to others. During the second world war she worked extensively for the Red Cross knitting scarves, hats, long helmets and gloves for our boys in the service. She headed up such a group, and women came to our home often to pick up the yarn and other supplies to knit these necessities and then to return the finished items. My Mother in turn returned them to the Red Cross for shipment overseas and elsewhere. I am proud to say as a little girl I too knitted some of these necessities with the guidance from my Mother as she worked on her own knitting.

JEWEL CREATIONS*

Always smiling—not a frown
Bustling 'bout her shop in town—
Managing then a jewelry store
Where people continually came for more.

It was a friendly place to be—
The customers certainly did agree—

They valued Violet's sage advice,
Her creativity—the moderate price.

Costume gem stones of every hue—
She placed in settings with special glue—
And right before their very eyes—
Lay jewel creations of every size.

When Church bazaars would come around
Her generosity would abound—
She'd donate jewelry by the score,
Sit up late hours creating more.

She taught her customers how to make—
Lovely jewelry that was fake—
Yet each stone shone and came alive
For authenticity she would strive.

Everyone wore her gems with pride—
From Grandmothers to the blushing bride,
Even elite and rich relations—
Chose Violet Gray's fine Jewel Creations

A little lady with colorful name—
To this small shop brought much acclaim
Why don't you wander right on down—
Perhaps this store is still in town,

But Violet left there long ago—
She lives with Jesus—did you know?
She's making now jeweled crowns so fine
For those who share His Life Divine.

Dedicated to my Mother   JGK
Violet McKay Gray
Died Sept. 26, 1978

*10th and Sansom Sts. Philadelphia, Pennsylvania

She was also the manager of a large costume jewelry store in center city Philadelphia. Customers bought the parts and stones of the jewelry and assembled them to create pieces of their own designs. My Mother spent hours of her own time at home creating display models for the store but also creating jewelry to be sold at benefits that helped many causes. She gave freely her own time and donated the money generated from the sale of the jewelry at these functions completely to the cause at hand, keeping nothing for herself. She was loved by all whom she worked with and by her customers. I saw great evidence of this repeatedly through various channels. All of these loving things she did and the constant outreach to people and her love and laughter and talent hid a mystery within her—numerous ones really.

When I was a little girl and for as long as I can remember while living in my childhood home, my Mother would not allow herself or me to enter into our home if we had been out at night together with my Father. In the incident I have shared with you in the opening of this chapter my Dad arrived home first by car from another direction, my Mother soon after. This happened each evening. But when the three of us had been out together my father first had to perform a little ritual. Whether we arrived home by the back door or the front door, it was my Dad who would go in at first. At the back door my Mother and I would stand outside the door in the basement area waiting. If it had been decided we were to enter the

Back of our house where my Mother and I would wait whille my Dad checked the house.

front door, my Mother and I would stand in the tiny, enclosed inner vestibule. My Mother would insist that my Dad go all through our entire home room by room, closet by closet, examining everything to make sure there was no burglar. Not only did he check every room and closet, but he had instructions to look under every bed. Any conceivable area that a person could conceal himself, my Dad would check out before returning to the door where my Mother and I stood. When he would smile, that was the all clear signal that we too could come in.

In my heart, however, it did not always matter that my father had checked the entire home, even though I loved him very much and trusted him. I was only a little child and the nagging doubt often entered my mind that he had missed a closet or neglected to look under a bed. Surely he must have been tired of having to go through this procedure every time we three returned home together. Maybe he was confident everything was fine and he just did a hasty room to room check to please my Mother. And so fear crept into my innocence and I would imagine at times someone hiding in my closet and I would cry to myself and sit in my room not knowing what to do. Often I would go quietly to my Daddy and ask him to come open my closet doors with me. He never got angry. He understood.

Many times I would envision someone under my bed and would spend fearful times over this. I would leap into my bed so the alleged intruder could not grab my ankles and I would lie in bed in fear and quiet so I would not bother him. Even though I was usually tucked into bed as a little one, the fear did not always leave once I was left alone in the room and the lights were out.

In recent months I have twice seen reruns of a remarkable skit on TV done by the late Gilda Radner, someone we admire for her great talent, humor, and gentleness. It was as if I was reliving my past, for Gilda's role was that of a little girl having been put to bed, the lights turned out, and she is alone with her fears. All the things I ever imagined and more seemed to happen to Gilda, and even the repeated calls to her parents brought her no satisfaction. Her bed moved up and down, later people came out from underneath it, and other frightening images continually appeared in her room. While the skit is hilarious and Gilda is remarkable in her child role wearing a little night cap and gown, my inner child could identify with *"the child Gilda."* It helps to laugh now at such exceptionally done scenes and portrayals also of childhood fears, but this skit does reach back like a giant hand and firmly grabs my heart. And though Gilda makes me laugh I am also experiencing her fear.

As I grew a bit older some of these fears diminished and only came occasionally. For years whenever I was sent upstairs for any reason in the evening, I had to turn the hall light on for the top of the stairs by the switch at the bottom before I would ascend. Upon entering a room immediately my hand went to the light switch.

All of these things I am sharing here with you were written in some form or other in childhood diaries, for writing helped me to cope. Sometimes it brought understanding, often tears. But I felt like I was capturing my life, that it mattered.

I also had fears caused by self consciousness over my hair. I had naturally curly hair and as a little girl everyone compared my hair to that of Shirley Temple's. She had been a child actress in the movies for sometime when I was small. My Mother would curl my easily curlable hair around her fingers and I would end up with a headful of Shirley Temple look-a-like curls. When that phase passed my hair was extremely frizzy at times and could not be well controlled. All of my friends had straight hair that I longed for with all my heart and so I felt extremely shy over being the exception. Everyone would tell me how fortunate I was to have curly hair—especially my Mother—but I did not feel fortunate and was not even certain they were really being truthful but merely trying to be kind. I even considered at times my Mother had put some of my friends up to their flattering words to me.

Girls and women in the present days including two of my own daughters, just let their naturally curly hair go wild and free and it is considered so lovely and beautiful. But when I was small—and even when I was a teenager—such hair was always in need of control. Since I knew no other person with hair like my own I had fears of being laughed at, or talked about when I was not within hearing distance. My Mother too, would often create strange hair dos for me that made me not want to leave my house. To a shy little girl things often grew out of proportion and I felt very ugly, something I have never been healed of. I had no grandparents in my life either to turn to, to find comfort in or consoling words, or a bit of fun. I was very alone in my home, in my fears and inadequacies.

MOTHER, MOTHER!

Mother, Mother, say my name!
Mother, can we play a game?
Mother can we toss a ball?
Oh, you won't speak to me at all!

Mother, can we take a walk?
Maybe then you'll smile and talk.
The birds and flowers along the way—
Will help you love me just today.

Mother, look what I have found!
Oh Mother, please just turn around!
Take your hands down from your ears!
Open your eyes and see my tears!

I love you, Mother.

Janice Gray Kolb

I also had fears of being a bad girl. I tried so hard to be good but I was
an only child and my Mother was very strict. She did her best I am sure,
but she wanted me to be the best because she felt she had to show off a
perfect child. She would compare me to my friends and hold them up as
having better behavior or grades, and scold me in front of them or when
I was alone. After I was scolded and told I could not go outside for a
certain length of time, or period of days to play, she would extend the
punishment by not speaking to me. Depending on her disposition at that
moment or to what degree she thought I had been bad, the punishment
of her silence could be from one hour to several weeks. In those periods
I lived in fear of making more mistakes to further displease her. I tried
extremely hard to be good so her silence would end. During these long
periods often decisions and situations arose as I grew older that needed
dealing with pertaining to school, church, or my personal friendships. I
would ask my Dad whenever possible for help but if a decision needed to
be made at once when he was not available I had to make it on my own.

It all frightened me to do things or go somewhere without my Mother's blessing. Whatever decisions I made always proved to be wrong when she again was *"back with me"* completely, and then one or more of these would often cause another period of silence. My Dad's intervention did not help me even in long weeks of silence.

In my life too was something that should have brought notes of beauty and loveliness but instead it was an instrument of pain. Our family was given a piano by my maternal grandmother shortly before her death so that I might take lessons. I began these lessons at age five and they continued until I was sixteen and a junior in High school. At that point I begged to stop and surprisingly was granted permission eventually. During those years of lessons and study and hard disciplined practice I could play the piano like a concert pianist even at a young age. At my eighth grade graduation at age 13 I was asked to perform. Normally frightened to play publicly, though I was forced to do it frequently by my teacher and mother, I accepted. I knew I had no choice. However it was the one bright moment in all my years of *"the piano"* for I felt I played the most beautiful piece in all the world, Richard Addinsell's *Warsaw Concerto* and all by memory, and I knew I had performed from my heart flawlessly. It was received with such great love and appreciation from my young classmates who were dear to me and the entire audience and my Dad. But my Mother's criticism awaited me. Yet God had given me an assurance in my inner being I had not failed, and I clung to that then and at other dark times.

THINGS CHANGE

Little girl not long alive
Began piano at age five.
Lessons followed through the years.
Enforced study—many tears.

Her playing sometimes did astound—
Performed concertos quite profound.
But she was shy—though would comply
But inwardly she did defy!

She longed to play out after school.
An hour's practice was the rule.
She often did not make the mark—
And had to sit there until dark.

Now came the day that girl was grown
Her Mother saw what had been sown.
Six grandchildren she comprehends!
"Don't make them practice"—she defends!

Can you believe this is the same—
Mother, who on me laid shame—
Who wouldn't let me out the door—
'Til I perfected scales once more?

Who is this Mother turned about—
Who does not nag or even shout?
"They're only young once—don't you see?
Please don't be strict —let them be free!"
—Mother ????

Dedicated to   JGK
my Mother
Who was a wonderful
Loving Grandmother

Years later when I first met Bob and in that one year before we married, he would often ask me to play the piano for him but I never could. He had taught himself and played by ear. He had been denied piano lessons growing up, and when older he was interested in non-classical piano so he could play in a more spontaneous way like his father. He could play wonderfully in my eyes, so free spirited, and he actually enjoyed it! I had only had a fleeting period of enjoyment—at my eighth grade graduation. I was met with silence if my practicing did not please, and so I was always under stress while practicing my hour a day or much more. This had to be accomplished before I could play outside after school and if it was not met with approval I never got out. I have to admit

My Dad (Ellis George Gray) sitting at the piano I used to play
(with my wedding picture to his left and my high school picture to his right)

I hated the piano! And so I never played the piano for Bob when he asked. Finally, one day when I was alone and Bob was overseas in Japan and I had just our little baby June with me, I sat down to play. I turned on the tape recorder that Bob and I used to send messages to each other and I played the Warsaw Concerto for him with all my heart and being. I mailed it to him and to this day he tells people about the gift of that tape and my playing. He shared it with his shipmates and it fed his soul while we were apart six months. But that was the only time he ever heard me play when I was such an exceptional pianist. I say that not bragging for it is as if I speak of another person—another world. All I can play these past years are hymns—and not too well. Yet Bob and I have had fun playing them together, he on piano and I on our small organ. And he wrote all the hymns we play! But that is another story.

By the time I record the Warsaw Concerto for Bob I already have a brand new adorable little Mother who never again uses silence against me. But I still choose to record the piece for Bob when my Mother is at work for I feel then a total freedom, even though I know she loves to hear it. This new Mother now acclaims my playing and with great joy and enthusiasm! And all during this period of Bob's overseas duty my love of writing is there and used to extremes! I write him long letters every day of his six month absence and he too writes to me. At least in this one period his love of writing also increases. We still have those approximately 400 letters stored away.

PRISONER

I come from the alley of seriousness.
I see it from the window of my small room
    where I sit crying.
My room is in the house of silence
    and doom.
I am trying
    to break free
    to be me.
        I am a prisoner of silent violence.

JGK
(Written by her "inner child")

Until 1992 I had never known another person who had experienced extended periods of silence as regular punishment in childhood and teen years. Then on one of many frequent trips north to our lakeside cottage I purchased a book by Christian author Marilyn Morgan Helleberg in a favorite bookstore I browsed and shopped in each time we crossed over the border into our wonderful New Hampshire. Upon nearing the completion of the book I was stunned to read that she too had been punished with silence by her Mother. I sat and read through tears, crying for her. I knew I had discovered a kindred soul who understood. She wrote that her Mother's silence often went on for days on end and young Marilyn would follow her around, crying, begging and pleading for her to recognize her existence and to forgive her for the particular wrong she had done. She acted as if Marilyn was not there. It seemed I was reading about myself. Often if I continued too long in begging or crying, pleading with her to speak, my own Mother would cover her ears and turn her back to me to emphasize this punishment of silence. Marilyn writes that unless you experience this *"silent violence"* as a child you cannot realize how devastating it is. She relates how she took courses in psychology in college and discovered that this form of emotional abandonment can cause very serious problems. She went on in later years to receive counselling, and new thoughts were revealed to her about herself. Marilyn had felt emotionally abandoned for years. Through prayer and direction from the Holy Spirit she went onto glean new insights about her

Mother. She began to see that the Mother who wounded her had been a wounded person also.

I wrote a letter to Marilyn upon completing her book and received a very moving and beautiful reply in May of 1992. This brings tears each time I read it. I keep it in her inspiring book which is titled *God's Best For You—Discovering God's Ideal Purpose for Your Life* (Collier Books—Macmillan Publishing Co. 1988). She wrote that we are "*sisters in the spirit*" and she too had never known of another who received this form of punishment until I had written her. She shared many other personal things in relation to this silence that I could relate to so deeply. We exchanged loving letters and also books we had each written, and I feel extremely blessed that God helped us to discover each other. Again, through writing additional healing was given, for through her book and revelation, and our letters written revealing much more on this subject, we were helped and comforted that another in this world understood what each had carried within them for so many years and what each had experienced. Not long before I had written to Marilyn I had written a poem, again in an attempt one day to touch my inner child in some way. Again "*writing.*" How could I live without it? I sent this poem to Marilyn in my first letter. She understood.

Two years later after my contact with Marilyn I sat down and wrote a book on this subject of "*silent violence.*" Marilyn had referred to our common experience in this term. So intense were the feelings that rose up while writing and centering in on it that I completed the book in four months. It was an experience I will never forget and it brought much healing. The poem that I had sent to Marilyn is in the beginning of this book and is titled "*Mother's Wall.*" I think if I could not write I would probably die for the need is so great within me. Bob and at least four of our six children have read this book but only Bob has talked to me about it in depth, for of course, he typed it and we have discussed this subject at times in the past.

One of my daughters talked to me very briefly about it only touching things on the surface, after Bob gave her a copy and requested she do this after reading it. Our son called Bob upon completing it and they talked for over an hour. One other daughter read it partially with no comments. Another daughter has decided to not read it at this time in her life. Our two other daughters have not made mention of it. Again silence abounds, but I feel there are reasons within this silence that they find difficult to explain and because we love each other so, I honor that. I do understand.

This book also includes more silence that entered into our lives after our marriage, not between Bob and me but from another source. It is far more painful than the silence of childhood and affected our children and our marriage. Writing that book released years of memories that had been buried. Writing can do that in enchanting and magical ways even in painful situations. Writing can bring healing of emotions in incredible ways. It is as if it all pours out from my heart and soul down into my hand and out through my pen. I know this can happen to others who turn to writing in their search for healing.

There were other fears but these were the main ones that affected my early childhood, and indeed have affected my entire life. My Mother totally changed once I married two weeks after I had turned twenty-one years, and she apologized again and again in the years that followed for her strictness over me as a child and teenager. It was at these times I had to repeatedly assure her of my forgiveness and eventually she was able to accept that it was genuine and true. I was so happy to have my Mother back, a Mother that never again used silence against me as punishment. I too apologized deeply for any problems that I had caused her. In fact I had been doing that frequently all my life up until then. The fears remained, but we had a loving relationship from the time I turned twenty-one and married until she died many years later. In that interim she was also the finest and most loving and unstrict grandmother to our six children. She truly was a loving Mother when I was small to the best that she could be, but because she was controlled by fears and other problems I shall never know, she had to be as she was to me. She must have believed she was making me a stronger person by her strange instructions and actions. Perhaps she feared I would embarrass her.

Mother in 1955, taken while
Bob and I were in San Diego—
our pictures are on either side of her

WOMAN OF COLOR

Dear Mother with a colorful name—
I often wished I had the same—
First name as yours.
This name endures—
Coming from your Irish background.
More recently I've truly found
It has a great significance—
And I never had the chance,
To tell you so—its afterglow
Remains a floral cameo.

A delicate leafy violet plant—
Somehow—someway—can so enchant—
And speaks to me of you—
For you're a Violet too!
And add your Welsh last name of Gray—
Such color you gave every day !

Dedicated to my Mother   J.G.K.
Violet McKay Gray
on her birthday—
celebrated in Heaven

Years later while still a young Mother of six and one year before my
Mother's death, she sat in the seat behind me in our van as I waited to
pick up several of our children. I wore soft bangs and my hair long and
pulled back in a barrette. She reached forward and gently pulled my hair
and said *"what's this?"* —indicating disapproval. She continued lovingly,
saying she thought I was too old now to have long hair. She did not speak
harshly as she did when showing disapproval when I was a child or
teenager—for she was no longer that former Mother. My heart sank and
immediately my *"little girl"* surfaced, though she was not evident to her.
I told her I liked wearing my hair in this way. But it seemed I was in
childhood. Her gentle disapproval had affected me, and though I fought
giving in, following her death I began to pin my long hair up on the back

of my head using a similar barrette as when I wore it long. For ten years I wore my hair pinned up! Always! Her remark had made me question my own decision on how I had worn my own hair. I actually had enjoyed my hair long then, the first time I had ever enjoyed my hair at all. Finally I unpinned the barrette and let my hair down and began wearing it again as I had ten years or more earlier. At least in this matter I was at last freed. And she loved me, and I am sure she would have approved.

Perhaps, like Samson, if I had allowed it to remain down and long I would have had added and needed strength to face and endure that terrible period of the 1980's, a matter I will write about later. My Mother's behavior and my fears were legacies from my childhood that entered into all the years of my life, and that I am still working on in the present through prayer, writing and meditation. I have been healed in many ways of numerous fears and will continue on this spiritual path. This legacy of fear that gave to me a poor self image and weakened me in numerous areas of my life, also gave me insights into helping others through the years. I wanted to be an instrument of healing used by God to bring health, peace and joy into lives that once had fear, and He has quietly used me again and again in this way. Scripture tells us that when we are weak He is strong. My fears in turn gave me the legacy of compassion, for I could relate to others that were fearful even if their fears were not the same fears that I had been instilled with as a small child.

My Mother, too, was a compassionate person and helped many people in her lifetime, but as a young woman when she was surely in need of help and healing herself, she often caused me to be filled with fear. Only God knows what caused this in her being. She had been the youngest living child of nine children born to her parents who had been born, raised and married in Ireland. Perhaps the mystery lies somewhere in her background. I never discussed this with any of her brothers or sisters while they were alive for I was young and felt it would have been disrespectful to do so, even though she did not hide what she did. I even corresponded for years with one of her older brothers while he served in the Navy overseas and we had a wonderful relationship, but I never touched on this subject of silence in our home. Nor did I speak to another brother and sister of hers about this that lived close by to us or to any other family member. All are gone now and at times I wish I had learned what could have possibly caused my Mother to resort to silence.

I do not feel that I am betraying her memory in the sharing of all of this because she knows how I love her and she was not secretive about it. And because she utterly changed and became a new creature in Christ when I became twenty-one, it is as if I am speaking of two people. I believe she would want others healed also if her story could help them. She was a very giving, loving and spiritual woman.

Only through continued prayer will I perhaps ever learn the secret that brought on her periods of silence, and through my continued writing. Often things come from the depths of our beings unexpectedly when we pray and keep our pen moving on the paper.

VIOLETS

So many violets in the grass—
    And over there a purple mass
Of gentle ones in earthen spot
    Of only dirt—where grass is not.

And by the steps a lovely group—
    Grow up the hill and take a loop
Around a giant log that lies—
    Along the walk—and they surprise—

Observant eyes who see them growing
    In sidewalk cracks—thereby bestowing—
Special grace to each who find,
    These tiny treasures—and who mind—

Their footsteps so they will not fall
    And crush these beauties here who call—
With only color as their voice
    To help each human make the choice—

To let the flowers live and stay
    Between the cracks to be and sway.
Shy, gentle violets sent from God
    To grow in grass and cracks and sod.

I knew a Violet like no other
  Upon this earth; she was my Mother.

Dedicated to my Mother   JGK
Violet Gray
and to the violets in
our yard in Jenkintown, PA.

Joys

    In extreme contrast to the fear I feel upon discovering my Mother at the corner bus stop, her back to me in body language I know to my core, and added fear my little friend will see her and thus add to my pain through the embarrassment of it all, is the joy I feel at other times. Expressed in these poems is the childhood enchantment of summer evenings when I am carefree and go to that same corner store to bring home ice cream at the request of my Mother to share together with her, my Dad and neighbors. And the simple pleasure of catching fireflies out on my front lawn and sidewalk and cement steps with neighborhood playmates; my Mother's laughter and delight on the night air accompanying these never to be forgotten enchantments.

CHOCOLATE JIMMIES

Chocolate Jimmies on ice cream—
Yes, I remember summer nights—
When we children like a team,
Were given the exclusive rights—
And each an empty bowl quite large
To take down to the corner shop—
And there while feeling quite in charge
We asked that each be filled to top—
With many flavors—all assorted,
For those at home and for us too—
And always we swiftly transported
The glorious dips of every hue.

The families all sat on their stoops
Under stars ate their ice cream—
I had jimmies on my scoops—
And now it all seems like a dream.

JGK

God is teaching me to live in *"the sacrament of the moment,"* and though in childhood I have never heard that term in my spiritual life, I am being shown it instead. I live from moment to moment accepting each, but expecting the unexpected, and know my role and duty when there is abrupt change from utter joy, to fear, despair, and silence.

FIREFLIES

I remember the fireflies.
    O the joy and cries
    of delight
        of a childhood night!
Equipped with jars
    beneath the stars
        our dancing feet
           in summer's heat—
Took us on flights
    to gather lights.

We'd catch our fill—
    and sit so still
        to gaze in awe
           at what we saw.
And then we kids
    would lift the lids—
        and with loving, heart-felt hugs
           freed our little lightening bugs.

Dedicated with love to Connie Gilman

JGK

Heart Gifts

Fear can be turned to good, and in my life it was transformed into the legacy of compassion for not only human beings—but compassion for all of God's beloved creatures that share this world with us—for every living being knows fear.

I also have spent my life time writing so that I could help others and myself through the written word, for a personal letter or poem can touch hearts in deeper ways at times than the spoken word. In times of darkness and unrest a piece of writing can be a light to the soul that is filled with fears. It can be brought forth and read again and again in time of need and give peace and inspiration and strength. I know, for I have experienced this many times through letters from others and from my many books. Books often too can seem like personal letters. Therefore I write because I too still need healing of fears and because I do understand how others need to receive written pieces. How wonderful it would be if they turned to writing also. Writing is a form of healing unlike any other and I am still in the process of being healed through many forms of this gift from God.

MORNING TRANSPORT

I remember way back when
    I was a child—my Mother then
Would come and take me by the hand,
    And from my back room slumberland—
Would lead me through the hall to where
    The sublime morning breeze and air—
Drifted into their front room
    And in their bed I could resume
My drowsiness—unfinished sleep—
    While o'er my being then would sweep
Glorious gentle wind of dawn
    With scent of flowers from the lawn.
Each morn my only blanket there—
    Was the magic summer air.

My Mother dressed and up to stay
    Would go downstairs to meet the day—
With Daddy—soon he'd leave for work.
    And I could smell the coffee perk.
Then I from my back room so warm
    Would lay me down there and conform.
And I would curl in sweet repose
    In lovely room of my transpose—
Dreaming in the Land of Nod
    'Neath fragrant zephyr blown from God.
And to this day I reminisce
    About the spot of childhood bliss.

Dedicated to that   JGK
room in my childhood home
at 6231 N. Third St.
Philadelphia, Pa.

CLOVER

The scent of clover sweet at dawn
That drifted on the morning air—
And drew me to my little lawn
To pick the soft white blossoms there—
Comes back to me in memory,
As I view clover now in grass—
All in profusion—growing free,
Gracing eyes of all who pass.

Like soft white lambs they flock together
Yet some have strayed to separate places.
And I recall in summer weather
Those childhood days and happy faces—
As we picked the flowers there—
From our lawns on city street
And made the chains to dress our hair—

And necklaces from clover sweet.
Chains of blossoms linked by stems
Speak now to me of earlier years—
And link me to those days—like gems,
Of innocence—that now bring tears.

Dedicated to   JGK
the clover
that grew on the lawn
at 6231 N. Third St. Phila. PA

Reflect and Journal

☞ Did you have fears in your childhood?.

☞ Do you still have some that remain or have you acquired new ones?

☞ Pray and meditate and ask God to help you to rid yourself of these fears.

☞ Write in your journal that you prayed and asked for help and date it. When any fear returns use this entry as a basis to boost your faith and thank God that He is there and helping you. Write more in your journal if you wish.

☞ Try to pray daily about this if even for only a few minutes. Always thank God He is helping you and is there for you even if you still feel fearful. Even if the answer has not come yet, still thank God in advance that it has come. This is scriptural and shows your faith.

"What is faith? It is the confident assurance that something we want is going to happen. It is the certainty that what we hope for is waiting for us, even though we cannot see it up ahead."

—Hebrews 11:1

Perhaps write this on an index card and put in on your fridge to see daily or memorize. Many, many other people before you have done this, myself included.

CHAPTER EIGHT

Death of a Beloved President

"We have nothing to fear but fear itself."
—Franklin Delano Roosevelt

MY CHILDHOOD PRESIDENT I admired very much, Franklin Delano Roosevelt. It is not because I knew anything about politics. A child senses things often in different ways than adults, and I believed him to be a good man and worthy to be our President. The above quotation by him concerning fear has been repeated all through the years and it is excellent. I should have grasped hold of it at that early age and applied it to my life.

I remember the fear and the sorrow I feel when I learn of his death. He has died at 3:35 PM on the afternoon of Thursday, April 12, 1945 of a massive cerebral hemorrhage at Warm Springs, Georgia. The announcement of his death comes across the airways shortly before 6 PM breaking into the airings of such childrens' radio programs as *Captain Midnight* and *Tom Mix*. The nation and the world are in shock! My parents too are in shock and I am sad and frightened. I write about it in a little diary that I wish now was still in my possession. I think he is kind and brave and am in awe that he was President with immense duties yet also was crippled from Infantile Paralysis and in a wheel chair. This is a disease dreaded by all children and adults in this period many years before the Salk vaccine is discovered. He has my admiration and his death is frightening to me. I know he was a gentle man also, for he had a little black Scotty dog named Fala he loved dearly. The little dog was often in pictures with him in the newspapers or on newsreels seen when attending the movies. Television is not yet in our home.

The next morning in school the teacher tries to minister to us and we have free time to listen to her and share our thoughts and move around the room. I stand by the window alone staring out and not seeing. His death affects me and frightens me. It saddens me greatly. These are war years and I felt he was in charge and would make it all go away. A little girl in the city of Philadelphia, and in innocence and sadness, truly feels the enormity of his death. I write more about him in my diary and think of the great mournful procession from Georgia to Washington carrying his body during the night, that train that slides by solemn crowds paying their respects. It is written that all the cars of the train are in darkness with drawn shades except the dimly lit rear coach. This car seems to shine by contrast it is reported, and a flag and four still sentries are visible. The thoughts of Mrs. Eleanor Roosevelt revealed later in things I read touch me so. To think of her on that train so sad and brave, and accompanying her husband's body, breaks my heart as a child when I hear these reports. To learn that the President's valet is walking the President's dog, little Fala, along the train platform before the train departs brings tears to me, that now Fala is separated from his beloved master and friend. It upsets me even now as an adult.

To write briefly, as a child would, of this enormous event in history about a man who had been my President since my birth, helped that little frightened girl in a time when she found herself unexpectedly grieving. That I turned to writing then comforts me even now. Whenever his name is mentioned or I see his picture I relive that period of his death and also things of my childhood, and I admire him and feel a connection to him.

Some years later and early in our marriage Bob was attending a Dental Convention in New York City and was waiting for a hotel elevator. When one arrived and the doors opened he stepped inside quickly with the woman within. They were alone and he instantly recognized her as the doors closed. It was Mrs. Eleanor Roosevelt! He said "*Good afternoon Mrs. Roosevelt*" and she replied, "*Good afternoon, young man."* He left the elevator before she did. Bob realized later this was the hotel in which she lived.

We have always treasured that encounter and I wished I had been with him. It has been remembered lovingly many times through the years.

In more recent years I discovered books of great interest to me. An old volume of Mrs. Roosevelt's autobiography found in the book basement of a favorite store, the Ossipee Owl on Route 16 here in New Hampshire brought delight. Then in Jenkintown, Pennsylvania while still living there I discovered and bought two volumes of Mrs. Roosevelt's letters in new editions. I gave all of these to Bob as gifts but I read them, of course. All these years I had admired her, as did Bob, and it was a joy to learn she too knew the enchantment of writing and had written hundreds of letters, as have I , and her autobiography. Perhaps there are other books written by her I am still not aware of. I know her letters were of far greater importance than mine, but it is lovely to think we have had the love of writing in common. So much history can be gleaned from her enormous capacity for writing and she gave great feelings of good will and peace through her letters. It was a joy to discover these, like the letters of a friend written for myself alone.

Several years later it was exciting to also come upon a shelf of mystery novels written by Elliot Roosevelt, the son of Eleanor and President Roosevelt. I only read mysteries on occasion and have several favorite authors of mysteries. That day I was looking for the latest in the delightful series by Lilian Jackson Braun, author of *"The Cat Who—"* series of which I own every one. Rochester coming into my life inspired me to read these, of course! In browsing, the wonderful books by Elliott Roosevelt were suddenly before me and thus began an enjoyment of a new author. (to us) These books are filled with exciting mysteries all in the era when Franklin D. Roosevelt was President. All are mysteries that take place in the White House or in other official buildings or grounds, and Mrs. Eleanor Roosevelt is the chief sleuth who solves the mysteries. Each book has knowledge in of the Roosevelt era and one learns so many personal things about the President, his family, relationships, and the period of World War ll. Since it was also the time of my childhood I have truly enjoyed all the personal knowledge I have learned about a President and his wife I admired, and all written by their son. Each book is truly a "*mystery with history*" and I recommend them. Each time I read one it returns me to the period of my childhood. Even President Roosevelt's son Elliott had known the enchantment of writing and revealed many personal things in his family through the sleuthing of his famous Mother in these mysteries. Sadly I learned after reading many of his books, that Elliott Roosevelt too had died not long ago, but he has left a legacy of many more historical mysteries in this series and all will eventually be published. Perhaps in writing about his family in the genre of mystery it helped Elliott to heal wounds within his heart and soul.

Reflect and Journal

✏ Did you have anyone in your life that touched your soul in this way as Franklin Delano Roosevelt touched mine?

✏ Perhaps write a paragraph or so about the person or make it an entry in your journal.

✏ Pray and try to recall others that maybe you had forgotten about and that you would like to remember in writing, if in only a sentence or two.

CHAPTER NINE

The Air Raid Box

*"As children, we had lots of energy and were constantly creating.
We told our friends incredible tales and built kingdoms for our adventures.
We flew with angels and fled from trolls.
Language was a constantly available toy; we invented songs
and rhymes to repeat to ourselves."*
—John Lee from "Writing from the Body"

A SPECIAL PLACE my friends and I liked to gather during the war years of our childhood was on the large gray air raid box. These boxes were placed in strategic places in all neighborhoods and in ours it was on the side of the end house on our block. Since I lived the third house from the corner on Third Street this box on Laveer Street was close to my home. On summer days, or after school, or in early evening of gentle nights a number of us would gather on this wooden air raid box. It held about four of us young girls side by side, our backs against the stone wall of the house and our legs stretched down its slightly slanting gray top. It was on this box that we shared secrets, fears and stories. In the box was stored essential equipment to be used by designated air raid Wardens in time of an air raid, either for a practice drill for one or for a real air raid that we fearfully prayed would never come. When the sirens would blare at night and our parents had to obey by pulling down all the shades so that no light could be seen in the windows, it was a frightening thing. It was preferred that all house lights were turned off and this made it even more terrible. Search lights would often be seen flashing across

66

the night skies while we were in the process of obeying the orders of covering our windows. I knew these were used to detect enemy planes and it was terrifying.

But in the friendliness of daylight or lovely summer evenings these large gray air raid boxes were a meeting place for children of the war years, and our box was unique and personal because of the private times we shared sitting upon it. It was a comforting spot. There was nothing frightening happening while we sat there, but left on its own it was often opened in the dark to the wail of the sirens and the mysterious items within it were removed and used, items we never saw because we were behind drawn curtains.

During the quiet time of friendship upon this locked container of war defense articles it seemed we could keep the war away. It was then we unlocked our hearts and confided fears and secrets. And always my friends liked me to tell them stories that I had made up in my own heart and mind. And I did. At that period in my life these stories seemed to flow without effort and they cheered my friends and myself. Often at home I would write a story down after spontaneously speaking it out for my little girl friends, and that in turn comforted me to have it in written form in a note book, to reread when I was alone or afraid. I was transported in spirit back onto the air raid box with my little friends, and their laughter and enjoyment then became gifts to me in my solitude. Through the spoken word of my spontaneously created stories, I later captured the essence of them through the enchantment of writing. These stories and the actual writing of them onto paper, helped to minister to an often frightened little girl. What would I have ever done without my writing? Pencils and paper—bandaids for the soul.

Reflect and Journal

✏ Was there a special place in your childhood where you and your friends gathered?

✏ Perhaps in writing about it in your journal, the writing about it will help additional memories to surface and you will have it written down for all time.

✏ Return to read it from time to time and perhaps it will recall other memories in connection with it. You can add these new things to the original. You are creating a *legacy of childhood* for yourself.

Things Remembered

The poems that follow capture some of the essence of things I have shared with you in the previous chapters. Poetry can bring delight and healing to the soul.

INNER HEALING

Often deep within one's being—
There is pain and hurt and grief.
This is when one needs God's freeing,
And His Help to bring relief.

Find time and place to welcome quiet—
And the moments to invoke—
His gentle Presence; don't deny it,
In His flowing Spirit soak.

Feel Christ's mark upon the soul
While knots within become untied.
Let the wounds that took their toll
Roll in Love's tide—with Him collide!

O let His Holy work within—
Fill each with power and resolve,
As suffering, guilt and old chagrin—
Beneath His Healing Touch dissolve.

JGK

If you are not a Christian and would choose not to invoke the presence of Christ to help you, then turn to God or to the One that you do go to for love and strength and healing.

This depicts the *"inner girl"* of my Mother

THE UKELELE

Before my mother was married
With friends she would go to the shore—
And more often than not usually carried
A ukelele—it was part of the lore.

And their speech there was turned into song—
As they'd sing on the beach in the sun.
All was right—life was good—nothing wrong.
O the twenties—so alive—filled with fun!

Beside breaking waves she would strum
Such memories were made in those days.
But soon the small uke became mum—
Gone were those ole flapper ways.

For many long years the uke stayed—
In its case—for there were no more flings.
But now with new hands it is played—
As my daughter strums rinky-tink strings.

Dedicated to   JGK
my mother
on the 15th anniversary
of her death
September 26, 1993

And this speaks of the young girl in me now—the one who loved to go to the corner store and bring ice cream back in a bowl to eat with family and friends on the front stoop!

THE GIRL INSIDE

Now that I'm a wee bit older—
I've noticed I am somewhat bolder.
I don't care if people know
A kid lives in me. Does it show?
With no intent at all to nourish—
Today with graceful arm and flourish
I poured and shook a steady stream—
Of chocolate jimmies on ice cream
And ate it all—and with no guilt—
Enjoyed each spoonful to the hilt!
The girl in me was very proud—
I let her live and be allowed—
To savour things out of her past,
Sweet memories she still holds fast.

JGK

Further Memories

Never will I forget my Dad; soft spoken, loving, and quiet but with a sense of humor that simply broke me up. Very especially as I grew older I appreciated his humor because it was subtle and unique, but as a child and teenager I thought he was rather wonderful for all reasons. He and I especially shared memorable days on the beaches of Ocean City, New Jersey as an earlier poem also speaks about. He was a precious "*Daddy*" to a little girl and I always think of him with such deep love. As a young man I know he was quite handsome too (although he was always handsome to me), and he played the drums before I ever knew him. I have his drum sticks as keepsakes but never heard him play. Apparently I was like him in many ways. If a set of drums was sitting in our living room next to the piano that I tried not to play, I am certain he would be too shy also to play the drums there. Perhaps in his youth he was more free-spirited. He is deeply missed. I write poetry for him continuously. This one speaks of a day on the beach at Ocean City, New Jersey.

AT OCEAN CITY IN MY CHILDHOOD

I am the spray of the ocean
    falling on father and daughter—
Standing hand and hand on the sand
    in the breaking splashing water.

I am the foam of the ocean
    lacing ankles and shore—
Retreating then back to the sea,
    returning to them once more.

I am the salty scent of the ocean
    the scent they shall never forget—
Little curly head child—sun-tanned father,
    so delightfully and completely wet.

Written with love   JGK
for my Dad
Ellis George Gray—
on the 20th anniversary
of his entering Heaven—
August 21, 1997

All sorrows can be borne if you put them into a story or tell a story about them" (Isak Dinesen).

When we love deeply we always keep the loved one near in spirit, at least I am that way with my loved ones. Poetry helps me. Shortly before the last anniversary of my Dad's death Bob and I were in Wal-Mart and had separated to get some shopping done. On the intercom music played and suddenly I was listening to Elvis Presley singing "*I Can't Help Falling in Love With You.*" It begins "*Take my hand*" and is very beautiful. Immediately my eyes welled up with tears and I began to cry and could not stop, and had to hide my face and try to find aisles without people. It had moved me so much. Elvis died several days before my Dad the same year, and twenty-one years later I hear a song and burst into tears for my Dad, and yes, for Elvis too. He died much too young. I know this for we are a year apart in age. When Bob and I met again he had no idea why I was crying. It was the anniversary of Elvis' death and he was being remembered through his music that day in Wal-Mart. And yet for me it was for my Dad too, music from an era filled with memories. But memories constantly surface and ever shall. They give no warning. My dad is only a "*heartbeat*" away.

HEARTBEAT

For ten years after he died—with pride—
I wore my father's large watch.
And though I often cried—the watch somehow denied
His death to me. His absence was like a dark blotch
Upon my life—and to see this watch there
Upon my wrist, to hear its soft sound,
Was like unspoken prayer—
And comfort to me each time it was wound.
A part of him went everywhere with me
And helped to regulate my existence.
A mere touch or glance upon the face and I knew it was he
Giving his time—his love—from an unknown distance.

Then one day his watch died too!
And I knew—it was true.
I would have to go on without this blessed reminder
That had not ceased whispering since he lived; this physical binder
Of his life to mine—
A very tangible sign—
Of this man most cherished.

His ticking watch had nourished
My soul.
Symbolic of his beating heart—it played its role.
At least I still have this lifeless gold
To hold.

Dedicated to my Dad, Ellis George Gray
Died August 21, 1977

Silence also came from my Dad's side of the family though my Dad never "*used*" silence. He was my friend throughout the long periods of silence within our home. In all my growing up years I never knew my Dad's parents. I asked about them occasionally when I was little and then stopped. The answers I received are blocked from my memory.

On the evening of our wedding as Bob and I stood in the reception line greeting so many guests, there was suddenly a woman before me, and in only these words she greeted me, "*Hello Janice, I'm your grandmother.*" And then she was gone. She disappeared! It was a moment I have always remembered. Even my Dad's reaction to this is blocked from my memory or if he even saw her. I cannot remember what she looked like, nor had I ever seen a picture of her or my grandfather.

This incident was recorded in my diary but I never wrote about it in a poem, nor do I recall speaking about it further except to Bob and my parents. I feel certain I told my children about it years later but for reasons I do not know I let it rest after it happened. And now many years later I am writing about it again. At some point long after, I know my Dad and his brother made it possible financially for her to be cared for in a fine nursing home. This was not disclosed or discussed, only made mention of when it initially took place. Perhaps now I will write about it in my journal. Because it has come to mind for the first time in a decade or two through writing here about my Dad, perhaps it is a sign to explore it in writing. This is an example of what happens when we put pen to paper. We often do not know what will come forth on the paper. These last paragraphs surprised me! I will never truly know or understand this mystery and there is no one living who can tell me. One thing I do know. My Dad was a man of honor and I have never questioned "why" but accepted how he wished to live his life. That he was protecting his family was how I always chose to view it. Now that I am older I trust his decision even more deeply, for I have lived and continue to live through unusual experiences of my own, and wish I had his strength and wisdom—and too, his protection.

I close this era of my life my early years—with another poem. This *"little girl"* still lives within me here in my wonderful New Hampshire and spends her days writing. I am glad she can be seen by others.

This poem was inspired by a sweet friend who too attended daily Mass in Pennsylvania as I did, and who loved to write poetry, letters (I have been the blest recipient of so many through the years) and to keep journals. Her death has saddened me so and came during the writing of this book.

A Smile Through Time

"When you smile you have the face of a little girl"—
A friend—after Mass—said to me.
I thought of a child with many a curl—
The little girl I used to be.

With misty eyes I genuflected—
And leaving church—deeply reflected.
What joy! My inner child is detected!
Perhaps a true sign she is not neglected.

I cannot express how my friend's words astound me!
(By sharing her feelings she lovingly crowned me!)
And now to others that are around me—
There is a perfect gift that I can give;
A smile! and let this little girl live!

In gratitude   JGK
to Janet Smith
my sweet friend—
and in memory too of good times,
love, conversations, and letters shared.

Legacies of Marriage, Home, Children and Ministries

*"No matter what we do, we can make it our ministry.
No matter what form our job or activity takes, the content is the
same as everyone else's; we are here to minister to human hearts.
If we talk to anyone, or see anyone, or even think of anyone, then
we have the opportunity to bring more love into the universe."*

—Marianne Williamson

CHAPTER TEN

My Places Apart

"I want to remind myself and others that our homes can become sacred places, filled with life and meaning. We do not need cathedrals to remind ourselves to experience the sacred."

—Gunilla Norris

URING CHILDHOOD and my teenage years I did most of my writing in my room on the second floor in the back of our brick row home. When Bob and I married and travelled for two years due to his Navy tour of duty, I wrote wherever I could, usually creating some special spot in each temporary home. Letter writing was foremost and each morning after Bob left for work at 4 AM to go to his ship in San Diego harbor, I wrote. It was exciting to get up in the dark in a new apartment (new to me), in a new city. The apartment was two blocks from the Pacific Ocean on Sunset Cliffs Blvd. With a cup or two of Folger's coffee and my pen and paper, I wrote daily to our parents. One day to Bob's parents, the next day to mine, alternating and never failing. They could also compare news. As to the Folger's coffee, it was big then, and had a very quirky commercial for it constantly sung on the radio. The show I listened to then for obvious reasons was *"The Bob and Jan Show."* Syncronicity! The commercial sung was (for those who may remember): *"A Folger's man to your door may come, And ring your doorbells one by one. . . ."*. It was cute and people often sang it anywhere.

Writing to my friends was also on this daily agenda in the peaceful dark and quiet of early morning. Prayer and reading were part of it all too, before beginning the normal day in connection with friends.

Eight months into our Navy duty Bob had to leave on his ship, the USS Piedmont, and sail off to Japan. I will never forget our tearful goodbyes as he boarded the ship in late August of 1955 followed by my driving to keep then my vigil on the tip of Point Loma near the Cabrillo National Monument. Standing there I waited as the Piedmont came in view from its departure point and sailed past where I was standing high above it waving and crying. Bob was somewhere with the other men waving also, a tiny unseen dot on the deck. I was seven months pregnant and stood there watching until the ship disappeared on the horizon of the Pacific Ocean. It was a sad and dreadful day. I then returned to Philadelphia to live again with my parents and to await our baby's birth. June was born in October and my parents made our stay with them so wonderful and did everything possible to honor and await June's arrival. They helped and provided for us both in precious ways I shall never forget. Their hearts were breaking when they took June and me to the airport to fly back to San Diego to meet the return of the ship and Bob, and for me

My father-in-law,
Robert A. Kolb,
holding baby June Leslie
in her nursery,
October, 1955

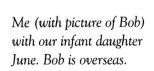

Me (with picture of Bob)
with our infant daughter
June. Bob is overseas.

to present him with his little June. More and more wonderful things happened while I lived with my parents and such healing took place with my Mother and myself. They were months I will never forget—months recorded in my journals of "*new birth*" of June and in my Mother's and my relationship.

In these six months apart from Bob I also wrote letters to him every single day as did he to me. Often he would not receive his until his ship came into a port, but then he would receive many all at once. This too happened for me for he could only send them and receive while in port. I wrote and poured myself out to him and shared great details about his new baby daughter. If ever letters written were important it was during this six-month separation. They are treasures to us we still have stored here in our cottage. The written word and prayer held us together while we were thousands of miles apart. I also wrote to my friends in San Diego, the wives of Bob's close friends on the ship with him. And when on the West coast, I wrote letters to my family and friends back home continually. Writing never ended.

Bob on board the U.S.S. Piedmont *in Japan, 1955, receiving a telegram (from me) announcing his first child, June's birth.*

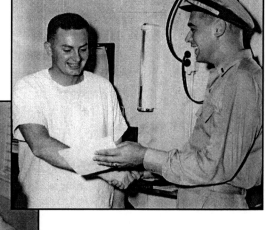

November 1955, in my parents' home, writing one of my daily letters to Bob during the six months he was overseas.

Once back again in Pennsylvania from California and the State of Washington, we lived in two other lovely homes over a period of five and a half years before settling into the home we would reside in from 1962 until December 1995. Our family had simply grown too large for the previous homes. We moved into a century old three story home with seven bedrooms. In 1962 this home was amazingly affordable for us, but in the present would not be so at all.

Bob, baby June, and myself, April 1956, in San Diego, California, after Bob returned from overseas and we were all re-united

OUR BIG GREEN HOME

The big old house of rooms and halls
Holds echoes still within its walls—
Of joy and laughter through the years
But sorrow too and pain and tears.
Six little children without cares
Played and sang and climbed the stairs
With three little dogs right at their heels
As giggles, screams and yells and squeals—
Made this old house a home apart—
A home that lives within my heart.

Dedicated to   JGK
239 Wyncote Rd.
Jenkintown, PA

On a quiet street with other large homes all containing large families and each home different, ours sat up very high from the street. Several sets of cement steps and a long walk bordered by green grassy lawns, led

Our big green home

up to an open porch with a wooden railing on three sides. The porch stretched the width of our home. Huge old trees surround our home and abounded on our property. There was a huge side grassy yard and back yard also, with a barn that also housed a three car garage on a private dead-end alley where children could safely play. When we moved in we had four young children, June, Laurel, Barbara and George, the youngest six months old and the oldest almost seven years. Before long we were blessed with two more children, Jessica and Janna, and all seven bedrooms were filled, six for the children and one for us. My dream I had had since my lonely childhood, of wanting six children, had come true! It is in this home we lived until permanently moving to New Hampshire in January 1996.

Our three Cairn Terriers: Crackers, Muffin, and Lizzie (the mother)

STAIRWAY OF STARS

I have five daughters truly fine—
And yet two daughters who are mine—
Are just the opposite—you see—
In height—and it's a mystery,
How the oldest is so tall—
Five feet seven over-all!
And the youngest—short in height—
Is five feet small and pure delight!

Sweet and slender is the older—
It's a joy just to behold her!
The younger's filled with fun—surprises!
And those she loves she energizes!
And the three that are between—
Add compliment to daughter scene!
I cannot adequately critique,
Or speak of three—each is unique!

In graduated heights they stand
A perfect stairway—a special brand—
Of joy and laughter—love and fun.
And add to all—one glorious son!
Though fourth born—a man of prayer
By far the tallest step on stair!

Dedicated to   JGK
June, Laurel, Barbara,
George, Jessica and Janna

For years after marriage, though I always did some bit of personal writing daily and too, always letters, writing could not be first in my life, and I had no special place in which to write. Because I was a wife and mother other important things in life were expected of me and I did them with great love for my family because this was the wonderful large family I had dreamed of having since I was a lonely only child. I was no longer

*An earlier "Stairway of Stars," when the children were much
younger and I am expecting our sixth child, Janna*

lonely and could rarely find time alone but life was fulfilling, exciting and
permeated with love.

Turning to sewing I made my daughter's clothes and also clothes for
their dolls. Many were special matching outfits to my daughters' clothing.
I embroidered several heirloom samplers for each of my children, samplers for all family members and for every friend far and wide. When the
creator of one of the lines of samplers I bought and embroidered saw my
embroidery, she selected my work to be hung in the needlework department of the very huge downtown Philadelphia John Wanamaker store. It
was awesome for Bob and me to go there and see my work displayed. It
was hung there to encourage and inspire others to buy these kits of
embroidery and too, so they could see the finished results.

During this period two of the people I made samplers for were both
our Mothers. When my Mother saw all of my work she began to
embroider samplers also and to give them as gifts. A very special one I
made for her of an old well known saying was:

Who ran to help me when I fell,
And would some pretty story tell—
My Mother

It depicted a silhouette of a Mother in old fashioned long dress with a child. She treasured this sampler so in light of our past together, followed by our healing that took place through God because of the drastic change in her. This sampler now hangs in our daughter June's home—the home in which the sampler had been embroidered.

Sampler
I embroidered
for a wedding
anniversary of
my parents

Sampler of our family tree

Another item I created on my sewing machine was a *"get well pillow case"* and each of my children had one. These pillow cases were only permitted to be used when the child was sick in bed. The cases proved to be delightful and often took the child's mind off his/her sickness. I chose unusual patterns for each pillow case, bright and cheerful. George had colorful racing cars, Barbara an array of many sizes of polka dots and the others were equally as cheery. They were so successful and desirable with our children I began to make them as gifts for other children.

On Christmas Eve our six children also had special pillow cases for that one magical night. I chose colorful Christmas designs in images appealing to children. Each child had a different case.

Along with all these creative projects I always read, but it had to be saved for later at night. Since I had so little time for reading, far less than I desired, I read only spiritual books. Because of our large family I felt I needed this inspiration and nourishment to be a better wife and mother and for my own soul. The reading caused me to want to write more but there was little time for that.

While pregnant with our sixth child, our youngest daughter Janna, I read the entire Bible from beginning to end. Feeling so blessed and fortunate to have had five children born healthy and sound, I was afraid that perhaps I could not be so blessed again. And though I had always loved Jesus since I was a child and read my Bible, I turned to Him anew in this pregnancy and received the spiritual strength and help I needed. I encountered Him again as if for the first time in an experience as I had had several other times in my past, when I had turned intensely to Him. There have been other encounters similar to this since and I pray I will always know His Presence. Janna was born unlike our other five, so quickly, and this time with Bob permitted to be with me. As she arrived into this world the chimes from the Presbyterian Church next to the hospital played "Faith of Our Fathers" at 6 PM ushering her birth. One year later as we had a birthday picnic for her in our yard, the chimes from our own Methodist Church played Janna's song, "Faith of Our Fathers," filling us all with gratitude and God's presence and awe at this synchronicity. All of these events I did record in diaries and related to close friends in my letters. Taking pictures was also something I did to daily record our lives with detailed reports of explanation written under each photo. Over the years I filled many diary-like albums for each child. Never did I stop writing. It was essential to me.

My children and myself on vacation in Massachusetts, 1971 L to R, back row: June, myself holding Janna, and Laurel front row: Barbara, Jessica, and George

Following Janna's birth my spiritual life grew more intense and along with faithfully attending our Methodist Church with Bob and our children, we both became involved in our church's charismatic prayer group. After several years when it was no longer permitted to continue there, I began to attend a very huge charismatic prayer group at the well known Chestnut Hill College not far from us. These spiritual happenings in our lives had me craving for a spot in which to be alone to pray and write. At last I created such a quiet corner in our bedroom. It consisted of an old rocking chair of my parents and a long table next to it. The double tiered table held my pens and books for writing underneath and other little related treasures. The top of the table was for a framed 5x7 picture of Richard Hook's Christ, just His Head. His eyes seemed to stare into my soul! Some artificial flowers in a pretty vase were near this, my Bible and my tape player. This was my little Holy Place I retreated to as frequently as I could to help myself emotionally and to become stronger spiritually. And each short period I could spend there was like a mini-retreat. If Bob had a meeting at night and had to be gone for a few hours, it was to this quiet space I went after our children were in bed or the older ones were reading in their own rooms. Many memories are in my heart in relation to this quiet corner where I felt God's presence and where I could write down thoughts.

A quiet corner to pray and write

On two occasions when I came downstairs into the kitchen after only brief visits to my corner for prayer, I was told by several of my children that my face was aglow. I could sense this but did not realize it could be seen. It was an opportunity for them to realize that God does indeed touch us when we go apart with Him. My children have had their own spiritual experiences since then and know this truth. All too attend church faithfully, and their children also. My Holy corner inspired more writing and always prayer. I believe its existence inspired my children in a quiet, subtle way.

Whispered Notes

In this prayer corner I existed through an exceptional period of time when I was *"given"* a group of special writings. While writing these meditations I felt *"held"* in a way that is unexplainable, and *"released"* when the writing stopped. The *"Whispered Notes"* bypassed my intellect, and I took dictation from the Holy Spirit with closed eyes. The words and sentences formed like soundless whispers within, and my hand flew across the page, for I was writing with great speed. This continued day after day. First there was a scripture passage indicated, then a devotion-like message, followed by a closing prayer, and each morning I was drawn deeply into prayer through the power of the Holy Spirit. Each morning I was given a new writing, sometimes several.

This continued until I had received forty-five writings, each complete with the appropriate scripture and closing prayer. These meditations were given to me to go with hymns that Bob was receiving in spirit. He could not read music, yet gradually he had been receiving a large group of beautiful hymns from the Holy Spirit, both music and lyrics. He would receive the hymns when falling asleep or would wake in the night with one in his head, or while driving, or at home. They came unpredictably. He would put them down as quickly as possible, then refine them later. When forty-five hymns were completed, he received no more in that way. When he asked me to write meditations for each hymn, I did not think I was worthy or capable. The Holy Spirit, however, took over when I sat in my rocking chair and asked Him to help me write accompanying meditations for Bob's hymns. After forty-five were given, no more came—as with the hymns. A mystery!

There were unusual happenings associated with the meditations in the years that followed. These meditations were lost for a total of seven years (I had no other copies of them), and in a period then of thirteen months, my Dad, Mother, and beloved Uncle, and a close friend all passed away. (I will tell you

The meditations I "received."
When they were lost and then found,
I wrote them all out in this notebook

next about our friend's death.) Had we had the meditations in this extreme time of grieving for our beloved family and friend, they would have been a great comfort to us. To read the full account of these mysteriously given hymns and meditations, one can turn to my *Journal of Love* or our *Whispered Notes*.

Finally, ten years later, the meditations were returned to us—lost no more! I was given seven more meditations. (Fifty-two now to go with seven more of Bob's hymns.) These I *"received"* here in New Hampshire. We felt they should be published after all that had transpired, and through prayer this finally happened in 1990. We know this book has blessed many people and continues to bless them. It blesses us also as we continually use it, for it was a gift from the Holy Spirit.

Though, as I have written in *Journal of Love*, this was the end of these fifty-two messages, I have always been able ever since then, through writing, to receive guidance, and comfort, and answers, from messages received from the Holy Spirit, after praying deeply *"in spirit,"* directing all love and intentions to the Spirit. Writing, *always writing*, opens up the unknown to me and allows Holy mysteries into my life.

A Mysterious Communion

One day when retreating to my quiet corner briefly I suddenly became overcome with sadness. Tears soon followed and I did not know what was wrong with me. The experience caused me to stay there longer than planned and I sat there grieving and not knowing why. I wrote down simple notes when I began to recover so I would always have this incident recorded and so I could pray about it to learn why it happened. In my mind a passage of scripture from Eccleasticus came to me and it proved to be disturbing when I read it. Finally I went downstairs and as I did the phone rang. It was a call to tell Bob and me that an extremely close friend had just suddenly died. He had been mowing the grass while visiting his son in another state far away and came inside and collapsed. He died on the way to the hospital. All this had occurred in that short period in which I was in my prayer chair and corner. The Holy Spirit had spoken to my soul and I had sat there grieving in tears and praying in Spirit—yet did not know why. We were devastated at our friend's death. I have continued to be in awe that I was led to my prayer chair at that very time and allowed to grieve while he became ill and entered Heaven. I share this because God does speak to us and I pray this comforts others who need to believe this. And the utter blessing of turning to writing at that time also has allowed me to have memories and notes written down of a most significant passing of a dear friend that I would not normally have had if writing had not been an important part of my life since childhood. I later added the details of his death to what I had already written during that most mysterious passage of time.

Silence and Most Significant Departures

In August of 1977 I grieved deeply over the death of my Dad. I have tears to this day for I miss him so. Insidious silence entered our family in a new way in February of 1977 when my Dad had to have his larynx removed. Seeing him following his operation after hours of waiting and praying for him with my Mother in a waiting room of the hospital, is a memory that lives in my mind and heart and brings deep pain to this day. His head and neck were swathed in bandages, only his eyes so filled with fear stared out, and the hole in his neck. I would never again hear his voice, the voice that had been so kind and gentle helping me through my childhood and teenage years. He remained in the hospital a month, Bob and I visiting with him daily and my Mother staying throughout the days by his bed. All of this could have been prevented had he not smoked, something he had done since he was a teen. After I had children he never smoked in front of them but would always go outside away from their being able to see him. He tried to stop but could only do so for brief periods.

He came home a different withdrawn person from the hospital only able to communicate by writing to us on a child's writing pad, the type that after the message was received the sheets could be lifted up and the message disappeared. Around their home were notes in pen written to my Mother and occasionally we received these too.

Writing—we could not live without writing! Writing entered into his life in a new way finding significant importance, for we needed his communications to us. It was a frightening, sad, and eerie period of his life and ours. My Dad who had been such a significant part of my life lost interest in his own life. To lose his true self was a deep loss to me. He died after this horrendous event and all his struggles to communicate within six months. SILENCE!

His death was followed within several weeks by our friend's death of whom I have just shared about and, in early November, my wonderful Uncle Elmer's death.

Nine months later in September of !978 my Mother died suddenly, and this too was added to our grieving. We believe she died of a broken heart, for up until the sudden deaths of her husband and her brother she had been vibrant, healthy and totally active doing all the things she loved at church and in groups of which she was a member, and too, being with all of us. We brought her to New Hampshire over Thanksgiving but upon

My Uncle Elmer, Dad, and Mother at Laurel's graduation in 1976

returning to Pennsylvania she was hospitalized with a heart problem then released. Within the year she too was gone.

HIGHER MEMORIES

My Mother came to Higher Ground
just once; it was Thanksgiving.
Such calm, and peace she found;
her sadness softened—and misgiving
That she had left the home she shared
with Dad before he died—
That this *first* holiday—she *dared*
be *here*—and though she cried,
She made it through the memories
of Thanksgivings past.
At times when grief her heart would seize
our Lord would hold her fast.

She did not come again next year—
so silently without a sound,
She slipped into another sphere
with Dad—on HIGHER GROUND

Dedicated to my Mother   JGK
Violet McKay Gray
on the 14th anniversary
of her death, September 26, 1992

   She mourned my Dad and Uncle continuously and deeply in the few months she lived, and like my Dad her personality and nature were never again the same. On their 50th wedding anniversary I had to once more suddenly take her to the hospital. I received her call and found her sitting on the front cement steps of 6231 waiting for me and weeping. Jessica was with me and helped to comfort her as I drove. She died one week later on the day she was to be released—not long past midnight, just as my Dad had done. Bob and I were with her.

THE LAST ANNIVERSARY

I remember other years—
And then they entered through *that door*,
While we shed so many tears—
Held memories that went before.

The last one ever I'll remember
Was the year that she was left.
Their fiftieth was that September—
And she sat there so bereft.

O her soul was sad and lonely—
Her heart was broken then in two—
For she wanted him then only—
So she died before the dew.

Dedicated to   JGK
my parents   September 19, 1993
Ellis and Violet Gray
on their 65th anniversary
(celebrated in Heaven)

Bob and I and our children have many wonderful memories, and those of visiting my parents in their row home on Third Street are fond ones. So many festive occasions took place there and very loving ordinary times of quiet visits. The poem that follows expresses how I felt upon returning to my childhood home on June 2nd of 1994. It was my Dad's 90th birthday and the home had just been sold.

UPON VISITING 6231 AFTER IT HAD JUST BEEN SOLD

I drove up Third Street last week.
The attached row homes speak
To me. The large buttonwood trees at the curb
Cause sweet memories that disturb.

I drove up Third Street.
It was no ordinary day.
In years past my Dad would greet
Us—as we made our way
Up the cement steps and walk—
To his door—and there we'd talk
And he'd welcome us in
And kiss and tease all his kin.
And my Mother would be preparing the food—
Always so excellent—always a joyful mood
Prevailed—and we'd be together for awhile.
Just thinking of it makes me smile.

No, it was no ordinary day.
With camera—leaning out the window of the car
I paused below the former home of Ellis Gray
To take last pictures from afar—
And to quietly say—
Happy Birthday,
Dad

Dedicated to my Dad   J.G.K.
Ellis George Gray
on his 90th birthday
June 2, 1994
(died August 21, 1977)

Jessica and my little granddaughters Maxine and Renee were with me on my Dad's 90th birthday. Jessica and Michael and girls had lived in this home from 1987 when they married until 1994 when they bought the Hitching Post Village Inn in Center Ossipee, New Hampshire. The Inn is twenty five minutes from our home in East Wakefield. We were making a last visit to 6231 before we all returned to New Hampshire.

I took four pictures of my childhood home that day as written about in the poem, and once back at my home in Jenkintown before leaving for New England I took several more photos of my two little granddaughters to end the roll. When the film came back to us every picture on the roll of twenty-four was beautiful and perfect except the four I took of 6231 N. Third St. The pictures were totally blank! Not one of the four held an image of my dear childhood home. Since I have been taking pictures for years and have marvelous photos, these blank photos were not understandable. There was no reason why they should not have been beautiful. It hurt me very much that this happened, but in prayer I soon came to the conclusion that I was being told by God or my Angels that this was now the end of an era. No family member now owned the home nor did we any longer. It was over.

6231 N. THIRD STREET, PHILADELPHIA

Within these walls a family of Gray—
Lived out their lives from day to day.
How ironic a family of Black
Has now moved in to keep on track—
This line of color—deepen the shade
So traces of Gray will never fade.

From Gray to Black in this same place—
Yet one's a name—the other a race.
How proud I am this home's a sign—
Of Brotherhood—for it once was mine.

Dedicated to	J.G.K.
Jessica and Michael	June 16, 1994
who made it possible	

Though I returned to Pennsylvania numerous times between the end of 1994 and January 1996, I never went back. We have lived in New Hampshire four years now and I have never been back in that period either. Perhaps in order to move on in life and healing we have to close some doors. I was fortunate to have my childhood home in our family for sixteen years after my parents' deaths. It was loved and lived in by several of our children. Laurel and Bob and infant son Jesse had moved in one year after my Mother died. Several years later they moved and Rob and

June owned 6231. Then with the marriage of Jessica and Michael in 1987—my parents' home again had new owners. As their living period neared its end in 6231 I wrote this poem for Jessica. She believed my Mother had sent her a sign and reply to her prayer through a scent.

A PRESENCE BREATHED IN

My daughter stood in her kitchen after preparing bread
And sensed not only the aroma of it baking—
But the scent of her Grandmother—who also fed
Her family in this kitchen—and in years past stood making
Delicious meals too.
I was her child—I knew
The food, this room—the special grace—
That passing time cannot erase.

But my daughter had been asking her Grandparents help in prayer.
And they who are with God and no longer there
In that lovely home and kitchen—heard!
And not being able to reply in word—
Sent a scent
That my daughter would recall
From her childhood—and it meant
Everything! It crossed the invisible wall—
That veil—and brought new faith rising—
Like the bread. For never disguising
That it was she—
This Grandmother—now free
Of visible earthly ties—
Brought faith and hope that all worldly explanation defies!
And my daughter never doubting this scent from her past—
Knew now her Grandmother—held all her needs fast.

Written for Jessica Mae (Kolb) Drakely
Child of the past—woman of the present.

Now this era was over. The door of 6231 is closed. Perhaps one day I will return but I know it is not yet time to revisit.

In this same year of 1994 when Jessica and Michael moved to New Hampshire and Janna and Bill were married here by our lake, I too made a commitment —to honor anew my Dad.

GRAY

I have decided to take my Father's last name.
Always I have worn it in my heart—and hidden,
And now there is this need to be one and the same—
As if mysteriously called to it—and bidden.

His name could not be carried on by a son.
Having only a daughter—I am the one
That must see that it is carried.
And I shall do that now—though I am married.

Dropping two middle names into my inner being—
Will spiritually signify that I am agreeing—
To raise up then his name given to me at birth;
To bring it forth anew—and show its worth.

Those middle names are no more lost than was his name.
Within my heart they'll replace his—that I reclaim.

Dedicated to Bob, who encouraged this change—
officially made June 2, 1994
on my Dad's 90th birthday

One precious way we can return to places in our memory and to people we loved on earth but who now reside in Heaven is through journal writing. I have truly found this to be so.

SONGLINE

I believe we are connected
 with those we love—those resurrected
To His Higher Holy Place—
 and though we cannot see a face,
Embrace or kiss or hold a hand—
 for they are in another land—
Yet a Spirit line can bind
 those far away—those left behind.

Each time we pencil down a story
 or a letter, of one in Glory—
Or we pen a poem and write
 about a loved one out of sight—
And make an entry in a journal,
 we are creating something eternal—
That links us to the past—and yet,
 to future too, so none forget.

In speaking of dear ones above—
 we keep alive their precious love.
We pass along wisdom and feeling—
 soul-links—that are most revealing—
Impart their Spirits—they keep us strong—
 it all becomes like whispered song.

Dedicated to   J.G.K.
my loved ones
In Heaven

  A year or two before Jessica and Michael moved from 6231 to New Hampshire they presented me with a heart gift—a treasure. They handed me the numbered address sign that had adorned my childhood home there since before I was born for they had bought a larger numbered sign. The original is cherished! Bob did special work on it of cleaning and restoring the glass and where the 6231 numbers are housed, and also on the exterior of the glass. With a special little ceremony we placed it above the door of our small cottage here in the woods. It has and will ever remain, though it is only a "spiritual" and honorary address here from time past and remembered.

1978—Another Era

In 1978 I was received into the Catholic Church and I have written about this briefly in my book, *Higher Ground*. There was a definite calling to this and also other significant reasons caused it. It is not important to be detailed for this particular chapter. Eventually Bob suggested that he make our son George's former second floor bedroom into a "*Prayer Room*" for me where I could have more privacy to write and to pray. George was then attending Villanova University in Pennsylvania and lived on campus by his second year. He had also claimed a room on our third floor as his after June and Laurel had just married. There was an ulterior motive to Bob's suggestion which we can laugh at in recent years but could not quite do so back then or in the six years that followed. My table in our bedroom next to my Prayer Chair had slowly filled with other religious objects. They were gifts to me when I became Catholic, and rosaries, statues and icons and the like were not a comfortable presence in our bedroom to Bob. We transferred all of these into the beautiful prayer room he created for me with blue and white walls that resembled a small cathedral. In the room I had this same table from our bedroom (I called it my altar table) with the spiritual gifts, two book cases, and two adirondack chairs we brought from New Hampshire that were identical to my green prayer chair on the platform by the lake. When sitting in the special one of the two I chose to use consistently, I could close my eyes and in Spirit be transported back to my prayer chair on the platform by Lake Balch. It was so real and comforting and yet always caused me to yearn to return to the woods of New Hampshire.

HEART'S LAKE

Within my heart there is a lake.
It's radiance is for my soul's sake.
It laps and laps the woodland shore—
And those soft sounds I can't ignore.
I'm drawn within to woods and trees—
And feel the blest prevailing breeze.
I hear the loon wail from a distance,
Dear little birds sing with persistence.
The sun is glistening—water's blue—
The heron wade and egrets too.
Squirrels and chipmunks run and chirp
While the birdseed they usurp.

If suddenly I'm forced to roam—
And for the natural lake I sigh—
My soul can ever be at home
On my heart's lake with inner eye.

Dedicated to   JGK
Lake Balch
and Higher Ground

Bob stained these chairs brown to match my desk. A small deacon's bench was in the room also. I wanted the furnishings and room to look austere for I was in my *"Monk-like"* period of spirituality. This is spoken of in my book, *Higher Ground.* My children often came in and we would talk for long periods when they had problems and we often prayed together. On occasion two came in together. Precious moments.

Only one of my daughters would not ever enter the room. Although Bob and I had talked at length with our children before I took a step to become Catholic, and all gave their consent to me, one had had some reserve. Had I known I would never have entered the Catholic Church just as she never entered my prayer room. We would always have our conversations in other rooms in our home. Later when she married, after a long decision she too became a Catholic (our only child who did) for the man she married attended the same church as I did. She and I have never shared our Catholic faith however, for I respect her privacy, nor sat together within the church as we did in the Methodist Church when we always sat together as a family for years. Our entire family did though attend the Mass for her entrance into the Catholic Church and we did all sit together there as we did always in the Methodist Church. Our daughter being received into the church sat up front near the Priest. When my daughter and I speak of spiritual matters, and we do, it is always as if we are both Protestant Methodists as we were when we grew in love for each other as she grew to womanhood. A mystery.

For six years following my becoming Catholic I still attended the Methodist Church also to sit with Bob and our family. Janna was still young and we felt she needed my presence there. It was my joy to do this, attending first an early Mass then rushing several blocks to attend the Methodist services. These were unusual years.

It was at this desk in this prayer room, a desk that had been my Mother's, that I did all my letter writing and journal entries. It was a room or place apart to write and pray and it helped me through some extremely difficult years. This room and contents gradually became less important to me after Bob retired early and we began to come here to our cottage in New Hampshire for longer periods. It was here in my beautiful writing room on "*Higher Ground*" that I felt whole and came alive to a new life of writing and living surrounded by nature in the woods. Somerset Maugham has written a passage in his "*The Moon and Sixpence*", 1919, that totally speaks my heart about our cottage, my writing room, and life here in the woods shared with Bob and Rochester. I felt this from the time it first became ours in 1976.

> "*Sometimes a man hits upon a place to which he mysteriously feels he belongs. Here is the home he sought, and he will settle amid scenes that he has never seen before, among men he has never known, as though they were familiar to him from his birth. Here at last he finds rest.*"

THE HEALING WOODS

I come to the woods to restore myself.
My spirit to be nourished and healed.
My calling to write I take down from the shelf—
And through writing my thoughts are revealed.

Solitude to me is life-giving,
In silence I do what He bids.
I am back to fulfillment in living—
All debris within me He rids.

Surrounded by nature again—
The wildlife, the lake—all things green—
My spirit is calm now and sane—
In His woods I am peaceful—serene.

Dedicated to   JGK
"Higher Ground"

Yes and Amen!

The blue and white prayer and writing room in Jenkintown, Pa, no longer exists, for two of my grandsons sleep in it now. It has been newly decorated and June, Rob and their six children live there in our home—now their home. For two years previous to this from 1994 to 1996 Janna and Bill lived there following their marriage that took place here by the lake. We shared the home with them since we were mainly living in New Hampshire.

The years pass but my desire to write has only increased daily. It is a dream come true to spend my days writing at my desk that overlooks Lake Balch. As I write now it is winter, the sun is setting in glorious orange shades and snow mobilers are driving in a line across the ice. A woodpecker is at our suet (or his suet) and chickadees are at the feeders, a Blue Jay is on the wood bar singing and God is present. Some years ago a poem was given to me as I sat in the dark in my writing room following a full day of writing. I have never forgotten that evening in every detail when I reread this poem and the magic returns once again. Each snow storm is different and with its own memories.

WHITE ON WHITE

White valences of delicate lace—
On windows at my writing place—
Enhance the view within my sight
Where I sit at my desk to write.
The air is filled with glorious snow—
Fragile flakes float down below.
Three white birches in the night
Are set aglow by soft porch light.
And I can only gaze in awe
Upon this beauty without flaw.

Mystical vision before my eyes—
Millions of flakes sent from the skies.
Spellbound in darkened room—I'm filled—
With wonder, as the snow is spilled
Into the night—enchantment reigns—
Right outside my window panes.
Magic window—white on white—
Curtains, flakes and birches bright.
My wish—to just remain here waiting—
In dark and silence—God's creating!

JGK

And now—let me tell you about this Holy room where I write my heart out and share life with Rochester and we meet with Angels.

"*Don't be satisfied with stories, how things have gone with others. Unfold your own myth*" (Rumi).

But first—let me tell you about a friend named Emily who entered my life to inspire at the most perfect moment. Then—we will go to my room.

Emily of New Moon

About ten years ago two of my daughters Laurel and Janna, discovered the Anne of Green Gables stories by L.M. Montgomery. We were all here vacationing by the lake and had rented several of the Anne of Greene Gable videos, thus my daughters were led to the books. They had not read them in their teens as some do though both were avid readers. Because of their enjoyment of these books and my occasional surprise of one of the series for them, I discovered at the bookstore a trilogy by the same author and I treated myself to the set. These stories were about *Emily of New Moon* and I identified with her greatly, for she too wanted to become a writer. This was in the very time of my existence I had just begun to write as my life's work and dream.

I put no limits on books as to age and am often moved by a book written for a child. But for me to read this trilogy at this point in my life was extremely unusual. I had been reading only spiritual classics and other spiritual books by present day writers for years. I was drawn to this type reading and there seemed no release. But I forced myself to read *Emily of New Moon* and was blessed and inspired. She was a lonely child like I had been and I identified with her longings in regard to writing. I have since bought the series for others as inspiration.

Later I was pleased to read in *Walking On Water*, an inspiring book by well known author Madeleine L'Engle, that she too had loved "*Emily of New Moon*" and had "read and reread and reread" them—to quote her exactly. Madeleine, like myself, had been an only child who loved to write and she felt Emily was like a friend, as did I. Madeleine writes how Emily walked to the beat of a different drummer and had a touch of second sight. She explains this gift as one which allows us to peek for moment at the world beyond ordinary space and time.

Like Madeleine and Emily I too was in touch with this world of imagination and it is another legacy from childhood I am grateful to have.

Madeleine writes that it was *"this world"* that gave her assurance of meaning and reality for like myself she knew many fears.

The poem that follows is one I penned in love following a second reading of the first book in the trilogy about Emily, several years later. By then Emily had become my special friend. Even her last two names are significant, for *"birds and stars"* are a holy delight and enchantment to me.

TO EMILY BYRD STARR

I've read a novel of a child
   who was so very much like I.
An only child—and quite beguiled
   by writing; it would fortify
And clarify—the things of life—
   oft times so hurtful—filled with strife.
She'd take her pencil—and her book
   with pages blank—to garret nook
And write to satisfy her soul;
   the writing helped to make her whole.

With little cat—companion there
   she wrote her most unusual fare—
Of poems, letters—an observation—
   set down in truth and imagination.
Often scolded—misunderstood—
   yet tried to please and be quite good.

I wish I'd had her for a friend—
   such wondrous things we would have penned.
On wings of dreams we'd both take flight—
   and write our poems by soft *star*light.

Dedicated to   JGK
"Emily of New Moon"
by L. M. Montgomery
—friend of my inner child—

And yes, Emily had a dear cat who shared her days and nights as Mitzi shared mine as a young girl. Now my beloved Rochester shares all of life with me and inspires and guides.

Reflect and Journal

➥ Reminisce and record things in your journal abut the homes you have lived in.

➥ If there has been only one then write about this significant home.

➥ Explore in your writing what appeals to you most within your present home and in writing also consider the corner or room you would choose for your private writing place.

➥ Have you ever wondered about your own personal background and did any questions arise? Have you ever written about them?

➥ Perhaps now you may want to explore these feelings and questions in your journal.

CHAPTER ELEVEN

Jan of Green Gables

"Writing requires concentration and silence.
I can only get that in total solitude. If I don't have that sort of womb
where I work and I can retreat completely, then I can't write."
—Isabel Allende

THERE IS A PLACE in our small green cottage that is filled with the light of Christ, the Angels and all the beauty of the woods and lake that can be viewed from its windows. Please ascend with me now the green carpeted stairs from our living room.

We are arriving at a small landing at the top. You have a choice of going left or right, but I am begging you to turn left and enter beyond this door into the front room. It is the room named *"Enchantments"* and it is my writing room. You see the lavender wooden Angel on the door? This room is where I spend my days and part of the evenings. It is Holy to me and a gift to me, a place apart to write from my heart. I feel like a Fairy Godmother tapped my head with a magic wand and transported me into this precious place, but in reality I fully realize it is a gift from God. I cannot await to ascend the green carpeted stairs each morning for they are like my *"stairway to the stars,"* another realm. It is from these windows at twilight when I am nearing completion of my writing for the day that I often pause to gaze out over the lake and to feel anew my gratitude for living here and for sharing in all the wonder of nature outside. Many poems are written in this room as well as my books, and one early evening most unusual inspired *"Shadow Visions"* from my heart and pen.

> Up from the waters dense mist arises—
> And in descending twilight—trees in their disguises
> Are shrouded—appearing like tall men in the haze,
> Causing flight of fancy and illusion—and the imagination plays!
>
> Unknown woodland night sounds from creation—
> Add to the mind's improvisation—
> Of myth and fantasy—and unreal things.
> O such imaginings a misty night brings!
>
> All this from my window as I gaze out on the lake.
> Such visions and whimsy a dreamer can make.
>
> J.G.K.

But I am not alone here in this room even though the significant quotation by Isabel Allende that opens this chapter indicates, but I am the *only* human. I share the gift of this room with Christ, my Angels, and my Rochester, who is visible Angel. The hours and hours I spend here are my joy and delight as I experience and live out the enchantment of writing. Rochester is ever by me on the bed that is next to my desk and has claimed as his own a soft wildlife quilt folded in quarters and covered with patches of deer, moose, bear and other creatures along with patches

*Rochester on
wildlife quilt*

of color, a quilt made for me by my daughter Janna. It is upon this he literally sinks down into for his cat naps. But he is also on my desk stretched out at times and from either position we commune, converse and I gather his thoughts. He remains with me all day, occasionally leaving only to attend to food or litter box downstairs. At times he sits in the open screened window in which my desk is also placed to catch the prevailing breezes, or on the corner of my desk to view the lake and trees. Below our window but in my vision as I write are a row of fine bird feeders hanging from a wooden bar all made by Bob on our front deck. As I write now Rochester and I see a Downy Woodpecker enjoying the suet, and a Mourning Dove on the wooden rail from which the feeders are suspended looking in at us. Rochester is all love and a totally committed soulmate—a joy forever.

COLLABORATION

Today we wrote all day.
I at my desk in the sun—
    He on the bed.
        I heard
                each dear word
                    he said—
                            every one.
A spiritual bouquet—
        a nosegay
of his thoughts, phrase after phrase.
    And I in love—and praise—
            with elation and admiration—
                took dictation.
            Collaboration!

Dedicated to Rochester   JGK
with love.

This soft green carpet in our room is intended to be enjoyed barefoot in the warmer weather and the soft pale green walls compliment it. The walls are gables and I sit beneath them, and a portion of my long blonde wood desk extends under them on the right side.

The gabled roof converges to the middle, an area which is about two feet wide and the only portion of flat ceiling. Two windows framed in natural wood holding sliding glass panes (I sit at the right one) afford the view of our beautiful Lake Balch, green grass seeded and nurtured and cut by Bob, my seven colorful flower gardens each surrounded by rugged rock walls built by Bob, my prayer chair on its platform by the lake and Bob's chair above the large tri-level dock that he built about eleven years ago. Birds daily at the feeders and other wildlife abound and an occasional boat on the lake, all of these add to the joy of my writing. In winter we are shut off from the world and secluded in this woods by mounds of deep untouched snow, and trees that are mystically draped in its white essence and it is other-worldly and Holy. We must wait to be ploughed out and often we are snowbound several days to our delight. The incredible New Hampshire snow storms always inspire poetry. This particular snowfall captivated Rochester more than ever.

SNOW GAZERS

My friend and I sit side by side
Gazing out of the window—we just cannot hide—
Our pleasure and joy at what we behold—
Millions of snowflakes out there in the cold.
He turns and looks at me as if to say—
"I cannot imagine a more wondrous day."
And then we continue to lovingly stare—
(He on my desk and I on the chair.)
His uplifted eyes try to follow each flake
And he guides many down to earth and to lake.

He turns once again to me—blinks in deep love—
Then his eyes seem to draw down more flakes from above.
Framed in our pane is a work of great art—
The Creator has sent it—it brightens the heart.
And while my blessed friend and I sit in the quiet—
Inside our beings is an unutterable riot.

Dedicated to Rochester   JGK

Above the two front windows at which I sit is a long shelf installed there by Bob and that holds my collection of Angels of all varieties. There is too, one small ceramic cat resembling Rochester surrounded by smaller angels beneath a crucifix that holds a Christ figure with liberated arms held upward. Under the shelf hangs a glorious Angel about a foot high all garbed in peach robes with shaded peach wings. Her countenance is very beautiful and her halo is peach also. She is holding a peach scroll and peach flowers lie in the folds. When my windows are open she floats about and is most inspiring and lovely.

The porcelain angels on my shelf that are weather proof I take down to put in my gardens in Spring through October. Each of the seven rock walled gardens has at least one angel and usually more to oversee the flowers. It is very spiritual and beautiful to me to see the combination of God's flowers and angels everywhere by the lake—along with precious wildlife, butterflies and birds.

Over my desk is a framed pencil sketch drawn after my deep spiritual encounter of meeting Christ that is written about in the chapter "*Poetry*" and also in much more detail in my previous book, *Journal of Love: Spiritual Communication with Animal Friends Through Writing.*There is also a framed picture of Rochester, a calendar page actually, of when he was chosen and then appeared in the Humane Society's Cat Desk Calendar for 1996. I had submitted his picture and he was chosen from thousands of entries to be on one of the pages for that year. If that was not enough joy in itself, he was placed on the page that commemorated Thanksgiving Day! Everyday in my heart is one of Thanksgiving for him, so it was extremely meaningful to me. This page with his picture also appears in my book, *Compassion For All Creatures: An Inspirational Guide for Healing the Ostrich Syndrome.*

When I first wrote this particular chapter it was like a book unto itself because I described for you everything within my room. I wanted so much to share it all with you. But now you have accompanied me here and that is not necessary. I can simply point out the three wonderful book shelves (our entire cottage is filled with them) built by Bob, packed with precious books of all categories, and the bed for guests, for this is also our guest room that is much enjoyed. The bed faces the windows and the glorious view through the windows is its only foot board. On a small cot is my stuffed animal collection that was written about in my *Journal of Love* and is added to lovingly and often by my granddaughters, and other significant treasures are within this dear room. As I write the loons are wailing out on the lake within my sight. In addition to my straight desk chair there is a high backed small wing chair, "*wing*" being appropriate for it is also my "*inside*" prayer chair and I often feel transported to another realm by my angels while in deep meditation. In my room too are framed pictures of my Mother and Dad and of dear friends in Heaven written about in my chapter on "*Poetry.*" There is also the childhood picture I have written about earlier in this book. Other significant photos are here too including one of the first time one of my books *(Higher Ground)* appeared in a store window. This was in Jenkintown, Pa. and my daughter June took pictures of it for me with her children on either side of the display. Bob has since recorded in pictures other displays of our books in store windows in New Hampshire and Maine. It is something still quite unbelievable to us and that is never taken for granted. Never! We always pray the books will touch and reach hearts that need them. We are grateful to God they are acceptable to be used.

In my room is also a sweet present from Bob, an adorable night light in the shape of a pine cone. It is made to look like a miniature home with little protruding gabled windows, a door and chimney. One might suspect a little woodland creature is living within it and snow is around its base. It is especially child-like and magical when it is lit in the darkened room which I do occasionally when I am sitting at end of a writing day thinking and giving thanks. The present was given to me when I completed my book *The Pine Cone Journal.* Guests do seem to enjoy it too.

Often we have heard the phrase that one is "*not out of the woods yet*" when a person is still not totally healed. For myself I have needed to be "*IN*" the woods to become healed. It is in this precious room *writing* that my soul, heart and spirit have been given healing again and again. I *need* to write! I *need* to be in this room of "*Enchantments*" daily. I *need* to be in the woods!

The desire to be here was so great that before we lived in the woods we left Pennsylvania every chance we could to return to New Hampshire even for a three-day weekend, which gave us so little time, but enough to refresh our souls.

NOMADS

Nomads, nomads—travelling far—
Life style perhaps—somewhat bizarre—
To those who oft' remain at home—
With hearts not so inclined to roam.

Up to New Hampshire brings elation
Inspiration—dedication—
To Our Lord and to vocation
When entrenched in woodland station.

We know that travelling back and forth—
From Pennsylvania to up North
To others might seem like patrols,
But we're just gypsies in our souls!

JGK

There are no gypsies in our souls any longer. They left when we moved to "Higher Ground" permanently. We have come home.

Now that you have experienced my writing room you can understand my desire to climb those green carpeted stairs each morning with Rochester leading the way. The atmosphere I have created is truly child-like because I am still a child at heart. My own childhood I lived on the edge. Here in this room I am at peace, deep peace. I am living in and creating a place of beauty and delight and charm for my "*inner child*" that is extremely conducive to writing and I have never been more filled with joy. At times I sit here and cry because of the gift of this room, and the life shared with Bob in this tiny cottage in the woods, and my life with Rochester. It is the most precious place of healing as I sit and write page after page.

Many writers enjoy writing in cafes and restaurants and this is understandable to me. It is very appealing. Always I carry a note book and pen in the car or when I go down to my prayer chair or anywhere else in order to capture thoughts and poems. These are then absorbed later into my writing. But writing elsewhere cannot quite touch my soul like writing alone in this charming room. All my life there were obstacles to my aloneness and being able to write in privacy. Though I had a room of my own as a child and began my writing there, it was more a place of refuge from storms within my home, a place of temporary contentment, and I was always waiting for something to take away any peace I may have momentarily acquired. After marriage there was barely time for long periods of writing and many family members were always about. Distress and wounds to the soul and heart also eventually intruded upon my life at times and writing had to be done almost furtively or whenever there was not anything else I first had to attend to. Even the blue and white prayer room in Jenkintown came to me at a very difficult period in my life that I will share with you later, and so often it, too, like my childhood room, was a place of refuge and tears. To now have this deeply spiritual and child-like room in the woods is like the happy ending to a fairy tale.

Here is still yet another poem written in that era of when we returned to New Hampshire more and more often, four years before moving here permanently.

ON RETURNING TO THE WOODS

The birds are singing, chirping, shouting
All the wood is filled with song!
There is not once that I am doubting—
I am back where I belong!

Wildflowers grow beside our road—
Springing up 'round this abode.
No, do not call these flowers weeds!
Their delicate beauty feeds my needs!

Loons cry out their plaintive wail,
O, that sound can never fail—
To lift my spirit—help me shed
Fears and cobwebs in my head!

Take to the woods and you will know—
The sights and sounds that make one glow.

Breezes blow—lapping lake—
All snap my saging soul awake!

Dedicated to   JGK
the woods on
"Higher Ground"

    I understand now why our son George as a teenager always loved this room and spent many quiet hours in it reading or playing a creative game "Stratomatic" that related to his interest in sports. His sisters chose the back bedroom here and all crowded into it with numerous trundle beds for summer fun while vacationing here. George still loves to sleep in my writing room now with wife Valerie and little son Jameson, as do several of our daughters. You can only imagine its enchantment! It is night now as I finish sharing my writing room with you and we can hear the peepers singing their hearts out down in the cove of the lake out front. They just arrived last night at dusk, April 19, and now it is officially Spring here in the woods. One year we decided to record their incredible song. As Bob approached the shore of the lake the peepers gradually became silent until there was not a sound from them. After he placed the recorder on the shore and began to walk back, slowly one by one the peepers began to sing. As he arrived at the cottage they were again in full swing. It was remarkable and memorable and so funny and the tape recording turned out perfectly, titled *"An Hour of Peepers on Lake Balch."* The Peepers too have inspired poetry.

JEEPERS CREEPERS—
WHERE'D WE GET THOSE PEEPERS

Peepers, Peepers—Everywhere!
Their jam session's on the air.
Warm Spring evenings—twilight hours—
Peeper music then is ours.

Tonight's performance—titled no doubt—
"Singing In the Rain"—and they're all out—

With such enchanting song and sound—
Performing live on Higher Ground!

Walking close the better to hear—
Makes the tenors disappear—
Into the water—they're all air-borne!
The lake's like a pan of popping corn!

They've returned—they live to sing—
They jump and swing and have their fling!
Ah—such an evening concert here—
It's filling all the atmosphere!

Dedicated to all   JGK
the Peeper Frogs on Higher Ground
and to the memory of Kermit Gottlieb—
a little frog, from "Higher Ground"
our grandson Tim had for a year in Pa.

Here is this room my dream of writing forever is at last being fulfilled, and I am so grateful that at times it is truly inexpressible. I pray I may always help others through my writing just as I was helped all through my life by others' writings. Books and writing are inseparable and without either I could not survive. God speaks to us through the written word. I often find myself writing words and sentences I know did not come *from* me, but *through* me. When we sit and open ourselves to God and put pen to paper wondrous and mysterious things can happen.

Reflect and Journal

✏ Perhaps you can find or create a corner or area or a room in which to write in, where you can be alone to create.

✏ Make this writing place desirable so that it calls to you in your spirit when you are not near it.

✏ Make it a place you cannot pass by without entering even if only for a moment to greet it or say a little prayer.

✏ Perhaps keep a favorite pen there and your journal.

✏ Think about it. Plan such a place that will be conducive to your desiring to write, a place where the Angels await. A place or room of your own.

CHAPTER TWELVE

Altars

*"Sacred space is a physical place where the divine or the supernatural
can be glimpsed or experienced, where we get in touch with
that which is larger than ourselves."*

—Peg Streep

N A PAST CHAPTER I have spoken of a piece of furniture that I called my *"altar table"* and described the items that were upon it when we lived in Pennsylvania. As the years passed other religious pieces were added to it and the altar table itself was moved from our bedroom to my own personal prayer room as I have written. To have an altar table was extremely necessary to my spirituality and was conducive to prayer and meditation, and one has been a part of my life for the past twenty-eight years or more. I realize now there were other altars even before that and back to childhood, but I did not think of them as *"altars"* but as a place where my spirituality had a more intense focus.

In New Hampshire my altar is on my desk and has been for years. When the collection of significantly important pieces grew and were centered under a picture, with some expansion of the pieces spreading out to the right under the eaves, I realized in a moment of time an altar was upon my desk.

Though I had had other spiritual items before this on another smaller desk that had belonged to my son, and the desk sat at the same guest bedroom window (my writing room) overlooking the lake, it was not until some changes came into my life that I realized the true import of what I had created and that I had an altar here.

After I met Christ in July of 1992 and made the sketch of Him and framed it in an 8.5x11 peach frame and hung it above my desk, that was the beginning. My desk was too small then for writing my books and in 1994 Bob bought me a handsome blonde wood table with a butcher block top. It had been a kitchen table, but in my room it looks like the finest of desks, quite large and rather marvelous. Almost half of it sits in front of the window from which I enjoy the glorious view of the lake, woods, birds, gardens etc. and the rest of it extends under the gabled roof on my right. On the wall next to the window, a triangular piece of wall due to the slanting ceiling, is hung my picture of Christ along with a framed picture of Rochester, the calendar page from the Humane Society Calendar in which he appeared. There is also a white porcelain head of Mary with her delicate folded hands beneath her face, (a gift from our daughter Barbara), and a lovely artificial chickadee sitting upon the maple frame of Rochester's picture. There is a plaque of two tiny fawn also; the picture of Rochester, the bird, and the fawn all representing my deep love for God's creatures. Deer are known to be a symbol of Christ.

Directly below the framed pictures is a slim wooden statue of Christ in a pale orange robe that is simply a slightly darker shade than the picture frame holding the sketch of Christ.

The wooden figure of Christ is identical to one I gave my Mother following my Dad's death, except hers had on a light purple robe. She treasured it and after her death it became mine. Later, years later, when our son George married his lovely Valerie, I gave the statue to Valerie since it had been a love object of my Mothers and she and my Mother would never know each other here on earth. When I found later this peach robed Christ now on my desk in the same religious store, it became mine.

There is also a slim statue of an Angel (from Barbara), a glass deer (from my friend Rose-Beth) and an unusual statue I found of a Unicorn, with a little girl who appears to be no more than twelve. She is standing on the right side of the Unicorn in a long flowing blue and white dress and her left arm with the delicate long ruffled sleeve is extending over the Unicorn's back to his left side. Her face, framed in a ruffed collar and soft brown hair, is at the Unicorn's neck looking over to the left of the Unicorn also. The Unicorn is pale blue with golden horn, mane, tail and hooves. When I first saw this Unicorn and child I instantly felt in my spirit it was meant for me and had a message. I waited eleven months before I bought it in one of my favorite stores, the Ossipee Owl on Route 16 here in New Hampshire. It seemed extravagant for me to purchase and yet I checked on it from time to time hoping no one else had purchased it. Finally one day I walked in and bought it and it is meant to be here on this desk. I must still learn why. At times it seems I am to write a story about it and one has come to mind but I still hold back. I believe I will know eventually why I have it just as I knew the moment I was to purchase it. I think of the little girl as my *"inner child."* Unicorn like deer, are also believed to be a symbol of Christ.

Other objects on my desk inspire me also. Beneath the drawings of Christ and in front of the statues I have written about is a sweet tin box covered with pictures of beautiful cats. Its coloring and trim match the three statues beneath the drawing of Christ. In this tin box I place prayer requests and concerns and leave them there to be taken care of by Christ and the Angels.

Beneath my soft green and white lamp that matches my walls is a circle of stones. Each stone has meaning to me. Some are from our property, some gifts to me by friends who know I love rocks and stones, several are lovely Amethysts in the rough and two others are from Medjugorgie brought back to me from this Holy place. (I also carry rocks in my pocketbook and it has been lovingly suggested by loved ones they are also in my head.)

There are small pictures in frames on the far right of my desk containing photos of family members, Bob and me, and an Angel. There is a photo postcard framed of Ernest Hemingway, the writer who has brought inspiration to me, very especially when I began writing books. Too, there is a small box holding secrets with a white unicorn and flowers painted upon it and a small oval box protects a treasured Rosary. A little ceramic statue of a small child holding a *"lamb of God"* is in the palm of an upright hand and is symbolic of the *"child in the Lord's Hand,"* spoken of in Isaiah 49:16 KJV—*"Behold, I have graven thee upon the palms of my hands"*—A handsome small, round and chunky brass cat sits on my desk too, a gift from my friend Dottie shortly after Rochester came into my life. A framed picture of a woman writing at a desk with an Angel inspiring her from behind was a greeting card sent me by Janna with an attached angel pin. I framed the card and wear the pin. There are other objects also, but what I am trying to express is that I have small significant treasures upon my desk that are an extension of my centered Altar area that is beneath the drawing of Christ and the other meaningful pieces on the wall with Him that I have already described. My desk is so large none of these interferes with my writing area! It is an enormous writing area. The treasures are along the back and at the right end of the desk under the eaves like little guardians all at the edges. Each has meaning, each a personal "*find,*" or a gift from a friend, or a piece from the past. There are others too I have not mentioned.

I have been told by my spiritual friend Dan that my framed drawing of Christ is an Icon. It has been written by the Russian Orthodox Archbishop Anthony Bloom that an icon participates in "*the energies of Christ,*" and John Chrysostom in the early Church advises us to stand before an icon and close our eyes before starting to pray. In meditation I look *through* my Icon, not *at* it. An icon is a sign of God's presence and we are helped to pray by simply being in its presence. Each morning before I enter my writing room I genuflect out on the square landing at the top of the stairs and greet my Christ image as if I were greeting Christ Himself, with a "*good morning dear Christ*" or any loving greeting that comes to mind. As I leave my room each night I again genuflect and thank Him for all the help He has given to me in my writing and otherwise. I am not praying "*to*" the drawing of Christ but to *Christ Himself.* The drawing is "*symbolic*" only, as are any statues. There is never *worship* of statues, only to Christ Himself and gratitude and messages to my Angel images. I know that Angels are in my room with me and I have experienced them. The images of them are simply reminders. I greet them too as I enter and leave my room.

Often I kneel down before my Icon of Christ in reverence or to ask special help and guidance. The icon and the statues act as a revelation of the nature of the Divine and their Presence here. My animal figures act as symbols of strength and energy and symbolize guardianship. Animals are empowering to me. The natural world is filled with signs and symbols of the divine and are available to all to learn from.

> "*Sacred space, is a physical place where the divine or the supernatural can be glimpsed or experienced, where we can get in touch with that which is larger than ourselves.*"
>
> —Peg Streep from "*Altars Made Easy*"

My altar acknowledges the sacredness of the space my beloved Rochester and I inhabit daily. *"Altars do not make sacred space sacred; they work by showing us what has been there all along."* (Peg Streep) Altars can release energy within us and help us focus on things spiritual. Mine does this for me.

My altar was created gradually and this is usually the correct process. My altar is to reinforce my spiritual life and is present at and on my desk because writing consumes me and is an enormous part of my life. It is how I express myself and I ask God to bless my writing and inspire me. To have an Altar on my desk is most appropriate for me and it is a part of my writing life. I leave my finished writing for each day beneath the Icon of Christ and ask His blessings and to reveal to me anything that needs correction or change when I again return to my desk the next morning. That my altar is on my desk is intentional and it is meant to be not just part of my spiritual life but my entire life, and writing consumes my life.

As I have written in the previous chapter, I also have a long shelf above my front windows above my desk, filled with an Angel collection. It has a Crucifix centered above it with a Risen Christ upon it in victory. Beneath the cross is a ceramic figure resembling my little Rochester surrounded by Angels, and a glorious Angel in peach robes hangs

centered from beneath the shelf and floats in the lake breezes to the left of my desk. This shelf too is an altar I have learned through my reading and this is added blessing.

The altar shelf and Rochester

For me, altars are essential in my life and most certainly my writing life, which is essential to my soul. Perhaps creating an altar in your writing place would inspire you also in your writing. You can make any sort of altar that speaks to your own soul, your own spirituality. I have shared my Christian altars with you, but altars can be made to suit your own life's path of whatever inspires you in heart, soul and mind. I have seen so many unusual altars depicted in recent spiritual magazines, altars for all faiths and some centering on nature. They can be made anywhere in your home not only in your writing space or you can have more than one. For several years I had a small altar (or shrine) in the unused ash tray of my car. The lights in that inside area when lit at night were so lovely and I kept small statues of Jesus and Mary, a Cross, and an Irish bogwood rosary. This altar was created during the difficult 1980's I have written about later and since I spent a great deal of time praying in my car, this little sacred spot was comforting. The inner lighting around it made it seem far lovelier and enhanced the plastic figures. I always had my notebook and pen with me. My car was a chapel on wheels.

Your spirituality and your writing are companions, they go hand in hand. You discover more and more about yourself and your life and spirituality the more you write. Creating an altar is not necessary to your writing life but it definitely will enhance it and inspire it. It is comforting also to have symbols of the Divine present, but if you are not so inclined this can be substituted with photos of loved ones, (humans and animals), treasured objects of meaning, flowers, anything that speaks to your soul and causes you to focus and realize you are not alone. An altar gives incentive to your writing and is enlivening. For me, my beloved Rochester is also symbolic of the Divine, an angel in fur, and God-given breath

of life bestowed on me at a time when I needed both an Angel and an enlivening prod to begin my life of writing. My Angel often lies on my desk beneath the Icon of Christ and is breathtakingly beautiful, his presence a blessing on myself and my writing. A precious animal like Rochester with his love, warmth and affection, who loves to be near you and petted, is a Holy presence where God can meet you and heal you.

PURRING PAPERWEIGHT

What could be more beautiful than this—
Dear cat contemplating in silent bliss.
Upon my desk in unmoving pose.
So pure of heart—free of life's woes.

Profiled in window—backdrop of trees—
Wafting through screen—the gentle breeze—
Entices closing eyes to slowly raise
Upon blue lake in meditating gaze.

He nobly sits—so utterly trusting.
Because I love him—I am adjusting.
For on my papers he has been alighting—
Until he moves—I cease that writing.

I take my pencil and waste paper scrap—
And pen this poem on my lap.
Sweet honorable companion—eternal friend.
In your faithful presence—I choose to bend.

Dedicated to Rochester   JGK

All of outdoors here to me is additional inspiration for my writing, either seen from my windows at my desk or actually being outside. My prayer chair and the platform it resides on is like an altar where I offer myself daily and receive words from Him, and the birds and all the loveliness of lake and woods and prevailing breezes are around me. In each of my gardens are Angel figures and one garden too has an eighteen inch statue of St. Francis of Assisi with a dove in his left hand, a book in his right and a goose by his left foot. A small shrine.

All the glorious walls of rocks that surround my seven rock gardens are spiritual to me and the flowers of every variety. Trees are like tall altars reaching to the heavens vibrant with birds singing their songs, and squirrels and chipmunks chirping their own music in the only way they know how. All of this is so conducive to writing and in summer I do write often in my prayer chair, or on our screened in porch, or even on a special rock that is in the wooded hills behind our cottage. Our screened in porch is alive with the mystical sound of many wind chimes that combine with the ones on our front deck that transport angel music everywhere around us. Paperback books fill a row of shelves built by Bob that inwardly surround our screened in porch on three sides high above the screening. These too are a spiritual sight to me inspiring me to write. When I needed the book entitled *Germans* that I refer to in this book, I went right to the spot where it stood on that shelf. Books inspire other books to be written and surround me on the porch and every other room in our cottage. We cannot write unless we read daily. Any book shelf to me in our home is like an altar, books chosen and placed upon them by us and for us to read and reread and to beget writing and light up all of life. Some of our family staying here in summer also love to read our books.

THOUGHTS FOR FOOD

Books are other minds on earth—
I must search the shelves to find—
The ones that have the greater worth,
The books that best will feed my mind.

When I'm within a room of books
I seem to hear the silent voices.
They fill the crannies and the nooks—
Deep in my soul—and it rejoices.

I wait to feel that gentle prod—
Before selecting ones to read.
That soft impression comes from God—
For He knows best the books I need.

JGK

My kitchen window too has a shelf beneath it made by Bob at my request and holds plants and other objects. This shelf space is in the process of becoming a kitchen altar as I carefully select spiritual objects to me to be placed with the green Jade plants.

The two wooden adirondack chairs on the screened in porch were transported here from my former prayer room in Jenkintown to return to New Hampshire where Bob had had them made, just as he had the other two green ones made by the lake. To sit there on the porch and write in summer on what I call a "*rain forest day*," when showers lightly fall on our green trees and wooded hills and lake and flowers, is absolutely incredible. I can write my heart out out there. Rochester is there with me too, on my lap or on the wide arms of the adirondack or on the table near me, always increasing and generating love and thoughts that need to be put into writing.

GOLDEN PRESENCE

He walks on marshmallow paws of white—
Padding silently through our home.
His golden eyes glow day and night—
His very existence is a poem.

A metaphor—love on four feet—
Golden presence like sunshine.
Constant giving so complete—
Enlightening, gentle and divine.

With love for   JGK
Rochester

Please consider an altar of your very own creation to inspire, and to help you comprehend that your writing is sacred and worthy. Perhaps you will more fully realize through an altar's presence that your writing is a *divine* gift, a gift that only you can open up and bring forth into being. The Angels will be there with you.

Reflect and Journal

✏ Perhaps write in your journal ideas for an altar in your writing space or room.

✏ Begin to collect objects of meaning for your altar prayerfully.

✏ If you create an altar leave portions of your writing there overnight to be blessed.

✏ Perhaps take a picture of your altar after it is completed and carry it with you or keep in your car. Each time you glance at it it will draw you back to your place of writing or cause you to write in your car or wherever you may be.

✏ Consider your altar sacred.

✏ After creating your Altar say a prayer of blessing over it in your own words.

✏ Feel free to change or rotate objects you have placed on your altar. You may want to change it according to seasons or in other ways personal only to you.

CHAPTER THIRTEEN

Letter Writing and Tapes

"Practice 'spiritual writing,' whether in journals, poetry, or letters.
Writing out words gives them body, and then they speak to us
in an enchanted way. Writing letters and journal entries is not just
a way to communicate or to keep a record;
primarily it's a form of contemplation, while the act of writing gives body,
sensation, and beauty to our thoughts."

—Thomas Moore
from *The Re-Enchantment of Everyday Life*

AS OUR CHILDREN began to grow older I was able to do more letter writing. Many of the letters were to personal friends, many the wonderful friends we had made when Bob was in the Navy and now were scattered across the United States. Other letters were to permanent shut-ins and some to those who were ill for a period and then recovered. As the years passed a letter writing ministry developed to many in nursing homes and even to some people I did not ever meet.

Every day I wrote letters and also wrote in diaries or journals, but I was not always as faithful to the journals due to lack of time. A dream was to one day write not only letters but books too, but during these years with our children growing up my writing was centered on mail. Bringing joy and friendship to others through spiritually centered letters also temporarily fulfilled my need and longing to write "*much more.*" And so the letter writing I had loved to do since I was a child was now growing and at times out of control, for there was never enough time for all the wonderful things in our lives as a family. The letter writing was something I had to work in through the cracks of family time.

With all my heart I can truly say that letter writing is a worthy precious way to lighten and brighten other hearts. And through the years blessings have returned to me over and over a thousand fold because in learning what a letter or card meant to an individual, I was blessed also by the often amazing words in reply. Most shut-ins never answered my letters and I never expected them to reply, and a large number of them were too ill to do so. This type of letter writing brings a special joy to the writer. To do something for love only and no returns is like a touch from an Angel.

Time, passing time and much writing, has allowed me to experience endless circumstances connected with the enchantment of writing letters. When I say "*letters*", I mean letters from the heart. These type letters give you license to use any writing implements you prefer, any writing paper or any style writing you wish. You are the author each time of an original work and many of these "*originals*" are lovingly kept forever by the recipients. They are reread, treasured, and often stored in special places. This I know to be true because I have been told so again and again and also have been the recipient of many such letters. Soon we will have to build another cottage nearby in the woods just for storing dear letters I have received and for the growing amount of books I continue to purchase over the years. It is true!

Recently in the bulletin of St. Anthony's Church in Sanbornville, New Hampshire was a very significant little paragraph tucked in between other notices. Father Edmund (Babicz) often puts unusual things in our bulletins and I felt this message most significant and hoped many would read it. I saved this message to include here.

THANK YOU

Gracias, Merci, Danke—in any language this phrase is a powerful motivator. Teach your children to write thank-you notes for every single gift they receive. Teach them by doing it yourself. The social art of writing our thanks seems to be falling by the wayside, causing a whole generation of youngsters to grow up thinking they have those gifts coming and that a proper, well-thought-out "thank you" isn't necessary. It is! Thank you isn't something we just teach our two-year olds to say after the nice lady gives them a popsicle. "Thank you" is something we say to everyone for everything all our lives. And when we've received an actual gift, even it it's as intangible as a weekend at Grandma's house, we need to say "thank you' and write "thank you."

Thank you Father Edmund!

During the 1970s for eight years we also had a spiritual tape ministry operating in our home. It was begun by Bob and me in our Methodist Church to record the inspiring sermons each Sunday of our two Pastors. We then made duplicates of the recording at home and I distributed them to shut-ins with brief visits. What began as a simple operation grew out of control and soon it was controlling a great portion of my life. Through word of mouth and many other channels the tape ministry spread all over the United States! Instead of two tape recorders copying a Sunday sermon we now had a row of tape recorders set up by Bob in our front closet so as to make as many duplicates at once as possible. I also recorded other spiritual messages. For eight years I spent hours each day in this tiny front hall closet under our living room steps. Often I would set up a row of tapes for duplication and then run to the kitchen to start dinner. If I would hear one of the recorders click I would go racing through the dining room to the living room closet to make sure all the tapes ended at once. If they did not it was a great deal of trouble for me.

Janna and her friend, Eileen

The synchronization was important! My daughters used to enjoy imitating my race from the kitchen to the closet and I have to admit *"their duplication"* was hilarious.

Also my little daughter Janna and her friend Eileen used to stand outside the narrow window of my tape closet and watch me. I felt like I was on display. Or they would rap at the window and ask when I would be done so I could come out and play. Though I loved doing this inspirational work I often felt like a prisoner in this small closet. At times daily it was also my "*prayer closet*" which was spiritually magic.

One humorous aside we will all remember is the night one of our older daughters was going on a date with a new friend. Because I had constant orders to fill I was in the tape closet when Laurel's date arrived. When I came out to greet this new friend my family was trying to stifle laughter imagining what this boy was thinking of a Mother being stowed away in a closet. I arrived last on the scene and most likely he did not expect my entrance through this small door.

But in this hideaway surrounded by shelves of cassette tapes, brown mailers, pens, a notebook and a poster of "*The Monks of Weston Priory*" (an inspirational group in Vermont who sing haunting songs) hanging on a slanted wall (the underside of our living room stairs) above my row of tape players on an old kitchen table cut by Bob to fit under the slant, I was filled with spiritual joy. I did not have to listen constantly to the tapes I was recording but listened most of the time. To be confined in a small closet with glorious music and uplifting thoughts was an incredible blessing. The volume could also be raised so that I could listen as I did work in the house near the closet. These were unusual years and this ministry fed my own soul and areas of my life that needed God's touch and healing.

On several occasions I was invited to give a talk about our tape ministry to church groups both Protestant and Catholic who were interested in perhaps beginning their own tape ministries. The message was always well received. After giving a loving message about the outreach and benefit of tapes to my charismatic Prayer Group I was then asked to be in charge of the tape ministry there also, and served in that way until I left in 1980.

One very joyful thing I practiced in my tiny tape closet was "*ecumenism.*" I would deliberately send tapes with Protestant speakers to the Catholics and Catholic speakers to Protestants. Not constantly but quite often, and every person in my very large tape ministry received such tapes. Never was there a complaint, but often there were requests for more cassettes of a certain speaker or clergy person of a different faith. It was exciting! These people may never in their lives have heard a person preach of another religion until these tapes. It opened hearts and doors!

I considered myself a Methodist Catholic. There are treasures in both faiths.

But what was just as important as the tapes I duplicated were the letters that accompanied each order I filled sent in a brown mailer. The letters were necessary for many reasons in regard to the tapes, but mainly they were to uplift each recipient. The majority of these recipients were people who could not get out to church. They depended on both the tapes and letters as a hungry person waits for a meal. They were so appreciative, and in return letters came telling me of how certain messages touched individual souls. In that period of my life letters in tape bags went out six days a week, so very many each day, for eight years. They waited for the handwritten letters more than the tapes and I felt connected to so many people out there that I never met or ever will. But we felt as if we knew each other because of the power and blessing of letters. The cassette tapes sent alone could not have connected us in this deep way. That I was able to also be a wife and mother with great love during those years is amazing. Bob and I were also deeply involved then in a healing ministry through the Methodist Church. It was a period we will never forget. Many of these cassette tapes were also made for the local people who were receiving prayer through this healing ministry.

By December 13th, 1978 as I have written about previously, I had also been received into the Catholic Church and I grew more and more silent in prayer. Remaining in my back pew after Mass was over to pray alone for a half hour or more for many years—this was what my soul desired. Gradually as the many tape players in my closet became worn and broken, Bob decided not to repair them and the ministry gradually came to a close. It was time for it to end for both of us. *("To Everything There Is A Season")*

Cassette tapes were a marvelous vehicle for sending hope and healing. A person could close his/her eyes and feel present in the church to the speaker of the sermon, or be transported to a glorious and huge charismatic prayer meeting in Atlantic City, New Jersey (We attended these for four years) in Convention Hall, or elsewhere, and feel the presence of the Holy Spirit through words and overwhelming music of prayer and praise. There is not enough good that can be said about the healing brought to so many through the listening of cassette tapes, myself included.

In a sense they could be called "*audio letters,*" especially for the blind, and several blind people were on my mailing list. But for me, they were never a replacement for a letter. Even to the blind persons I wrote personal letters when sending the tapes and some loved one always read them to the receiver. I often would receive letters from these people who were helping their blind loved ones saying how much the letters meant, and that because they were blind I did not deny them a letter. Combined with the cassettes they were blessed.

Cassette tapes of another sort however, have been extremely meaningful to me more in the last ten to fifteen years, but only at certain times, those of soft ethereal music that seem to transcend explanation but transport one to other realms to God and the angels. Living more and more in the woods changed me and I no longer attended the charismatic prayer meetings or listened to the sermon tapes. I found Him here in all of nature and in the stillness where the only music I write to is bird song, chirping squirrels and the rhythmic cawing of the crows, and the song of the Blue Jays. In the seasons when the lake is not frozen the lapping water is a song—and always the wind through the trees. This all surpasses recorded music for me. To write at my desk with nature's music and the purring of my sweet Rochester is both inspiration and pure healing. I feel so blessed!

While I know cassette tapes are marvelous in so many categories now, not only spiritual, my heart still goes out to the written word through letters. When cassettes have long since become tangled and broken or crisp and brittle through age and unexpectedly snap, letters remain through the years. They are always there to be savored, treasured and read whenever the heart desires. Cassettes were spiritual food in my life for eight years and in the lives of the many, many people I made cassettes for in my tape ministry in my prayer closet, but letters have fed my soul since I was a little girl—both the writing and receiving of them— and they always shall. There is nothing like writing.

A LETTER

An envelope—filled with caring,
a loving letter, baring
and bearing the soul of the writer—
Helps another soul become lighter—
made whole again—
by paper and pen.

JGK

Reflect and Journal

✏ Try to visit a stationery store or any store that sells stationery supplies. (a 5 and 10, a Wal-Mart, K-Mart etc.)

✏ Treat yourself to a special inexpensive pen that appeals to you, or several, perhaps in different colored inks.

✏ Select some paper that touches you. Note paper, writing paper, lined tablet paper, anything you personally like.

✏ Keep your new purchases in a separate box or drawer so that you will always find them.

✏ Pray and ask to be led to write a letter to someone, or if you already have a person in mind write to that one.

✏ Be open to writing to others too as time passes, and replenish your paper and pen supply as needed.

✏ Write what you did in your journal.

CHAPTER FOURTEEN

The Joy of Letter Writing, Rochester and Angels

"What release to write so that one forgets oneself, forgets one's companion, forgets where one is or what one is going to do next. Pencils and pads and curling blue sheets alive with letters heap up on the desk"

—Anne Morrow Lindbergh

THERE IS SO MUCH MORE that can be said about letters, and letter writing is so precious and important to me I want to just share more of my thoughts with you about personal letters. Letters are really like intimate conversations between loved ones and friends. In a letter you often open yourself up to the recipient in a way that you might not if you were speaking face to face. Letters have souls! Many become priceless to their owners. They are impossible to discard because of this Holiness about them. I would sooner throw *myself* in a fire than destroy Bob's letters to me in this way. I cherish other letters from close friends sent through the years. They are like living missals and too become a form of autobiography.

One outstanding published volume of letters I enjoy is a collection of author Ernest Hemingway's personal letters to his friends given to me years ago by my daughter Jessica. It gave me insights I have treasured. This man was constantly writing to his friends no matter where he was and no matter how involved he was in his writing of books. These letters were filled with greetings and invitations like *"Come on up!"* or *"Come on down"* depending on where he was at the time. To receive a letter from him was a gift and a joy! He gave himself to his friends through personal letters. He had a loving and generous soul and poured himself out in these letters to keep connected with those in his life who mattered to him. He also loved cats and those cats closest to him were all about when he was writing. But he also had a huge tower built on his property just for his many cats to play and sleep in and fully enjoy. Rochester and I have known about this for many years and appreciated this caring and love by Hemingway. The tower he provided still stands and ancestors of his cats still live there today at his residence. Occasionally one is permitted to be adopted.

Some people never write letters. They say they cannot or they do not want to and thereby cut themselves off from a joy that can barely be explained. They are happy to receive them but never have time to answer or simply will not. Some cannot reply due to physical limitations and I have touched on this in the previous chapter. There are many published volumes of letters by authors and other well known people. Several others beside Hemingway's that speak to me are the books of letters and journal entries by Anne Morrow Lindbergh. These are *"Hour of Gold, Hour of Lead 1929-1932* and *Bring Me a Unicorn 1922-1928.* Both are published by Harcourt Brace Jovanorish, New York. There are others of hers also available.

But letters are so magical and often they connect us to people we might never have met. Meeting someone through letter writing only is very real and often sufficient. It has been the basis for pen pal letters for many, and too for myself when I was a child. For years I exchanged letters with two little girls, one in England and the other in Mexico. I have a friend similar to this now though she is not a pen pal but a friend in Pennsylvania and in Spirit. We have corresponded for perhaps eight years or more, sharing our writing, family, animals, books and other interests. I am grateful to her for she was responsible for having put my second book, *Higher Ground*, into the chain of Encore Book Stores due to her position at that time with that company. Because of the content of my book, she wrote to me and thus began our friendship. It is interesting and lovely and more real than some face to face relationships because in letters one reveals their soul if they trust the recipient. We have never met or talked yet we share deep concerns. We have this mutual trust, Jeanne and I, and we are two writers who enjoy writing. Recently her beloved orange and white cat Tasha passed away and I was overwhelmed by this and understood Jeanne's grief. This dear little cat had been written about often in Jeanne's letters, and Tasha's picture is in my writing room. My friend Janis and I are also close friends in Spirit, even with the same name but different spelling, who communicate through letter writing and have never met but feel total trust. She lives in rural Michigan and our mutual and deep love of animals and our spirituality have been our living and loving connection. She calls me her "*sister*" and I am honored. I too feel this for her. Knowing her has enriched me. Her letters are long and wonderful filled with her life and our mutual interest of animals and faith. Letters are like angelic cords binding people soul to soul, heart to heart. Janis and I have written things to each other that just we could understand. We are so alike in many ways yet connected only by written letters and prayer—and only several phone calls through the years.

Craig is a friend whom I cam to know through a tragedy that occurred in his life. He has been such an example of courage to me as he endured and rose up and conquered this terrible thing. A young man from my former hometown had an accident here in New Hampshire, and thus began our exchange of letters these many years. We have never met, yet have a rich friendship through writing. He has helped me in ways he cannot realize through his endurance, bravery, and his written words.

I too have been blessed by sharing correspondence with two friends I have never met at Blue Dolphin Publishing, Chris and Jill, who do so much in preparing my books to go out into the world. I am so indebted to them for this. But we have discovered we share similar interests in areas other than books, and corresponding with them has also taught me about things in life that I have not experienced. These letters are saved to be often reread and appreciated anew.

Letters are enchanting! Letters are a gift! You can write to a friend and the letter can be kept to open at a time that is best for the receiver. Unlike a telephone call it is never an interruption. You choose when to open your letters. They are a treat and meant to be savored, and saving them until the right moment achieves this. Often in summer and other lovely weather I take my letters down to my prayer chair by the lake to read. In winter I often read them quietly in our living room with Bob while he reads his mail as we take a short break from our work to be together. But more than often I read them in my prayer chair here in my writing room. Always first I make a cup of tea or International French Vanilla coffee or cocoa to enjoy with the letters. After reading my letters I return to my writing at my desk here in my writing room. Letters are visits from friends and deserve respect and time to be read and received properly. I never just rip open a letter and read it and go on. It took some one time to write it and I give special time to read it. It is so nice to be with the friend who *visited*. One gives of oneself often in a letter more than is done in person. Yes, letters deserve respect and appreciation. Rochester shares letter reading with me when done in our cottage adding even more joy.

When you describe specific moments or surroundings in a letter it is almost like sending your friend a photograph if you do it in detail. And of course, it is thoughtful to enclose photographs of anything that might bless your friend in some way. I love sending pictures of the lake, gardens, woods, sweet Rochester, and glorious sunsets over the water. And I love to be blessed and receive photos too, and give them respect.

Poet Emily Dickinson knew the beauty of receiving letters and writes:

> The way I read a letter's this:
> [and she reminds me of myself on days that I take my mail up to my writing room when she continues:]
> And I go the furthest off
> To counteract a knock;
> Then draw my little letter forth
> And softly pick its lock.

This too expresses my deep appreciation for the thoughtful personal letters I receive daily. We are all meant to be living letters to the world.

I have had several very favorite movies in my life, one of which I will speak of in my chapter on poetry. Another is one I will mention now for it was so precious in friendship and in letter writing. In "84 *Charing Cross Road*" starring Anne Bancroft and Anthony Hopkins, an exchange of letters brings these two very close in heart. Helene, (Anne Bancroft) a writer in New York, orders out-of-print books from a London bookstore. One of the employees takes a special interest in her, Frank, (Anthony Hopkins) and loves her witty and charming orders and an exchange of letters begins that spans twenty years. They never meet yet are deep soul friends. The letters are read aloud in the film and we enter into this very moving exchange and their relationship. This film expresses the deep meaning that letters can have in peoples' lives. Perhaps if you have not seen this you can rent this to enjoy. Helene Hanff, the woman depicted in the movie has written three books you might like, one being *84 Charing Cross Road*, of course. The others are: *Q's Legacy* and *The Duchess of Bloomsbury Street*. The first and last are published by Avon Publishing and the second is by Penguin. Helene lived in Philadelphia as did Bob and I and she also attended Temple University briefly—as did we, though our stay was not brief.

It would seem that tea and letter reading or writing often go together. (or any beverage you might prefer.) I have often sent a tea bag in a letter so that the recipient can have a cup of tea *"on me"* while reading, and perhaps it will make us seem even closer in distance. I often send *"Constant Comment."* It seems appropriate. I too, have often suggested to friends who are sad or feeling lonely (although this is a lovely thing to do any time! You do not need a reason), to invite an Angel to tea. Set the table for two and put out pretty cups and saucers and light a candle in the middle of the table. Sit down quietly, and in prayer or any way you wish invite an Angel to join you. Believe that the Angel is there, for your Angel is. Your Guardian Angel never leaves you. Often you will see the candle flicker unnaturally at the moment you request the Angel to join you at the table, and also when you finish your tea. It does not matter the other tea is not gone. It has been appreciated in Spirit. While you are sharing this time with your Angel reveal your heart and any problems. You will feel comforted. It is a precious thing to invite an Angel to tea. It can be done whenever your heart needs this. After the tea is over write down in your journal all you felt in your soul and the consolations you received. Writing about the experience will comfort you at future times and take doubt from you that the Angel was there. We are told in scripture we each have a Guardian Angel. Believe your angel is there with you at tea. Then share the experience with a friend in a letter who too may need to have tea with an Angel. Moments like this are meant to be *"given"* to others through writing just as I have written of this to you. We all need realization of Angelic presence and we all need letters. To me letter writing is also a form of prayer. I believe to *receive* a letter is also prayer. Letters can be like angels!

It had been my custom for many years and long before I became Catholic, to actually make the sign of the cross with my pen on the top of each piece of paper I write on in a letter. (Or on anything I write, journals, brief notes etc.) It is asking a blessing on my words and on the recipient and is a reminder of God's presence. A cross is on the top of this page of this manuscript as I write as it is on all the pages—and on all written pages of all my previous manuscripts. I was moved years later after beginning this practice to read in a journal by a man who has inspired me in faith for twenty-five years or more that he too made the sign of the cross on all that he wrote. It was just another deep connection in Spirit to this marvelous Trappist Monk, Thomas Merton, who was received into the Novitiate of the Trappist Order on the same date December 13th as I was received into the Catholic Church though I in 1978 and he years before me in 1941. Other significant occurrences in December fell on the tenth for Merton. He marked his entrance through the doors of the Abbey of Gethsemane on December 10, 1941 and that of his sad and untimely death on a December 10 in 1968. The month of December held so many significant events for him and was another synchronicity connection. Both Bob and I have December birthdays as does my Mother. This deeply spiritual man was not only a journal keeper (those of his journals in print have such meaning to me), but a prolific writer of personal letters and of books. He has had a deep affect on my spiritual life. I have spoken of him frequently in my book *Higher Ground.* He too had a tenderness for animals, advocating in general non-violence for all!

Author and Priest Edward Hays feels letter writing is prayer also. He has suggested we breathe part of our spirit into the envelope, more than just a puff. He believes we send along with our message then, a part of our soul. He believes as I do, that rituals or signs help us to remember we are sending love to the recipients (from *Spiritual Literacy: Reading the Sacred into Everyday Life* by Frederic and Mary Ann Brussat, Scribner).

Neither my own Dad or my Father-in-law were letter writers. My Dad loved to read but rarely wrote. For years he was a draftsman and sat at a board writing and drawing all day therefore I suppose he did not like to write in his time at home. He seemed to be ashamed of his handwriting yet I thought it very unique, tiny and precise, so he usually printed. And that was very small and neat. I have no letters from him as keepsakes but I do have several dear greeting cards he sent to me as a young child and girl, alone, without my Mother's signature. In them were brief, sweet little remarks (he could be very witty) and expressions of love aside from his signature. That he took the time to shop for cards for me always touched me and he did for my Mother too.

My Father-in-law did not enjoy reading or writing due to absorption in his work as a stock broker, but we are grateful we do have two loving letters he wrote telling us his love (the best part), and thanking us for something we had given him and done earlier in our marriage. Because neither of our fathers were men of letters (or pens) we are appreciative to have these small tokens and keepsakes. All the more reason then that it is so important to write, to write for yourself and to connect with others. You may have to force yourself at first but in time you will discover its rewards. If you are ashamed of your penmanship, change it! If you practiced writing slowly, in time it would look better and you would be happy with yourself. Sloppy handwriting is no excuse for not writing! You have caused that perhaps in your hurry and disinterest in writing anything at length. It would be fun to create a *"new written you"* and you would feel so good about it. Never let poor penmanship stop you from writing! If you are not willing to try to change then just write anyway. It is for *your* soul! If you are touched by writing after making an attempt, your new spirit about it will be conveyed in the words you write in a letter to others and the handwriting will be less significant. But write! Do not deny yourself this spiritual joy and practice! (in any form!)

I always taught our six children to write thank you letters upon receiving gifts and almost every January gave them new diaries in the hope they would use them. Their letters were sweet and as a result they

My Dad and tiny daughter Janna

wrote other types of letters too. Not long after my sixth child was born I became involved in a healing ministry at our Methodist church that began through the healing of our next to youngest daughter Jessica when Bob and I *"laid hands"* on her in prayer. I have written of this earlier. I spent a great deal of time visiting people to pray with them for healing and brought my little Janna along for I had no baby sitter. At four years she was *"laying hands"* on people with me and saying prayers for them. It was so precious.

But at home she wanted to write to the sick people she prayed with so she would dictate to me what she wanted to say and I would print it out on a separate paper. She would then spend long periods copying what I wrote down from her own words into sweet note cards to send to those she met and visited. The words were so simple she chose, like *"Praise the Lord"* and *"God Bless You"* and *"Jesus Loves You."* I remember well some cute caterpillar note cards she used with pale green envelopes. The people were so moved by these notes from a tiny child (and she is still tiny but big in heart). She was filled with the Holy Spirit and loved to write these notes!

Not all our children kept their diaries but each one always had some days filled, or several months, then that was all. But it did not matter because I was trying to encourage them to write. Now they have these diaries of their growing up years as small treasures.

I still give each of our grown children a journal as a gift for this reason because I feel if they use it it will be a gift to themselves. My daughter June often gives me beautiful writing and note paper filled with Angels because she knows my love for Angels and paper. Also an entire box of Angel greeting cards were a surprise from her. And in mentioning greeting cards it is always lovely to write and add a personal message in a greeting card along with your name and not just let the greeting card company print your sentiments. One of my favorite gifts to give daughters June and Valerie, is a big picture tin filled with a variety of greeting cards for every occasion from the Renaissance Card Company in Springvale, Maine. This is a place I visit every two weeks or so and once I enter it is difficult to leave. The cards are very beautiful and unusual and I keep a large supply here in our cottage because I send so many cards, and due to winter weather cannot always get out of the woods or off our property. When I can, then, I have cards to mail even if they were made late by snow. But cards are meant to have personal messages written in them, they are really mini-letters, and a lot of love and sentiment from your own heart and hand can be written in them.

I want to tell you about my Rochester who has been a letter writer for many years. Because of my letter-writing ministry and in my attempts to send healing and encouragement to others, I began at times to send cards and notes with Rochester's name signed to them, instead of my own. I did this when a friend or acquaintance was ill for an extended period and confined to a longer recovery. Since I almost daily sent cards and messages, to lighten hearts and bring in a small change from the more serious topics, I would often send instead a card with note inside from Rochester. (with his approval, of course) He was always respectful in addressing my friends and would never call them by their first names. Sometime he might write, *"Dear Aunt Ruth,"* or *"Friar Francis,"* or *"Mister Ed"* or *"Dear Mistress Charlotte."* Soon his personality became more real to the recipients and he would share little personal tidbits about his life in the notes. Also I would continuously share about him with my friends.

Rochester near our desk (his and mine) and intercom where he "writes" a lot of his letters

Over the years of his precious life he has warmed and changed some hearts, and also some human views toward animals. I have spoken of all of this in my book *Compassion For All Creatures*, but it continues still to this day. One tender moment I have never forgotten. One of Rochester's beloved pen pals was *"Mister Ed"* and during frequent times of confinement in hospital or home, Rochester would write him or send tiny remembrances to make him smile. When he was well, my friend *"Mister Ed"* came to me in church at daily Mass in Jenkintown, Pennsylvania, one day and smilingly said, *"Will you thank my friend Rochester for me? And I have never even shaken paws with him!"*

Rochester continues to send cards and notes. In earlier years I felt I knew what he might like to say because we were so close, but now I *know* what he likes me to write because of our spiritual communication. Perhaps I was truly sensing it back then also. He has told me that I was.

The beauty of a letter is that you can write it anywhere and anytime of the day or night. You can write it on lovely paper or anything you choose. But write! Many of my letters through the years have been written late at night with Bob and Rochester sleeping there as I write. I write anywhere! But mainly I love writing at my big desk in my writing room as I look out at the lake and Rochester is with me.

Wherever I go (even in this small cottage) I have a steno pad with me and green ink pen. I am like my own private secretary! This is for sudden bursts of inspiration in poetry, notes to myself, and even an instant letter, especially if writing late at night in bed. I buy these steno pads in packages! But I always cut off the frazzled paper at the top after removing the written letter pages from the pad if I have written a letter. I have dozens of these pads filled with such private notes that I have to keep them all as I do my journals. I have several filled spiral steno note books just with notes in regarding things I want to write in this very book. Those jottings are there with everything else I put into these note books. I cannot be without one! It goes in the car with me also. Some of my finest note taking and letters have been in these books.

Postcards

Postcards are mini-letters and wonderful too. Granted, you cannot write as much but if you write small, lovely sentiments can be sent when you do not have the time to write a longer letter. You can buy post cards depicting the city or state you live in, or use ones you brought home from a vacation, or buy them with pictures on in any card shop. Or you can buy the regulation ones without pictures at the Post Office but they are not as colorful and fun. If you carry some with you stamped you can always drop a brief note to a friend if you are taking a break somewhere over coffee or tea. If you think about it, anytime, anyplace, you can dash off a note to a friend if you keep such cards with you, or small stamped note cards in your glove compartment or pocket or purse. Besides it is fun, and you often bring in the atmosphere of where you are writing, and the friend can enjoy that. Writing *is* fun!

And speaking of postcards you can make your own! This is something I have been doing for years, and my friends Ginny and Clara have been generous in giving me their old greeting cards for almost as long as I have been doing it. Ginny also gives me other sorts of paper and note cards too. Every once in a while a carton arrives from New Jersey! I love it! Ginny has felt a part of this ministry and I tell her the cards go out to the people from her also. I have told many shut-ins I send to about Ginny and Clara. To make a postcard from any greeting card simply remove the front of the card you like and draw a line down the middle of the blank side of it. Some cards you select to use for this often have writing on back. (This is thoughtful—someone wrote a note in a card—and just as I had suggested doing in this very chapter!) Surely though there is enough blank sided ones to choose from in your older cards. Instead of throwing them out create postcards that can be sent to shut-ins and anyone you wish. I began doing this for shut-ins and for the people I visited in nursing homes, but now I use them for quick notes to friends also. And many of my friends began to do it too. Marcella, "Mr. Ed's" wife and my good friend, creates wonderful postcards continuously. I receive them almost weekly. (Letters too!)

If the card is large you may have to put first class postage on it. Many of mine are that I use. But if you keep them a bit smaller you need less postage. (postcard rate)

There is sufficient space to write on, and if you divide the back unevenly giving a small section to the address, you have more room for the personal message. You will enjoy it! I am sure once you have read this you will view your greeting cards in a new way and maybe begin to recycle ones that you feel you can part with. (the world's worst *"saver of things"* is writing this!) Try it!

There is another fine use for postcards that will inspire you to write. As a child I saved postcards and had this collection up until I married. Once I left home, however, I never found this collection when I returned. I had wonderful imaginative play, and later inspirations from my collection for writing.

In recent years I have another collection of both real postcards and the ones I create from greeting cards. I just enjoy keeping them and they are used for responding to them in writing for myself. Just a glance at one can trigger a thought. Pretend you are looking through a doorway at the picture!

It is good to create a collection of them and when stuck in your creative writing, use one to get you started writing a poem or short story or anything you wish. Perhaps see yourself in the picture and then begin to write. After going through the collection over a long period, begin anew, for you will see new things in each picture. If you treat them with respect they will help you and they will be meaningful to you. Keep them in a pretty box (I do), or tie a lovely ribbon around them, or keep them in a wallet-like container or small bag. Whatever draws you to use them.

This is a poem I was inspired to write about an usually mystical painting our daughter Barbara created for us. However, I then apply what I wrote in the poem when viewing exceptional post cards I have collected of paintings.

ENTERING IN

When one looks at a painting—and has dared
To let his soul be bared
And by imagination steps across the frame—
The very threshold—to lay claim
To the scene once witnessed from beyond—
And now is within—creating a bond
And surrounded by all that is there—
Emotions, texture, and in mystical moments rare—
Is wandering through the landscape, the hues,
The findings—to sense the views

Of the artist; then that is letting go—
Abandoning oneself to the flow—
Of the magic—to mysteries and surprise.
And one will never again see only with the eyes.

JGK

That experience has caused me to imagine stepping into postcard pictures frequently, and also into larger art work including paintings in our cottage. It opens the door for free flow imaginative writing. Perhaps you will be enticed to try this.

In Summary of Letters

There is so much to write about letters and I am realizing now I could write an entire book on this subject. It is difficult to try to summarize and slow down in sharing. I will just add that whenever you write a letter it is a precious thing and you are sending an essence of yourself. It is especially lovely to write when alone, and somehow you write things you may not have written in a crowded place or even if with only a few nearby. It is comforting to think about the people you are writing to and see their faces and remember enjoyments you shared. Your letter will reflect the way you are thinking and feeling.

In recent years since travelling back and forth to New Hampshire continuously, and then moving here, I received many more letters than usual. These were from my "Muffin" friends from daily Mass at Immaculate Conception Church in Jenkintown, Pennsylvania. Since I do not attend Mass with them any longer or have breakfast with them in a little nearby shop, many write faithfully to me and I write to them. I treasure these letters and wish to thank these precious friends here and now in this chapter. Thank you, dearest Muffins.

And I wish to thank every friend who continues to correspond with me through the years. You know who you are and how I appreciate you. I wish to thank all the fine animals that have also sent me cards or notes. Photos too!

In writing a letter you reveal the vulnerability of your soul and that is what makes letters priceless and precious. I feel, in a sense, I am writing a letter here expressing the beauty and joy of letter writing to you. Perhaps you will receive it in that way believing that it is meant for you alone. In turn, maybe you will write and give of yourself in a letter to another.

Reflect and Journal

✏ Try to learn to truly appreciate personal letters sent to you if in the past you took them for granted.

✏ Slowly begin a small collection of writing materials that appeal to you so that you will be more apt to write letters and answer those you receive.

✏ Perhaps read the book mentioned in this chapter by Helene Hanff— "*84 Charing Cross Road*". Also rent the movie of same and see the joy and spiritual connection letter writing brings into lives.

✏ Perhaps you will see postcards in a new light and want to save some that speak to your heart to possibly use as inspiration for your writing in the future.

✏ Consider inviting an Angel to tea and record it in your journal.

CHAPTER FIFTEEN

Delightful Accessories for Letter Writing

*"Having a place and a variety of paper, cards, postcards, envelopes, stamps,
sealing wax and writing paraphernalia all symbiotically encourage
the act of putting a pen to a sheet of blank paper and
beginning 'Dear' or 'Dearest' or 'My Dear.'"*
—Alexanra Stoddard from *"Gift of a Letter"*

ACCESSORIES AND SUPPLIES for letter writing are easy and fun to keep on hand. If you do not keep these things available you will put off writing. Each person has their own tastes in cards and letter paper and pens and I will not try to persuade you. But suppose I share with you some of the things I have used and do use now, and perhaps that could possibly give you ideas for some supplies to keep ready if you have not been inclined to do so before. I am a bit of a nut (well, not just in this area) because I love everything that has to do with writing, therefore I am not very conventional. Because I have always written a lot of letters I know it helps if you make it fun and a pleasure to do. If you only have one kind of plain writing paper and one pen you are going to rebel against corresponding! That is boring!

When I was a child I used tablet paper to write on and pencils or a fountain pen. In my late teens I had gotten various kinds of writing paper but still enjoyed tablets also and liked the Big Chief writing tablets for letters as well as for other writing. Just about that time ball point pens came on the scene and I began to use these at once. Wonderful! As the years have passed I have used everything imaginable for letter writing. During the late seventies and into the eighties large legal pads were my favorite for long letters. Most of my letters were very long. At first only yellow lined legal pads were in stores but gradually these pads were made in many pastel colors. These pads made writing fun! There were also miniature legal pads, miniature (5x7) in contrast to the very large ones. These too are available in pastels. My friend Rose-Beth writes me her precious letters on such pads and has for thirteen years! Occasionally I use normal writing paper given to me or that I bought for shorter letters and thank you notes. In the past years and present, for shorter writing I also love the beautiful animal note cards sent to us from animal groups because of contributions given to these groups who help to save and rescue dear animals. I am so proud to use these and the photographs and art work of God's creatures touch my heart.

In recent years Bob has been creating exceptional writing paper for me and it inspires me to write and write. He uses the large 8.5x11 paper used for computers. With his computer he has produced such excellent designs pleasing to my soul! All are of scenes in nature or animals and all with my name and address at the top. (sometimes actually with the scene) But often he puts the design smack in the middle of the page because I am so *"far out"* and love this! Otherwise it is in one of the lower corners or at top., He has also produced the cover of my book *Compassion for All Creatures* onto writing paper, and too, a large tree that grows up the left side of some of my sheets; two favorites! Just this past week with his new color printer he has been able to make me the loveliest new designs; real photos of deer, birds and other wildlife. All these designs mentioned are the most magnificent he has ever created for me and the finest and most appealing paper to me I have ever had. I will be using them forever!

My choice of pens has changed from those mentioned I used as a child and teenager. Through the years many pens and many colors of ink appealed to me for letters and my journals. For a ten year period or so I used only a "Blessed Mother Blue" T-ball Jotter Parker pen with "Blessed Mother Blue" refills (My own caption for that shade blue.) I have written about this pen also in my chapter on Journal Keeping. This pen meant so much to me it seems I must have made reference to it a lot while writing and was a bit obnoxious about it as I look back. And so my daughter Barbara used to do wonderful exaggerated imitations of me doing my *"commercials"* for this pen. It was not easy being viewed as eccentric in a household with six children. They enjoyed overemphasizing my quirks (quirks only to them—I felt normal). I eventually stopped using my Parker pen because I learned the company that makes them, Gillette, tests on animals and this is against my beliefs. I could never use it again (or any Gillette products)and disposed of it.

Pens too have been special gifts to me from a number of my children. June has given me a Cross pen in the past and also a wonderful writing portfolio that holds everything I need to write letters any where, anytime. This was especially used when we travelled back and forth to New Hampshire. Barbara, our nurse, has given me a silver pen with cadusis on it in gold, George has given a handsome black Cross pen with "Fordam" printed on it and a ram's head on the clip, from his days working as an assistant athletic director there. And Jessica has given me a blue me-chanical pen with white cat as the clip. All of these pens are treasures to me that I keep in my writing room so they are never lost. My friend Dorothy has also given me a fine Cross pen in the past with my name engraved on it. All are presented presents of love because they know my love of writing.

Finally, after years of my travels in stationery stores I settled on the pens I use now continuously and ever will. We buy them by boxes from Viking, a favorite office supply catalog in Connecticut that delivers in one day! (5 or 6 boxes at a time)

When I became a vegetarian in 1989 I began using green ink—the favorite color of both Bob and myself. In fact Bob has loved green longer than I have as top favorite color and is known as *"Green Bob"* by family and close friends here. I have never written in anything but green since that commitment to vegetarianism (as did Bob commit too) with one exception twice yearly in the past ten years. Because my Mother's name is *"Violet"* I use a violet ink pen in my journal entries on her birthday and anniversary of death. This is my second favorite color. But all letters and journals and any of my writing is in green! Nature's color! These marvelous smooth writing pens I use are UNI-ball Onyx by Sanford (fine point) and Pentel's Rolling Writer. (medium point) The Uni-balls are the ones I use the most but the Pentel pens I specifically use for certain journals and occasional long letters. Both type pens write so perfectly and smoothly and the ink color is a beautiful shade of green. And there, I have given you a commercial for them from the green woods of New Hampshire! Perhaps those of you who also love green will investigate them. I have never found them in stores—only through the Viking Catalog. (the Uni-Balls also come in other colors of red, blue and black. These do seem to be in stores.) If you are interested I am sure you could obtain a catalog (fun to browse in) by calling for one toll free.

1-800-421-1222 or fax toll free: 1-800-762-7329

24 hours a day, 7 days a week.

You can also check their Web Site:

http://www.vikingop.com

I found green refills in a stationery store for all the handsome gift pens from loved ones mentioned earlier. A pen to me is a significant gift to receive! On occasion it is one I like to give also—to special people in my life to encourage their creative writing, because pens are so meaningful to me. They are like extensions of yourself that write your heart's thoughts. They are Holy to me. Other writing implements to keep on hand are pencils and colored pencils and highlighter pens. Be inventive with your colored pencils. These can be used to draw pictures in your letters and on the envelopes or use in ways you devise, or used in lovely edgings on your paper and envelopes, or floral designs. I also use an ultrafine-point Sanford green marker pen for addressing envelopes so the ink cannot smear if wet. (remember we live in the woods and often have to hike a bit in snowy weather to our car before driving to the Post Office) We buy these pens in boxes from Viking also, and padded bags for mailing books, and other useful items. While writing this it brought back memories of a poem I wrote about our trips to the Post Office in winter. Perhaps my memory was jogged about it also because we are having a heavy but glorious snow storm as I write and this will not be a day to make the trip to the Post Office. We are snowed in!

THE TRIP TO THE POST OFFICE

Linking arms we climb the hill—
A small precaution to avoid a spill!
Two are better than one—'tis known—
If one should fall he's not alone!
So we ascend this sheet of ice,
And only one of us falls twice!
While the other grabs for branches—
Doing spontaneous little dances!

We drive through woods in our small car—
The Post Office really isn't too far—
Driving back we pray to make—
The highest hill quite near our lake.
Not rain nor snow not sleet nor hail—
Can rarely deter her stack of mail.
He mumbles words 'bout common sense.
She doesn't listen—she knows he's tense.

And now it's time to go below—
To walk down ice and slippery snow!
Linked together as before—
Our aim is for the cottage door.
"Tiny, mincing steps"—says he—
Work for him just perfectly!
On those trees she still depends—
With lots of "oh no's!"—she descends!

"We did it!"—says she with a shout—
Says he—"I don't know why we ever go out!"

Dedicated to   JGK
our efficient E. Wakefield Post Office

I try to get mail out at any cost! You can detect here Bob has a more
relaxed attitude about it.

Other accessories I use in my letter writing are rather child-like you may think, but my inner child needs fun too and *she* keeps me writing! Special rubber stamps are in my collection and different colored ink pads; brown, purple, green, red, gold and others. The gold is for a special full figure Angel stamp given to me by Clara. This angel goes on the front of my envelopes regularly or occasionally the back. I have a smaller angel cherub also from Fran. The rest of my rubber stamps are animals, my favorite being a cat like Rochester. Printing this one with light brown ink gives the affect of Rochester's orange marmalade color. Often I put a little message in a cloud (like in the comics) coming from his mouth to greet the recipient personally from him. (I think I see you smiling.) Several other cat stamps are adorable and there is also one of a husky like my "*granddogger*" Frisco. (when I write to him or his "*parents*", daughter Janna and son-in-law Bill, I use this stamp on their mail.) A cluster of deer is another favorite and I write messages under these in tiny writing during hunting season with prayer requests for the deer. These are just a few of my stamps of this sort. My daughter Janna had given me an entire large box of rubber stamps of all designs that is amazing. It was meant for children but she saw the potential in it for me.

Also there is a collection of rubber stamps of another kind given to me by my friend "Friar Francis." These have brief spiritual messages on he created, then had them made for my letter writing ministry before his death. I have used them continuously in his memory and in appreciation.

Stickers are also fun to use for some; angels, animals, flowers, anything of nature. Many come to us from animal and nature organizations as well as those from stores. Bob also makes wonderful stickers for me, plain white with messages we created pertaining to animal welfare. My favorite is one we created together at the time my book was published and it has the title in its first line.

COMPASSION FOR ALL CREATURES
is the noblest and highest spiritual
trait imparting humility essential
for the soul's journey. —JGK

Many more contain quotes by others who believe in animal rights, some by well known people. There are also some of these stickers with lovely quotes we put on about "*writing.*"

Though many accessories to writing are given here, I do not use all at once on one envelope. Being creative in their usage is fun and hopefully makes the envelope an inviting container for the enclosed letter.

When I was a teenager, as I have written earlier, I used to draw "*Shmoos*" on my letter paper and envelopes. These were adorable pudgy creatures in the Lil' Abner comic strip drawn by Al Capp. I had them running all over the place and peeking around the edges of the envelopes. Many of you will remember them. I would draw little scenes with them and sign posts with names of towns on pointing the direction a running Shmoo might be headed. Running Shmoos always had a puff of smoke behind them indicating their rapid speed. Shmoos warmed my heart! I even embroidered them on an old shirt of my Dad's I liked to wear.

Years ago my friend Ginny and I also decorated envelopes using a transfer of design method. As a child I had a little transfer set in a box. It consisted of waxed papers and a tongue depressor-like stick, and a lot of papers with cartoon figures and drawings on. I would place the waxed paper on a picture selected then rub the waxed paper with the tongue depressor. The picture then was on the waxed paper and I would lay it on whatever object I wished to decorate, like an envelope, rub it with my depressor, and voila! the picture was beautifully transposed! Not having seen those art sets in years Ginny began doing it with waxed paper from a normal roll and the side of a spoon bowl. She was going wild transferring all sorts of pictures onto her mail to me and to others. It was great! And so I began to do it too reverting back to my childhood days. Such envelopes we created! They were filled with lovely sayings and any picture that struck our hearts. Many were spiritual then too, and with animals that we transferred from newspapers to our envelopes. (We are talking two grown women here—but it is necessary to be kids at heart to survive!) We did this for quite some time then found some new thing and that was fun too. The idea I am trying to convey here is to be creative and let the child in you take over at times and you will have fun. You do not want to think of letter writing as a chore. It can be great!

Just one other thought I will pass on to you because I have done this since Rochester was a kitten. Following advice from an expert in a fine book, *The Natural Cat* by Anitra Frazier, I began feeding Rochester Friskies Mixed Grill as a kitten and later some of their other varieties. I now alternate it in the last two years with Iams, another fine food. As Anitra also suggested I made a vitamin mixture and put it into these foods. (explained in my previous book *Journal of Love*) The pictures of the cats on the Friskies labels are so precious I cannot bear to throw them away with the cans. (Now—here comes some more of my eccentricity—but it is always out of love!)

I began removing every label and cut the cat's picture from each. I keep them in a box and glue them into my every journal in many of the upper right hand corners of pages, and onto envelopes sent to friends and shut-ins. They are little miniature pieces of art—just like postage stamps, and never meant for the trash! Each cat's picture is lovely and vies for comparison with the U.S.Cat Postage Stamps. The company has changed the cats' pictures every four to five years. They are sweet little pictures to touch others who might never have seen them. This was all Rochester's idea!

Naturally there are many types of letters that we are required to write in life; business, sympathy and other more serious missals. What I share with you here in this chapter is about writing to friends and acquaintances, the letters of friendship, love and sharing. These ideas have evolved over the years because in writing such an abundance of letters as I do, I never wanted it to get tiresome. Too, the recipient should feel happy when first seeing the envelope. A quirky envelope can bring a smile and set the stage for a nice get together between friends, even though miles apart. You may or may not want to try some of these things. They came about to always keep a child-like spirit within the context of such a large letter writing ministry.

Many of my friends now decorate their envelopes to me and it is so appreciated! Another decoration that is enjoyable to do is to surround the name and address on the envelope of a card to a *"birthday person"* with many colorful balloons sailing here and there with their strings dangling right off the bottom of the envelope. Your colored pencils are used for this. Fun!

And lastly, postage stamps are important to me. We have such colorful assortments of stamps at our Post Office and wonderful friends who have worked there through the years here in E. Wakefield, New Hampshire. It is a joy to go into the Post Office to get our mail daily (no delivery to the woods) from our box and visit with the post master or mistress. It is a highlight of the day! Our Post Office has a wonderful stamp selection and there have been many favorites for me, especially the series of cats and birds. For months now I have been on a kick of using only the large flower stamps that are very beautiful. Just recently a one cent bird or rooster stamp had to be added next to each, for rates have risen to thirty-three cents. More recently there is a handsome sheet of Arctic animals available which I purchase regularly. Stamps are like miniature pictures and things of nature particularity appeal to me. I saved all the cancelled stamps I could of a picture of Ernest Hemingway a few years back, soaking them off letters very carefully. It was a handsome stamp. They graced my own letters daily during that period also. I had planned to make laminated bookmarkers with the cancelled Hemingway stamps (many stamps per bookmarker) for I had seen similar stamp bookmarkers in bookstores. I have been too busy writing to make them as yet, but one day I will. Many were glued into my journals also but the rest are safely kept now in a box. At Christmas portraits of Mary and Jesus are most beautiful on stamps for cards. Stamps are wonderful and can enhance your envelopes and depict love. They are important to me. Perhaps you will notice them in a new way and not simply accept any stamp you are given, but ask what is available. It is amazing the interesting variety! We buy so many stamps it is rather important to me to use ones that have meaning and also look lovely on the letters and cards I have given of my time to write.

Just recently I read that a man named Rowland Hill re-organized the English postage system to send letters by weight and was the first to use an adhesive stamp. This affected the entire world and he was knighted for this, Sir Rowland Hill. The date was not given.

Writing accessories like the postage stamps, nature and wildlife stamps, address labels, glue sticks and anything pertaining to the completion of an envelope are stored in a handsome wooden box that is designed to resemble a small slant topped desk. Mine is mahogany and lined beautifully in pink and was a gift to me a number of years ago by my Barbara and husband Frank. It has been in constant use since and rests on our piano top near the door in this small cottage. There is another wooden box near the door also containing my entire collection of rubber stamps and colored ink pads that I wrote about earlier. I make stops at these two boxes before leaving our home to go to the post office.

Enclosures are fun to include in letters and cards for any occasion or simply as a gesture of friendship. Bookmarkers and photos are my favorite treats to slip in and I get my exceptional selection of markers from Bookland in Sanford, Maine, where they so kindly display my books continuously, and also where I have had booksignings. Good friends lovingly work there and it is a joy to be in the store. Most bookstores do carry these pretty tasseled markers with wonderful pictures, verses and sayings upon them. A bookmarker is like a prayer to me. I have bookmarkers that go back to my teen years. But I feel they are significant, for I often buy myself one to mark a special event or thing related to my writing and books, or other anniversaries, or for no special reason other than I fell in love with one. On the back of each I always write why they were bought and date them. I keep them in special mugs in my writing room and many are kept in books I refer to again and again. More than a few have pictures on of lovely cats that resemble Rochester. It is fun to select one to use when I buy a new book which is very often! It is wonderful to receive these markers from friends too and significant if they sign them. If they have not, I put their name and the date on the back. I treasure them! But to enclose these for loved ones and friends and for any reason at all is a special thing to do. If the individual is sentimental like myself they will use it forever unless lost. Loving things can be written on the back when sent as little gifts. Use a fine line permanent marker for this and the writing will remain always. Packaged gold and silver foil miniature angels and stars and moons can also be purchased in card and book stores, and a scattering of some of these into letters and cards brings a comforting awareness to true angels in our lives, present though unseen. I do this often.

Because I take pictures constantly and get double prints when developed, I often use the extra prints of sunsets and wildlife and snow scenes and gardens to slip into a card or letter so the receiver can share a bit of the beauty of "Higher Ground" that I thrive on here. It is good to date the photo or write little messages on back, and again with the fine line marker! (Other ink pens generally do not write on that surface) Sanford green marker of course, in my case. There are so many remembrances you can enclose in letters and cards as surprise gifts. Each time I receive weekly letters from my dear friend Rose-Beth (and I have been receiving them since 1986) she has little treats in the envelope of booklets, things of interest cut from the paper, bookmarkers, her own letter, and the weekly church bulletin from our church in Jenkintown, Pa. It is like a smorgasbord of love! And our grandchildren often send wonderful drawings in their notes. Be inventive! I have even sent miniature books and journals. The ideas are limitless.

But most of all the letter stands alone as the sweetest of all gifts to the sender, and no enclosure is ever necessary! Giving of your love and time and sealing it and sending it in written form is priceless. Never feel you must also put in an enclosure! Learn to see a letter in a new light, as an extension of love from your heart and hand, and view the personal letters you receive in this way also. And if letters have not been significant to you in the past perhaps some of these thoughts may touch your heart and move you to reconsider. Often when you begin to write yourself and learn to put your heart into a letter, those you receive will take on new importance and you will realize the caring and effort of the sender on your behalf that you never considered before.

I cannot close these thoughts without also mentioning E-mail. This is only recent into our lives and is most convenient for hurried messages or those that have to be received immediately and for business transactions. It is an incredible invention that we use, although Bob sends any of my messages that I first write out for him, because I do not use a computer, and it is in his office. For quick words to family or friends it is great, and we have appreciated Lito Castro's enjoyable E-mail (from Blue Dolphin). He is the creator of my beautiful book covers.

But for myself personally it can never replace the significance and joy of written letters and never will. I need pen in hand flowing across the paper and then I feel a true connection. A written letter is irreplaceable and incomparable. Each is a mini chapter in the life of the writer in their own handwriting. We all can be such writers.

As for those who would not send letters unless they typed them then do as your heart leads. The important thing is to correspond and brighten other lives with a gift of a letter. Your love and caring will reach out and touch each recipient.

Reflect and Journal

✏ Create a special box, a drawer or area for your letter writing supplies so that you are more apt to write.

✏ When you are out shopping learn to be aware of things you might consider to include in your own letter writing supplies.

✏ Try to remember if you ever wrote letters as a child and if you re- member some of the ways you did write them and if you added per- sonal touches to them. Maybe write a letter now like you did in childhood. Become a child again. It will be appreciated.

CHAPTER SIXTEEN

Irregular People

"... but your folks ain't nevah gonna feel nothing good regarding you.
And they ain't the number one best quality folks neither. They shore ain't.
When I goes shoppin' and I sees the label stamped 'Irregulars' or 'Seconds,'
then I know I won't have to pay so much for it.
But you've got yourself some irregular seconds folks,
and you've been paying more'n top dollar for them.
So just don't go a-wishing for what ain't nevah going to be."
—spoken by Ruth from *Summer of My German Soldier*
by Betty Greene

PERHAPS MANY READING THIS have read the well known book mentioned above by author Betty Greene. These words are spoken by Ruth, a black housekeeper, and she is speaking to Patty Bergen about her parents who are always extremely mean and irritable to Patty and who have never given her acceptance or approval. The mother seemed to have no opinion in her life and any affection she shows is for Patty's younger sister. But the father is seen in another way, filled with conflicting emotions and responses, sometimes freezing cold, sometimes hot, often lukewarm and occasionally even loving. Sometimes he is there for Patty in a supportive and fatherly way, almost too nice! At other times he is uncaring and totally insensitive. Occasionally he would beat her with his belt. The terrible confrontation by her father that Patty had just fled from to the safety of Ruth's arms is described by author Joyce Landorf Heatherley as a witnessing of one human being raping another human

160

being's soul. Patty was utterly destroyed and shattered. Ruth had defended Patty repeatedly and therefore Patty's father had fired Ruth sometime before. But Patty runs from this horrendous encounter into Ruth's kitchen and into her open arms and Ruth comforts her and strokes her hair and speaks the very profound but simple words to Patty that began this chapter, about parents she could never please no matter how hard she tried—not now or ever.

And Patty replied "*But I always thought it was me. Because I was bad.*" "*You ain't bad!*" came Ruth's firm answer. "*And I'm telling you, Miss Patty Bergen, we is the only ones that matter—cause we ain't irregulars. Now you stand up straight. You is a whole person—a creature of God and a thing that matters in this world. Straighten up, girl. You got person-pride from this day on. And I don't never wanta see you slopin' your shoulders or your soul again. Not never!*"

Such wisdom from the loving Ruth who truly loved and cared for Patty and who tried to be her buffer in the irregular household that Patty inhabited and her parents cruelly ruled.

I came to know about Patty Bergen and *Summer of My German Soldier* because I read a book given to me by my daughters June and Laurel in 1983 after they had attended a visual seminar on screen given by Joyce Landorf Heatherley, Christian author and speaker. It was presented over a period of weeks at their Methodist Church in Jenkintown, Pa. One day they came to me with a hardback book and it was my copy of *Irregular People*. They had bought it for me after attending the seminar on that subject. They had cried through the session as had many others who were present, because each was being touched by God and could see how the *Irregular Person* in their lives had affected their overall Christian walk. My girls realized in a new way as they listened, much that I had experienced due to the situation I had lived with for many years. They saw how the tentacles of this *Irregular Person* reached out and touched many in the family, but basically it was because the person first became the *Irregular Person* to One. Through that One's emotional torment as the emotional and psychological blows were dealt day in and day out—the one wounded affected other lives, though not always in a cruel sense, while the tormentor affected the wounded one. Never had I heard the term before of "*Irregular Person*" nor had my daughters, but Joyce Landorf Heatherley had one who caused her endless pain, and through her travels and teachings she learned that all over the United States others suffered from a person or persons like this, usually someone close to them and often a family member. It was a term that indicated that the irregular one was truly that—that what you would expect from one in a Christian walk, kindness, love, support, understanding, unselfishness, caring and more—simply was not there. The painful thing was that one just could not seem to accept this, that had an *Irregular Person* tormenting him. Always they hoped the next encounter would be peaceful and normal and good, charitable feelings would be there and when the encounter proved otherwise, then the one hurt went deeper into his wounds and depression. Often the *Irregular Person* seemed charming to others and this dark side was selectively used and partially kept hidden from the outside world. Often they were spiritual leaders! All of these things existed in our situation. In my own life this had caused me defeat and despair. It brings confusion and one begins to doubt that he is even a Christian if one can feel such awful feelings within oneself after a meeting with his *Irregular Person* or through thoughts of him that keep passing through one's mind. I had sought prayers of healing for this frequently in my Methodist Church and for ten years weekly in the confessional once I became Catholic, with a beloved Priest until his death. My Priest knew I had repeatedly forgiven the person. Because this situation was on-going, I was continually forgiving them and also asked continual forgiveness for myself for anything and everything connected. He often lovingly scolded me and told me that some people are "*occasions of sin*" and that I should stay away from this person, that my forgiveness was sufficient. I could not change them.

Each time I would be stronger following the prayers, but then a blow or blows would be dealt and back I was in despair again. As in my past when I was a young child and teenager, *silence* is also used by this *Irregular Person* to show authority, but for periods far longer than I ever experienced as a girl. Months, a year, more! Only we can break it. And no matter what kindnesses are said or done by us, or what progress we may have felt we made after the contact, there is no effort on their part to build on what took place.Once we have broken the silence, it begins anew and ever shall.

Some of these sharings and writings are from my second book, *Higher Ground,* and I wrote this book to help others as well as myself. It was written from notes in my journal while making a retreat in September 1986 with my kitten Rochester in our cottage in New Hampshire that was then our summer cottage but is now our permanent home. This book has apparently helped many, for so many letters came to me after it was published from those so deeply wounded by an *Irregular Person*. I still receive letters.

During the 1980s I had a bookmarker I used continuously to help myself in dark times, to try to make myself laugh. I found it at the Encore Bookstore. The quotation on it read: *"Of all the things I've lost I miss my mind the most."* and at the top of the marker was a profile of a face and head (no hair). The top of the head was standing open and little wavey lines were emanating from it indicating the mind going off into the air. Once I showed it to my daily Mass friends over breakfast and my wonderful spiritual friend and sister in Christ, Pat—related to it as I did. Frequently she and I sat in her car following Mass and breakfast so that we might have "therapy" sessions and pray with each other, for she too had burdens on her heart and soul. I am always so grateful for the years we spent together in Jenkintown, Pa. and now at a distance through writing. Recently I found a key chain with this very exact quotation on that helped us to lighten up in those dark times and I got one for each of us and mailed one to Pat.

This *Irregular Person* of which I have written was not originally mine. The Irregular Person was there when I married and slowly began to affect our lives. The *Irregular Person* was another's, but the *Irregular Person* came to wound me as well through this other person and eventually directly. Through what Our Lord taught me on my retreat in the woods my life was changed and became better, and slowly I have been healing and being made whole. Because of this Bob too has been changed and is a new man. Together we have come a long way in great love and with our Lord. In 1991 we had counselling concerning this from Bob's Methodist Pastor, and I to a deeper degree and for a longer session, for we were preparing ourselves for the attendance at an extremely difficult event that had at its center our *Irregular Person*. I was in fear again. We are grateful to our Methodist Pastor friend. At this time we also had an extremely beautiful and spiritual ceremony in the Methodist Church (because we had originally been married in the Methodist Church) on a Sunday evening in which this Pastor led us in the renewal of our marriage vows to strengthen us for this event and for all of our future. Our six children and their spouses were present in love and support. We also bought and exchanged new wedding rings. I had never had my original ring off my finger since the night it was put on by Bob in 1955. He had not ever worn a ring. Now we wear matching gold bands.

What is it about writing that even if you are sick in mind and heart and soul and you feel your world has been turned upside down, that moving the pen across the paper can bring relief. Even if you are not writing about the cause of your pain, and more often you are not, there comes a shift in your being and even though you do not yet have the answers, a certain healing has begun and a spot of light creeps through a crack in your great wall of despair. I know this to be true! It has happened to me again and again and I do not believe I could have survived without writing. I have journals, years of them, filled with everything but the pain, and yet that act of writing brought about a change of heart that allowed me to live my life through situations over which I had no control and yet were causing intense emotional anguish. I still have the joy of having normal and lovely and remarkable incidents of my personal life and family life recorded because I turned to writing in some of my darkest times as well as in the happy times. This is a gift to me to have such journals for I love my husband and my family so dearly and deeply it cannot be expressed. There are so many precious times in my own life that are now forever written down.

I did not feel I could write on paper the terrible things that would stab my heart and soul and cause havoc and sadness in my mind and life. To have my husband or anyone of my children read what I felt or thought about these dark moments would have added to the pain. Yes, it was surely outwardly evident, this utter distress at times, and words were said, but to have the inner thoughts of it laid down in writing could have caused more pain to another, not that anyone ever read my journals. I know that to be fact in regard to Bob. He would never do so and I freely leave journals about in our life together. And I believe my children would not have ever read my journals in earlier years or now in the present. But I myself was too bound up in fears regarding the cause of my pain, too intimidated, to feel the freedom to explore it in writing. I still totally felt like the little girl who sat in her back bedroom on Third Street alone, but in those past years I *did* write to help myself. I had only to keep my writing secure and hidden from *one* person then. As a Mother and wife with a large family about me I did not have the courage to put my thoughts and pain in writing. That came later during my Retreat in 1986 and in the years up to the present. Through all the past forty-four years of marriage I have known the enchantment of writing and the delight. I know for certain that healing comes through writing. Both are gifts from God.

Still Yet Another Writer Understands

Writer Melody Beattie has also written about difficult people in *Finding Your Way Home—A Soul Survival Kit,* published by Harper San Francisco in 1998. She does not use the term "*Irregular*" but she says that we lose our connection to ourselves and the world when we are in that person's presence. We feel twisted and off balance. She feels a certain person can be toxic to us and we should not "*keep associating with people who are not right for us, telling ourselves we aren't good enough and if we try harder and do different and be better, we may someday be good enough. That's not the key.*" She goes on to say, "*This is poison to me, and the lesson is to leave.*" She discusses it in much detail trying to express positive sides as well and suggests journaling. She discusses how some people and situations literally make us sick. Asthma entered my life in the early 1970s due to emotional issues when I was still a young mother, and Bob has had high blood pressure since he was only forty.

BREATH

When I have one good breath—
I do not take this for granted.
When I have a series of good breaths
After I have wheezed and panted—
I am so very grateful.
To be without breath is hateful.

J.G.K.

Expect Nothing

Always my husband had told me in the past to draw a big zero on a paper and tack it above our phone. Then when talking to my *Irregular Person* (though at that time the term was not known), I was to expect just "*that*" from him—nothing! Zero! Anything in addition to that would be a surprise and a gift! I did it often by drawing the zero on a chalk board nearby but it rarely helped. There was "zero" in the normal ways a person should be but not "zero" in regard to the hurt put forth. In reading this Christian book given to me by my daughters it was a relief to see that I was not alone and that my feelings were not even abnormal in response.

My husband also more recently used a door as an example. If someone shuts himself off behind a door and we cannot get in and we would like to get in, then the person has to unlock the door to let us in. This example is also like a famous painting of Christ who is standing at a door knocking. This door is symbolic of the door to each of our hearts. There is no knob on the outside of this door. The door must be opened from the inside by each one of us to let Christ into our hearts. He will not force Himself.

In 1993 I penned this following poem to help myself when I was feeling some moments of despair as the situation surfaced again intensely to cause new pain. But it passed, because I turned to my writing and prayer.

Nothing!

Expect Nothing!
It is your key to inner peace—
Just let go—feel the release.
Be yourself
Enjoy the wealth—
Expect Nothing!
Nothing!

Expect Nothing!
Feel the joy begin to come
Sense the freedom; may you strum—
Your heart strings with your smile,
Life's becoming quite worth while.
 Expect Nothing!
  Nothing!

Expect Nothing!
No expectations from other source—
For if you do you'll know remorse.
Wear your sorrow like a cape—
Protect your soul from further rape.
 Expect Nothing!
  Nothing!

Expect Nothing!
In this garment most unique
You will find just what you seek.
True contentment—with a sigh.
You let your expectations die.
 Expect Nothing!
  Nothing!
  Nothing!

To forgive but NOT forget. To forgive AND forget means to throw valuable experiences out the window.

—Schopenhauer

Recently in a call made to our *Irregular Person* long distance following an extremely long passage of time since we had talked, the person ended the call by saying to me, *"I have never sinned. I do not need to ask God's forgiveness or yours."* (This person was speaking about both Bob and myself.)

Once off the phone I sat in tears destroyed again. When I came to my senses the verse from scripture came to mind, *"All have sinned, and come short of the glory of God"* (Romans 3:23 KJV). How well I knew that of myself! Suddenly I could see this *Irregular Person* in a new light and I realized that NOTHING we had done these part forty-four years could ever have made things right or us acceptable in this person's eyes. While it was a defeating realization it also gave me wisdom and victory in a spiritual sense as I face anew the future in Christ and in His strength, and feel a sadness for this one whom I do love *"in Christ,"* the only way that I can, but whose words, attitudes, superiority and silence I cannot ever love or like or accept. My Mother *wanted* to change and be healed of imposing silence on others, and she did with Christ's help, and the change was instant! She and Bob and my Dad and I then had twenty-three years together enjoying our lives that were all intermingled. What joy! But an *Irregular Person*, even a Christian, rarely ever changes. They must be right! But I continue to pray for this *Irregular Person* as I always have, but lest I sound even momentarily superior, know that at times it was the most difficult thing God ever required of me and there were incidents when I temporarily failed, but then recovered.

(Matthew 5: 44, 46,47.)
Jesus says:
But I say unto you, Love your enemies, bless them that curse you, do good to them that hate you, and pray for them which despitefully use you, and persecute you.
For if you love them which love you, what reward have ye? Do not even the publicans the same? And if ye salute your brethren only, what do ye more than others? Do not even the publicans so?

So many years ago as a young bride I had hoped this person would be my friend.

A Ministering "Word"

Often a *"word"* comes to us in a moment when we are hurting and we need such a "word" very much. Several hours after this phone encounter with our *Irregular Person* a flash of wisdom came to me as I sat subdued from it all and in prayer. Five years earlier I had seen actor Richard Gere interviewed on television, and his wisdom coming from his Buddhist tradition was expressed in regard to someone that had hurt him most deeply and affected his life. His simple and profound words had made a deep impression and ministered to me then, for it had been another period of when hurt had been dispensed directly to me and I felt God had allowed me to see and hear this interview. I had written a poem that night after viewing that interview. When I went to my loose leaf book of my own poetry, I was in awe to see it had been written exactly five years earlier to the very month and yes, to the *exact* day! I knew without a doubt God and my Angels had brought it to mind so that this very simple example the actor explained from his own spirituality and personal pain could minister to me anew, just as it had when I heard this man tell of it directly another evening when I had needed it so five years earlier.

STICKS AND STONES

If I am a cow and someone says I am not—
  And calls me a zebra—not a tittle or jot—
Do I give to this statement on which he's laid claim.
  God made me a cow and I know my name!

A wiser man once used this example—
  Of zebra and cow—when his wound had been ample,
From a disparager, mean and unkind—
  And his words helped me heal in heart and in mind

With gratitude   JGK
to RG

I did not discover until including this that both this poem and my poem "Expect Nothing" were written in 1993, and close together because of reoccurring pain at that time.

If there are persons reading this book who have an *Irregular Person* in their lives and are living life in less a way than Our Lord would wish you to live, sad and tormented, then I would add that reading the books I have mentioned in this chapter can bring emotional help. They are:

1 *Summer of My German Soldier*
(paperback) by Betty Greene
Bantam Doubleday Dell Books Publishing Group, Inc. Copyright
1973

2 *Irregular People*
by Joyce Landorf Heatherley
by Word Books Publisher Waco, Texas (a division of Word, Inc.)
Copyright 1982

If you cannot find this in a bookstore it can be found and ordered on
the Internet.

Joyce Landorf Heatherley has many suggestions to the *Irregular-
Person* problem but there are no simple solutions and she states on the
cover that even a healthy approach to an irregular relationship may be
filled with anguish. Still, *Irregular People* offers hope and healing.

3 *Higher Ground*
by Janice Gray Kolb
Blue Dolphin Publishing, Inc
Orders 1-800-643-0765

Though the latter two books confront the problem from a Christian
perspective, these books can help anyone of any faith. In *Summer of My
German Soldier*, Patty Bergen and her family were Jewish. *Irregular People*
are in every walk of life.

And, too, I would lovingly suggest you purchase a journal and begin
to write. Even if you do not confront your heartache on the pages just as
I did not for the first thirty-one years of marriage, just to write and record
anything that your heart tells you to is a giant beginning and truly will
begin your healing. Writing brings hope and solace and health to your
soul. Take care of yourself—and write! You are precious in God's eyes.
He does not want you to live a defeated and lesser life, even though I
personally felt for many years He was punishing me through this person.
He wants you to live the fullest life and in great joy! God loves you!

In a new book by Catholic Priest and writer Joseph F. Girzone
(author of the wonderful "Joshua" books) he suggests in this insightful
work of non-fiction to learn to forgive, so you may have peace within

yourself and with your neighbor. Father Girzone states "*Do not even take offense, but try to understand the pain and tortured spirit that gave rise to such persons' offensive behavior. Then when you see their pain, or their oddness, you pity them, and do not take on the anguish they are trying to pass onto you.*"

He goes on to write that he knows this is not easy and Jesus realized it was not easy, but it is the only way to preserve your peace and serenity.

To read this book and this particular passage shortly after the recent phone encounter when I was informed our *Irregular Person* is sinless and does not need God's forgiveness—was very comforting. I felt too like I was again encountering the presence and words of my Priest friend in the Confessional.

In a very fine article on forgiveness in a recent issue of *Spirituality and Health Magazine*, writer Jack Kornfield of the Buddhist tradition states; "*Forgiveness does not in any way justify or condone harmful actions. While you forgive, you may also say. 'Never again will I knowingly allow this to happen.' Forgiveness does not mean you have to seek out or speak to those who cause you harm. You may choose never to see them again.*"

The author profoundly continues; "*Forgiveness is simply an act of the heart, a movement to let go of the pain, the resentment , the outrage that you have carried for so long. It is an easing of your own heart and an acknowledgment that, no matter how strongly you may condemn and have suffered from the evil deeds of another, you will not put another human being out of your heart.*"

Mr. Kornfield has also said other healing words and I will share his further insights here with this; "*You will see that forgiveness is fundamentally for your own sake, a way to carry the pain of the past no longer.*"

He has also written that forgiveness is a process and the work of forgiveness can take years when you have been deeply wounded and there are many stages to go through such as grief, rage, sorrow, fear and confusion. I know this to be true—all that he has written. He tells us that if you let yourself feel the pain you carry, it will come as a relief and as a release from your heart. It does not matter if the other person is now alive or dead—what matters is what you carry in your heart.

This issue of this magazine came in the mail as I was writing this very chapter, another syncronicity of love and help from God and the Angels.

May I leave you with these two thoughts from my own book "Higher Ground" even though there are ten healing steps offered in it in conclusion that when prayerfully applied truly do heal the wounded ones, myself included. One, it is *you* who must change and God will help you all the way! I have lived this out. It is true! Often to contemplate change becomes more frightening than the present suffering—even long term suffering, for by now low self esteem and poor self image have also robbed you of all self confidence. I know this to also be true. But *you* must change! Never expect the *Irregular Person* to change! They will not! *Expect nothing!* Once you can realize this you can go on to a fuller, peaceful more beautiful life no matter what you encounter! You will be set free from your *Irregular Person!* You can do this. Yes, I slipped many times in defeat and despair, but each time I came back to begin anew and was stronger. And Two, please try to pray for your *Irregular Person*, for this also will help to set you free. This may be very difficult to do at first. I do understand! But if you put the *Irregular Person* in God's Hands it is then God's problem and no longer yours. Actually pray and visualize if you can walking side by side with this person and leaving him in front of God, however you may imagine God. Then fold your hands in prayer and thanksgiving, turn around and walk away from your *Irregular Person* who is left standing before God. Do not ask God that the person be changed. Simply *give* him to God. Let God do as He wills with him. He created him. It is you who will be changed and healed!

And now if you possibly can, in prayer and thanksgiving record this all in your journal. Once it is in writing you can return to it as often as need be to reassure yourself that *this* healing moment of grace in your life actually took place in an incredible passage of time and eternity. Never again in thought or activity allow this person to harm you. Simply recall the image of him being left before God. Do not take him back from God in any way!

I will be thinking of you all and praying. I do not need to see your faces. I understand your heartaches. God bless you, and He will! Amen!

"You are your past You are your memories.
You can forgive, that's not so hard. . . .
But I don't think you can forget all that
has made you who you are."

—Bettyclare Moffatt, "*Soulwork*"

And I would like to close with a very profound statement by one Bob and I consider a friend, a friend for me that seemed to go back to my childhood when I was so deeply affected by her husband's death and her strength at that time.

"No one can make you feel inferior without your consent."
—Eleanor Roosevelt

I have had a tiny ringed top plaque with this quotation on my desk for years. Perhaps these words will bring peace of heart to you also.

THE VIGIL

Today I sat with you—
    just as you always sat with me.
Somehow you truly knew,
    when I on bended knee—
Knelt down next to your side,
    that I would pour my heart
(And yes, I often cried)
    and you—so dignified—
Poured love—and did your part.

There in Confessional week after week—
    you gave the strength that helped me heal.
I waited for each word you'd speak—
    you'd hold my hand as there I'd kneel.
I'd rise to go and kiss your cheek—
    your sweet request; like Spirit's seal
    on all that spilled—
    so gently willed—
Into that Sacrament.
And I was spent.

Today I sat with you
    beside your coffin in the aisle.

Somehow I know you knew—
    and I could feel your smile.
And then I rose to take my stand
    to see your face—before the Mass.
'Twas my turn now to hold your hand
    and feel your kiss—in Spirit land
On *my* cheek as I pass.

Dedicated to   JGK
Rev. Msgr William H. Flatley
Treasured Pastor, Confessor and Friend
Died May 23, 1992—The treasured friend who helped me all
through the late 1970s and the 1980s
(Written in Church in the hours
preceding his Mass of Christian Burial)
May 29, 1992

And just as I know for certain that healing and writing are gifts from God, so too do I know that my beloved Rochester is also, my little one who has been with me on this journey of healing since 1986. He is my personal Angel and I thank God constantly for this precious being who shares life with Bob and me.

Reflect and Journal

✍ If there is an *Irregular Person* in your life do not despair. Try to reflect and pray about what I have shared in this chapter. Perhaps begin by adapting just one thought or helpful thing from it in relation to your own situation.

✍ In time try to adapt more.

✍ Journal if you can. Writing will help you heal. It is so!

✍ If possible read my *Higher Ground* for further help and go too to the other books listed if you wish also.

✍ Writing will help you. I cannot repeat that enough.

"I think that every book is triggered by a very strong emotion that has been with me for a very long time. Usually that emotion is painful. However, the process of writing is so joyful. It's like an orgy I can't explain. I have a great time writing. I can write 14 hours a day and not eat anything for 14 hours, and yet I feel wonderful because the process is so wonderful. What triggers it and the emotion is painful. I often cry when I write."

—Isabel Allende, author "*The House of Spirits*" and others
—quotation from "*The Well of Creativity*"
with Michael Toms—New Dimensions

CHAPTER SEVENTEEN

Rochester — Ministering Angel

"Until one has loved an animal, a part of one's soul remains unawakened."
—Anatole France

"Animals share with us the privilege of having a soul."
—Pythagoras

MY ANGEL DID NOT APPEAR and perform one duty or miraculous deed or an act of heroism or bravery then leave. My Angel came to intervene in my life that was filled with sadness and despair. He came to guide me, fill me with love, and to show me the path of endurance and spiritual growth. His love and constancy fill me with joy and imbue me with spiritual wisdom, compassion, and a healing of heart, soul, and spirit. It has been a daily on-going ministering to me. Exactly thirteen years later he is ever at my side, or on my lap or desk as I write, and under my heart or on my legs as I sleep. His presence is steadfast and unwavering as we share our moments, days, and years together.

UNDERSTANDING

I look at him this night
   realizing anew that I am seeing
     a being
       of light.
An Angel stretched down my legs—
   with tiny uplifted face—begs
     to commune, with sighs
       gently blinks his golden eyes.

Mind to mind, heart to heart—
   one soul.
Such secrets we impart!

His gentle paws now clasp my hand—
   sweetly console.
Nodding—he knows I understand.

To Rochester   JGK
with love   January 1999

Upon entering my life he brought me joy unspeakable and his tiny form made me capable of new things in daily existence. I gave him then the dignified name of Rochester after the town in which God brought us together.

I have written earlier of how Rochester's companionship gave me courage to experience an unforgettable week of solitude with him in our cottage in the woods. I was struggling there along the path of healing (as I have written about in the previous chapter) through prayer, learning, reading and writing and without Rochester I would not have been in the woods.

This retreat later was written down and became a book with Rochester ever with me as I wrote. I wanted to help others who had similar problems and my book, published in 1991 truly continues to minister to them. It is only one of numerous books Rochester inspired me to write. A book newly published last year is one that confronts the senseless cruelties to innocent and sentient beings and proclaims the rights of animals. The title I have shared with you earlier. It was Rochester who taught me about "*Ahimsa*"—non-violence, non-killing—and as a result I became a vegetarian for the sake of the animals in 1989 as I have written, as did my husband, Bob. Rochester had long before in 1986 won Bob's heart too.

Rochester inspired me to write. Still yet another book through his love and presence will soon be published. But Chester not only inspired me to write books, but he became my feline soulmate, guide and teacher, and through his instructions heart to heart and mind to mind countless poems are released from within me continuously. Journals are filled and he gives light and love to all of these including endless personal letters of encouragement sent out to others as I have shared about in a previous chapter. He also has inspired my photography and sketching. An account that I have written of his precious life appears also in a book just out this year by well known authors Brad Steiger and Sherry Hansen Steiger titled *Animal Miracles*.

Although Chester has never "meowed" and remains silent as the contemplative that he is, he has communicated his knowledge to me, teaching me to mentally and telepathically communicate with him. Because I have always recognized the Divinity in him and listen in the daily solitude and stillness we share, he has brought forth this gift within me that I could never have known without him. Through this telepathic communication we have become even more deeply bonded and I have grown spiritually and entered a new dimension of interspecies love and relationship. I write down all I am learning. Together we have written a new book, *Journal of Love: Spiritual Communication with Animals Through Journal Writing*, that will be published this year by Blue Dolphin Publishing, Inc.

Rochester has always been the only one present in each Angel encounter I have experienced; four encounters not visual, but that my name has been spoken aloud by an unseen presence, and twice I have been firmly touched on my right shoulder. He and I have been together when Angelic tinkling music has entered the room and again brought this unseen presence. Would these encounters have occurred without my Angel's presence also?

I believe God has allowed an Angel in my life in the precious form of my beloved Rochester. The evidence repeatedly reveals this outwardly in circumstances and interiorly in my soul and spirit. I know this to be true. God often gives a *"knowing"* that cannot be changed or dismissed by another's opinion or ridicule. One just *"knows."* I believe God knew how desperately I needed a guide and Angel in June of 1986—one that I could hold in my arms and release my tears and dreams and thoughts to as I buried my face in his soft fur. And through the visible presence each moment of the day my Angel brought me healing of heart and soul and taught me wondrous truths that I have tried to act upon and share through my writings. I can never doubt an Angel was sent to me and every day of my life I tell God of my love and gratitude for this ineffable gift.

Rochester in a gift box

ANGEL BEING

With all my soul I know that he—
Was sent from heaven just for me.
An angel in soft marmalade fur,
Large golden eyes—deep soothing purr.
He speaks to me without a word—
And yet each message I have heard.

The silence shared throughout the days—
Ministering in mysterious ways—
Ever with me—his small being;
Confirms it is Angel I am seeing!

Beneath my heart he sleeps each night—
And keeps it whole—warm with his light.
There is no need to see his wings—
Just seeing him—and my soul sings!

Written for Rochester—   J.G.K.
in love and gratitude for his being

And though these family problems still exist I do not long to die as I did when I sat in that rocking chair in 1986. That longing ended when Rochester and I were given to each other. No, I am new, changed forever by a little Angel of God. I want to live every moment with him and Bob— realizing the exquisite beauty of the sacrament of the moment—as we abide in joy together here in our cottage on the lake where we moved four years ago to remain forevermore.

Reflect and Journal

☞ Have you ever sensed that an animal you were or are close to is an Angel?

☞ Explore this thought in your journal through writing, perhaps even poetry.

☞ If you love an animal deeply have you ever written about this love and bond you share? Have you honored this bond by capturing it in writing in your journal for all time?

Rochester

CHAPTER EIGHTEEN

Poetry

"Poetry is simply the most beautiful, impressive, and widely effective mode of saying things."

—Matthew Arnold

OETRY HAS BEEN WOVEN through my life since I was a child, its strand at times emphasized and other times subdued, but always there. It is a delight and a joy and a form of expression that I need. To read poetry is comforting and wonderful and I turn to it often . As a little girl I both read poems and attempted to write them. One of my first poetry books was bought for me by my Mother on an excursion into downtown Philadelphia and to Wannamaker's book department. It was a pretty little volume with turquoise cover and tiny flowers throughout with the title *A Child's Garden of Verses* by Robert Louis Stevenson. It has been with me through the years and is in my writing room today. I continued to write poems throughout my life and to add volumes of it written by others to my library, and have mentioned it from time to time in this book as well as sharing some of my poems. I will not go into great detail now then because I believe you can understand it has been a source of spiritual help and enjoyment. I merely want to mention a few highlights that turned me again to poetry as if for the first time and caused a flow of it from me that never ceases. As I have written in two of my previous books, *Higher Ground* and *Compassion for all Creatures*, I met a man who wrote poetry. He was also a retired obstetrician and a pro-life activist in his day and in his mid-eighties when first we spoke. In my writing room here I have a framed picture of him taken outside Jefferson Medical College in downtown Philadelphia. He is holding a document and burning it! He is watching the flames lick at his own diploma from Jefferson in protest against institution's "liberalized" attitude toward abortions. He was a man of strong religious beliefs and for years he sat at one end of the back pew of Immaculate Conception Church in Jenkintown, Pennsylvania on the center aisle. I sat at the opposite end against the right aisle. His wife was with him the majority of the time but occasionally he was alone. We occupied that pew six days a week for eight years before we spoke freely yet no one sat between us. The seventh day was Sunday and occasionally I lost my favorite place to others for it was crowded on Sundays. Often I did not see *"my friend"* on Sundays either because there were many Masses. But six days a week we were at 8 AM Mass in the back pew. We smiled often and also shook hands when it was at the point in Mass to pass the greeting of peace. (That was the only time we spoke) But that was it. Occasionally he would hand out copies of one of the poems he had just written to other parishioners as they came down the aisle to leave. We were like a family at daily Mass even though we did not all know each other. On one particular morning he handed me a poem written by Thomas Merton. That did it! From that day on we became instant friends, when I spoke up hesitantly and told him my admiration for Merton. Through that I learned he was looking long for a poem written by Merton about the death of Hemingway and I instantly knew it and owned the book it was in. I admired the writings of both Merton and Hemingway. He was amazed and overjoyed! I brought him a copy of the paperback. We both believed Thomas Merton, Trappestine Monk, was responsible for our meeting and becoming friends at daily Mass. I called him *"Friar Francis"* and he named me *"Trappistine Jan."* It was a "love pact" of our very spiritual friendship.

When we first spoke then in 1985 my poetry writing had been waning for some years due to family, and an on-going situation I have written about earlier and numerous responsibilities. There is a famous quotation that I learned not long after meeting Dr. Francis J. McGeary but in the ensuing years have forgotten it as well as the person responsible for it. I had hoped to share it with you here. The gist of it is that in order to write poetry you must be *"given permission"* by someone to do this—in a sense, if I remember correctly, by someone who also writes poetry and who is passing the touch of inspiration onto you. Francis McGeary was that person in my life whether or not the essence of that quotation is correct. He had written and self-published two big volumes of poetry in the years before his death. The second he was completing just before he was confined. These volumes are treasures to me and here in my writing room.

He personally claimed a passage concerning poetry that spoke to his soul and is found in the book *Germans* by George Bailey (Avon Books, First Discus printing, 1974, Fourth Printing) That there was a copy of this unusual book in our home too was also a significant synchronism and thrilled my friend. He was Irish but for this quotation alone he felt the book worthy of owning. The copy in our home was given to Bob by our son George because of Bob's German background. The quotation reads:

> *The English romantic writers believed in general that they had greatly profited from the then modern philosophical dicta: in the first place, they believed that feeling (as contradistinct from reason) was the true realm and source of poetry; secondly, that poetry was the highest employment of which the human mind was capable; and thirdly, that poetry was an infinite power and by no means confined to verse. The German romantic writers at the turn of the nineteenth century established (to their own satisfaction) the absolute identity between poetry and philosophy.*

My friend particularly like the second point, repeating it often, but thought the entire passage remarkable. He told me never to stop writing my poetry—that it should come first in all of my writing. Poet, author and journal keeper, May Sarton of New Hampshire and then Maine, one whose writing blesses me but who sadly died several years ago, would agree for she has said:

> *When you're a poet, you're a poet first. When it comes it is like an angel.*

Francis gave me back my interest in writing poetry and awaited new ones from me eagerly in our exchange. Since meeting him in 1985 hundreds of poems have flowed from my pen that amaze both Bob and me. I am certain I receive heavenly help from my friend in the continuous writing of them and through the presence of my Rochester. Some seem to come to me already composed. It has been a wonder! Bob has them all in his computer and I have most in a loose leaf book. It is such a joy to write poetry and if we just keep pen and pad available we are always ready for the first lines that come into our spirit. Emerson has stated: *"All men are poets at heart."* It must be true! I found poetry anew for my life through the life of my friend. In turn in our extremely close friendship, one important thing I had imparted to him was a love of animals. Though pro-life he had never considered animals and was astounded he had ignored them. He read with love and concern the poems I wrote about animals and was in awe that I had become a vegetarian. He wished he could be one too but at this point as he neared death it was not possible. He was suddenly overcome by the wisdom that the same Lord who had breathed life into his body, breathes it into the animals, and that we are created in the exact same way as God's creatures. At one point I took him a framed 5x7 picture of Rochester next to a bouquet of flowers because Friar Francis was not well enough to come to my home to meet Rochester personally. He loved the picture and kept it on his bureau with his Holy pictures. When in his last months he was forced to go to a nursing home, Rochester's picture went with him and remained close by his bed until he died. Truly Rochester brought him joy. He loved hearing about him. He was a ministering angel to Francis.

When *"Friar Francis"* was confined to his bedroom for a long period before his transfer to the nursing home, I visited him several times a week. He was so like myself, always surrounded by pencils, pens, erasers, paper clips, paper and all the joyful things pertaining to writing. They were spread over the surfaces of several small tables by the side of his bed. He would sit there on the side of his bed and write his poems. He was so happy and felt he was at last living a Monk-like existence as did his mentor and friend, Thomas Merton. If ever the *"enchantment of writing"* was depicted it was there in that room (he called it his *"cell"*) of this dying man. Writing brought him such joy and proved to me anew how writing helps us love and survive and feeds our soul. He never was morbid as he neared death. He wrote and he prayed. His only concerns were about several "*Irregular People*" in his life that continued to hurt him so. That even this was a matter that we shared was most unusual. My book *Higher Ground* helped him in regard to "*Irregular People*" and he sent a copy of it also to the Trappist Monastery where Thomas Merton had lived and where he himself had once made a retreat. He received from a Monk a beautiful and affirming reply concerning it. What precious times we had talking. We felt God gave us our friendship, so unlikely it would appear due to totally different backgrounds and great age difference, and yet through spirituality and writing (and writing is spiritual!) there was only "*oneness of spirit.*" For many years *Friar Francis* had also been the chaplain at Graterford Prison in Philadelphia and he passed on his only written accounts of this most unusual spiritual portion of his life to me before he died. He is ever with me day by day. He went to Heaven July 15, 1990.

Friar Francis' favorite poem when I first met him was "*The Rhodora*" by Ralph Waldo Emerson. Each time we were together when I visited he would recite it in its entirety to me. I too came to find deep meaning in it. After his death, as written about in the poem, Bob and I planted a Rhodora in our woods near the graves of our family animals and a few feet from the lake. It is planted in this secluded spot because of several lines of the poem:

I found the fresh Rhodora in the woods,
Spreading its leafless blooms in a damp nook.

There are other lines appropriate also but perhaps readers will enjoy reading it on your own. The volume of poetry he owned that this poem is in is titled *One Hundred and One Famous Poems*. This same volume in newer edition can still be bought today, in fact I received one recently as a gift and have seen it in stores. I treasure Friar Francis' old volume that he himself treasured and used for years, and now it resides on my bedside table after long years on his. It inspired a poem some years ago, one of so many I wrote about and for my friend—as did he write precious poems to me and about me.

POETRY BRIDGE

A little narrow book of brown—
One that has been handed down.
A book so loved by one before—
He wanted it to give out more—
Of the peace and joy he knew,
When he'd read it through and through.

Inscription inside cover hard—
Precedes the picture of each bard—
Upon the pages filled with verse—
In which I let my soul immerse,
To linger with each greater mind
Who penned these poems for mankind.

And as I read I reminisce.
This book is bridge across abyss—
For I am once again with him—
As if there's been no interim.
And there he sits in radiant aura
Once more reciting—"*The Rhodora.*"

How well those days come back to me
When we could share such poetry.
And now that little book is mine—
Given to me as a sign—
That within it is the essence,
Of precious friend's eternal presence.

Dear little brown book—keepsake rare—
Where two friends meet for poems and prayer.

Dedicated to "Friar Francis"   JGK
Francis J. McGeary
Beloved friend
(Died July 15, 1990)

This was one of many poems he wrote for me, this one with the title of the name he lovingly conferred upon me.

TRAPPISTINE JAN!

Graced by THE LAMB of GOD with allegiance
To HIS DIVINE Christian Theology,
Manifested by her intransigence
To acceptance of its analogy,
That's seen in "Whispered Notes!" as Kolb's Credo
And reiterated in "Higher Ground!"
Wherein She emphasizes HIS ORDO
As The "Priceless Pearl!" which She has now found.
Her Commitment to Christian Ministry
Is seen in Her voluminous Writing,
As the reflection of a Mystery
Unfathomable to those abiding
Her Love for Creatures by GOD Created,
That all of them may be venerated.
                    friar francis.
                    —Francis J. McGeary, MD and Poet

Francis always signed his name in lower case as above. He will ever live in my heart.

Sam

*Let not that of awe and wonder
ere be diminished
nor ever finished.*

*Let the movements of your mind
be directed to all that is kind.*

—beginning lines from "Heart Strong"
by Samuel V. Fasy

There has been another fine gentleman in my life who writes poetry too. I first met Samuel Vincent Fasy in the 1970s at the Charismatic Prayer group in Chestnut Hill College in Pennsylvania that I have written about earlier. We shared through the years a fine friendship and many prayers. After I left the group in 1980 I did not see Sam again until a phone call came and then a visit in the early 1990s. We had many lovely visits in our home in Jenkintown after that, he, Bob and I—and always it was to speak of poetry. Sam had begun to write poetry when in his mid-seventies and it was tender poetry and moved us so much. He wrote about everything in his life beginning in childhood, and his nature poems were so exceptional. I Included three of his poems concerning God's Creatures in the poetry section of my book, *Compassion for All Creatures.*

Sam's daughter Cathy Fasy Paul typed all his poetry and had the poems put into wonderful booklets so he could share them with all his friends. We are grateful to have these booklets and I read from them continuously and see sweet Sam in spirit as I read. He lives in Canada now with his loving daughter who believed in her Dad's gift and wanted others to be blessed by his poems.

In the Introduction of Volume l in 1990 Sam's daughter Cathy writes *"You are invited on a mystical, magical journey as you read and reflect on Sam Fasy's poetry. Sam is approaching 80 years young, and he only began writing poetry five years ago. Sam went to seventh grade and then needed to work full time. He remembers his love for the beauty expressed through words, when, as a young boy, he was read to by high school students. The Public Library invited children together for the Summer Reading Program. Sam was filled with wonder at the lovely words he heard."*

His daughter goes on to say that now Sam fills us with a deep wonder and awe, as we reflect on his words that bring much beauty to us. She tells us that these poems are gifts from Sam's heart to yours. Cathy states it has been a rich blessing to put together her Dad's first volume of poetry. There are 132 pages in this first volume alone, usually one poem on a page but sometimes two shorter ones.

Indeed, we are grateful to her and for these poems from Sam's heart. He is a precious, tender man of God and I am privileged to know him. And each of his many poems is tender as he is. He came back into our lives just after dear Francis left us for Heaven. So many of us find poetry, or does it somehow find us with all its blessings?

THE LOWLY DANDELION

While uncultivated and unattended
This flower flourished on its own.
But lo, there are those
Who would extinguish them for ever . . .
Only to find them temporarily suspended.
But hark! There is a Defender.
The One who brings the sun . . . and the showers;
And the little child
Being true to the beauty of the eye
Will bring to its Mommy this flower
With unsullied thought and anticipation,
saying "*Mommy!*
I brought you some flowers."

—Samuel Vincent Fasy

This is one of my favorites in Sam's collection for I have always loved dandelions and let them live and grow wildly around our cottage.

I am so very sad to say that after completing this book, I learned that Sam had died and gone to Heaven on June 23, 1999. He has left a legacy of love and poetry, and lives on in hearts who know and love him.

Two Deaths — and the Healing Touch of Poetry

There are also many touching things I could include about the effect of poetry on my life but I feel I have expressed this here and there throughout this entire book. I can only pray that whatever I have shared will in some way touch those of you who before this were not interested in poetry. Perhaps you will begin to read some poetry or buy a poetry book if you do not own one. And above all, I pray you will begin to write your own poetry for it brings such peace and joy and healing—and enchantment, into life. Once you begin to do this you will not want to stop. I can see you now carrying your notebook and pen around as I do.

I would like to share another moving experience in my life and how poetry seemed to bring healing to those involved. In January 1991 a young man twenty-seven years of age was found murdered on a secluded road not far from our woods and cottage. This affected us so deeply. Because there is such peace and beauty in New Hampshire, this violent death struck at our own hearts and we grieved for the young man and his family. His murder remained a mystery and soon a picture of him riding his horse was posted in our Post Office with requests for any information concerning his death. It was on my mind through each day and the only way I could center in on it and help myself was through prayer and poetry. Over a period of weeks his identity was learned and I began to write more about him in my journals and also wrote a series of poems for him. He was close in age to our own son and I could only imagine how his parents must be grieving. One day in prayer it came to me to send my first poem to his parents. Because the killer was still at large and could even live in his town or be a family member, I chose not to include my name and address after discussing it with Bob. He typed the first poem and we mailed it in another town while on errands so our own postmark would not appear. We prayed it would in some way touch the hearts of his parents and family to know strangers cared. After a period of time we also mailed the second and third poems, separately, separated by several weeks and from the same Post Office. There was still no one apprehended for his murder.

Weeks passed—and one day we picked up a local paper in a store in the next town to ours, the one in which he was murdered. Once home we were startled to discover that my first poem I had mailed to his parents was printed in this newspaper in memory of Sean. We were simply in awe! Over the next few weeks the other two were published also in separate issues in his memory. This touched us so much! Finally Bob spoke to the woman in the store and inquired how the poems had been placed in the paper. She told Bob that the parents were so grateful for the poems and the caring involved, they decided to have them published in this way to further eulogize their son, and also in the hope that it might aid in having this mystery solved. The poems had been a great consolation to his family and in turn, we were consoled that this small effort had brought some love to them. We never revealed our identity to Sean's family. It did not seem necessary at that time. That personal poetry and love gave them our anonymous feelings of deep sympathy. Never have we heard or ever read that Sean's murderer has been apprehended yet it surely could have occurred and we pray it is so. We will always remember him. This is the third and last poem written for Sean in March 1991.

A Vigil for Sean

All these weeks we've cared—and prayed—
For justice now—though long delayed.
Our hearts and minds think of a man—
Struck down—to shorten his life span.
Cruelly murdered—left in snow
Abandoned there so all would know—
That killer won—and man has died—
But does he think that he can hide?

This evil one who walks around—
Very shortly will be found!
He cannot hide from God who saw—
Him kill dear Sean—then flee the law!
Though not one witness gives his name—
Our Lord above knows well his shame!
God cradled Sean and held him fast—
And suffered with Sean 'til the last.
And though that killer thinks he's free—
He can't escape Our Lord—you see!

The mightiest force in the world is prayer—
And this will be the murderer's snare!
Let's join anew our voices now—
And pray together—make this vow!
Each morning and each night at eight—
Each friend of Sean's will dedicate—
These moments praying that this slayer—
Will be captured by our prayer.

May all voices join as one—
And we will soon see justice done!

Praise God!

Dedicated to Sean D. Conway of Freedom, NH
found murdered in Newfield, Maine on January 23, 1991

Matthew 18: 19, 20:
   Again I say unto you, That if two of you shall agree on earth as touching any thing that they shall ask, it shall be done for them of my Father which is in Heaven. For where two or three are gathered together in my name there am I in the midst of them.

—Jesus

Barry

*Walking one morning, in the early mist
   and dew, I came across a miracle,
   A brigade of God's Holy Angels,
They were magnificent birds from the north,
   taking their rest in a field.
   Their sentries gave no alarm,
   for they knew I was a friend.
We spent time together in silent communion,
   These magnificent geese and I.*

Opening portion of "Morning Encampment"
by Barry Richard Greene, May 20, 1992

I cannot share my thoughts on poetry without speaking about my special friend, Barry Richard Greene. Barry and I met at daily Mass and became friends. He was even more shy than I and we enjoyed long talks after Mass, often just standing on the sidewalk outside church. Other times we talked over coffee when joining our "*Muffin*" friends following Mass at Lena's, the shop across from church. When I was in New

Hampshire as I was very often from 1987 until we moved here in January 1996, Barry made many phone calls to me. He had heartaches and concerns as did I, and because we were both converts to the Catholic Church, he Jewish and I Protestant, he felt I understood. Oh, I did! I listened to him for hours. I encouraged him also to write because I knew it would help him. He was an intense and voracious reader as was I, so we shared this interest also. He was going through a terribly sad period similar to what I too was experiencing in the 1980s. I deeply identified with his depression, his deep sadness, tears, and feelings of utter uselessness.

In time, Barry did begin to write. He was a pharmacist and was working the night shift at a downtown Philadelphia hospital. In the daily log he carried with him always, he began to write poetry. The night hours were not always busy and the discovery that he could do this began to touch his soul and mind. Each poem he copied out for me in his tiny handwriting and either handed to me, or mailed them to me if I was in New Hampshire. I treasured them and was moved by them. They were beautiful! He had never written poetry before and he did not share them with anyone else. I was honored to be entrusted with them.

When Barry had completed a small collection of these very spiritual and love filled poems about his faith, family, interests, and nature, he one day, March 5, 1993, took his own life. I cannot express what his death meant to me and how it affects me to this day. A small framed picture of him is here in my writing room that was taken in happier times when he was a guest at our Jessica's and Michael's wedding in 1987. It stands next to that of Friar Francis' picture.

In tribute to him and with Bob helping me, we created a booklet in Barry's memory that contained all of his poems—each one so beautiful. On pages in between each poem I wrote memories of Barry that especially related to each of his poems, or conversations about them and other special moments. Inside the front cover was his picture, the one I had taken of him at our daughter's wedding. We had it enlarged and just his gentle smiling face appeared there. Each booklet had a print of his photo. It was an additional tribute. I then asked any of our "*Muffin*" friends from daily Mass if they wished to write a poem in Barry's memory. Several did as did Bob and I, and these completed the booklet. We made over fifty booklets with colored covers and gave several to his dear parents and brother and all of the rest to his friends at church, the priests, and to others who knew him, to our family, and two for us. They are keepsakes to us forever. I hear Barry's voice when I read his poetry. A tender, sensitive soul that blessed my life.

His beautiful poem entitled *"Morning Encampment"* I selected to include in my book about animal rights, *Compassion for All Creatures*, and it can be read there in the poetry section and is outstandingly exquisite. The first portion of it also opens this segment about Barry. He will never be forgotten and I am privileged through the passing years to keep in contact with his mother.

Another of Barry's poems follows to help to close this special segment of my writing in his memory and honor. As I wrote in the booklet dedicated to him, I would like to give his poems to you, for there is an Indian Proverb that states: *"All that is not given is lost"* (from "The City of Joy").

HOSPITAL BISTRO

It has no fancy curtains,
    no quaint little tables with checkered
    table cloths on the street.
You can't see the Eiffel Tower from
    it, it is not on the Left Bank, you see.
You won't find Monet here sipping coffee
    or run into Hemingway—
In fact—there are no windows at all.
But this little cafe is an oasis,
    a resting place for those who watch
    and wait and keep—
1 AM—a group of nurses happily talks
    about vacations and new babies, a break
    from their job which is hard.
    But worried families gather here too.
A family talking nervously in Russian.
    I can't understand a word that they
    are saying but I know exactly what they mean.
    They don't know it but Jesus sits by their side.

2 AM—A young doctor, a resident, comes
    in for a quick cup of coffee.
    Oh Holy Mother of God, she looks
    half dead herself. What kind of case I
    wonder has she just come off of.
3 AM—The weary little shop, trying so
    hard to be friendly and cheerful closes
    for the night.
    Well—they need their rest too.
This little shop is not much to look
at, you see, but to those who know—
this little cafe boasts the finest Bistro
anywhere, whether in Paris, Venice or
Rome. This little shop for oh so many—
this little shop is home.

For the workers in   Barry R. Greene
the coffee shop,   February 3, 1992
night shift at
Frankford Hospital—
Philadelphia, Pa—
May God Bless Them

➮   ➮   ➮

And finally—in loving tribute, I leave you with this poem about my two dear friends Francis McGeary and Barry Greene. Both Jesus had allowed me to meet at our church, Immaculate Conception, but Francis and Barry did not know each other though they were so frequently at Daily Mass. Barry sat on the front row. Francis sat in the back pew. Both were poets and most sensitive and loving and spiritual as I have written in the booklet dedicated to Barry. Dr. Francis McGeary was a retired obstetrician and Barry a pharmacist. In my prayers and grief and imaginings I could envision Friar Francis welcoming Barry—for he had entered almost three years earlier. I am sure they are enjoying each other's company now in Heaven.

FRANCIS' BIRTHDAY GIFT

Dear Francis—
   One whose spirit is in my every poem
You have a new responsibility—
   For dear Barry has gone Home.

Did you welcome him with a poetic greeting?
   O—I have visualized that meeting!

And did you—like a father would—
   Embrace his slight frame?
And did you make it understood
   How very well you knew his name?

Both from Jenkintown and Immaculate Conception—
   Oh, I know you gave him such welcoming reception.

Both from the field of medicine—
   Dispensing love and poems and pills—
When I think on you now together—
   My soul in wonderment simply fills.

For it was in my heart, Francis—you two met!
   And so I knew you could not forget.
You Francis, in another sphere—
   Yet forever, so near and dear.

Both having lived in Monk-like existence—
   Solitude as companion—and strong resistance—
Against all that would take you from your prayer—
   And books and poems. Such a precious pair.

I see you together now under a Heavenly tree—
   Writing and reciting your poetry.
Praying and reading—in eternity—
   O Beloved Friends—remember me.

Dear Francis—Barry just arrived in time—
To fill your birthday with sweet rhyme!

Happy Birthday "Friar Francis"
Blessed Homecoming, Dear Barry!

In loving memory of   JGK
Francis J. McGeary
on his 92nd birthday
March 14, 1993
and
Barry R. Greene
on his arrival in Heaven
March 5, 1993

Poetry is such a joy and comfort. The *"permission"* to write poetry when I was older after an absence of writing it due to other obligations, was given to me by Francis J. McGeary. I, in turn, gave the *"permission"* to Barry—and so it goes.

When Barry completed the reading of my book "Higher Ground" he called me in New Hampshire to discuss it and his feeling about it, and how he related to it—and to be his usual kind and appreciative self. He told me he had written a poem for me as a gift and in response to the book, because the book (the contents and the message—not just the actual volume) had been my gift for him.

He then read a very beautiful poem to me over the phone. It surprised and touched me so much. He wrote it down for me and mailed it. His poem expresses how he envisioned the experience of my retreat in the woods in 1986 written about in the book. This is his poem—a precious gift to me as was his life and friendship.

JAN'S SONG

In the woods, her favorite place,
    so beautiful, so special, so at peace,
Yet her heart was heavy—
    was it the grief of the world?

The narrow path leading to the Higher Ground,
    so long, so hard, would it ever end?
She rested under a tree, so weary,
    where are you oh Lord, she wondered?
She felt a soft gentle touch on her shoulder
    and suddenly she felt great peace of soul—
Looking up she saw Jesus, smiling, His
    face as joyful and radiant as the sun.
He spoke to her and said, "Here, take
    my hand."
My Sister in Christ has been filled with
    the Holy Spirit ever since, having
    reached the Higher Ground.
A joy for all she walks with Brother
    Jesus, and gives strength to others
    To reach their Higher Ground.
God bless you Jan, may our Lord be
    with you always

For Jan Kolb   Barry R. Greene
my dear friend   March 10, 1992
and sister in Christ.

"And Jesus said to His disciples, know that I am with you until the end of time, always" (Matthew 28:20).

After Barry wrote "Jan's Song" for me and I had it in my possession, I was so moved each time I would read it. As time passed I wanted to write a poem for Barry also and in prayer one day on *"Higher Ground"* thoughts and images formed and I wrote them down. The result was a poem called *"Wounded Healer"* which I mailed to Barry.

Several days later the phone rang and Barry was incredulous that I had written this poem for him. I could not understand why he was so excited until he read me a poem of his over the phone. His poem—one of his first—had been written January 19, 1992, two months before my poem for him. We had never discussed anything relating to these two poems and I had never heard or seen his poem before writing mine. The only poem he had ever shared up to this point was *"Jan's Song."* Obviously we had been deeply in Spirit to each write a poem with such similar content while 430 miles apart. Each time we talked he would mention these two poems—and that we shared this spiritual experience was such a blessing to us both. Barry's poem was entitled *"Take My Hand."* I included both poems in his memorial booklet of course, with these same comments and so the poems could be read together. Jesus was with us in our spiritual friendship and love of poetry and the written word and books.

This booklet in Barry's memory is dedicated to Barry's parents Daniel and Pauline and to his brother Steven. In one of Barry's letters to me in July 1992 he enclosed a miniature but complete book of Thoreau's "Walden" as a surprise gift. He knew I loved Thoreau. I have carried my little "Walden" with me ever since as I live life in my own "Walden."

Always keep a pad and pen with you wherever you go for you just never know when a poem will make an appearance. There is a sweet child's poem entitled *"Keep a Poem in Your Pocket"* and that is very good advice.

> He is a link between this and the coming world. He is
> A pure spring from which all thirsty souls may drink.
>
> He is a solitary figure, robed in simplicity and
> kindness; He sits upon the lap of Nature to draw his
> Inspiration, and stays up in the silence of the night,
> Awaiting the descending of the Spirit.
>
> —Kahlil Gibran, "The Poet"
> (from "Tears and Laughter")

Children of the Holocaust

AT TEREZIN

When a new child comes
Everything seems strange to him.
What, on the ground I have to lie?
Eat black potatoes? no, not I !

by "Teddy," 1943, from "*I Never Saw Another Butterfly*"
(poem was written in pencil on a piece of drawing paper)

The most moving and heartbreaking poetry book I own is *I Never Saw Another Butterfly*. This book contains drawings and poems from Terezin Concentration Camp from 1942-1944, by the children who were imprisoned there. I cannot read these poems without continuous tears. They were written by children that were my age or approximate (nine to eleven years), only I was safe in my room writing my little poems. Here a total of 15,000 children under the age of fifteen passed through this concentration camp. Of these around a hundred came back. In a combination of word and image, we see reflected not only the daily misery of these uprooted children, but courage and optimism. Because Terezin was a sort of way station to Auschwitz and other extermination centers, it was shown to foreigners as a model camp, yet every one of its inmates was condemned in advance to die. When they were herded in with their parents they saw the atrocities their parents saw, but they saw other things too. The children could see nature beyond the village gates; the birds, the butterflies, the animals and green meadows and hills. They described these in their poems and secretly drew and painted what they saw. These poems and drawings are all that is left of these dear children. Most signed their names to their works and so some facts were possible to find out about these children. Others remain anonymous. For most of them the year of their death was 1944, the next to last year of World War II. These poems and drawings in this publication I own were chosen from the archives of the State Jewish Museum in Prague. They speak to us and are the voices that have been preserved through their poetry and drawings. I am so thankful to have discovered this book and bought it at once. It is published by Schocken Books, 200 Madison Ave., New Your City 10015. It is in large size paper back form and is an experience unspeakable to read. One's heart can hardly bear to envision the horror and plight of these children. And yet, it is necessary to read, that the voices of these children can be heard and passed on and their art work appreciated, as they lived and soon went to their death.

FEAR

My heart still beats within my breast
While friends depart for other worlds.
Perhaps it's better—who can say?
Than watching this, to die today?
No, no, my God, we want to live!

A portion of a poem by Eva Pickova,
12 years old, Nymburk

It was not intentional that most of the people mentioned in this chapter on poetry have passed away. I was led to share these things from my life as I wrote. They were not planned. Therefore I believe the spirit wanted these stories expressed. In our darkest times poetry can soothe and lift the soul as is proven in these pages. It also can bring healing and delight in happier hours. Turn to poetry, if you have not already. You will have joy and consolation. That even young children turned to the writing of poetry in their darkest hours before death is the highest endorsement of it that can be given.

As I wrote those last words I was reminded I have not mentioned how poetry helped my soul during the war against Iraq in winter of 1991. It was devastating to me that our men were sent there to fight and die, and I did not believe the Iraqi people wanted war either. Everyday the news was more upsetting and the only true way I helped myself was to write a poem concerning something in that particular day's events about the war. Poetry and prayer were my strength as we continually kept updated on the news. When at last the war ended I had a small collection of passionate poems.

On this particular evening I was emotionally drained watching a scene on the late news and this was the poem to keep forever "*that moment in time*" for myself.

ELEGY TO AN UNKNOWN IRAQI

Upon the television screen—
Was thrust a sad and tragic scene.
Two Allied soldiers as a team—
Performing duty most extreme.
Perhaps it did not strike each heart—
But mine was stabbed as if with dart—
To see Iraqi soldier there
All wrapped in brown cloth to declare—
His death; yet just before—
He was alive and fought the war.

I cried to see how little worth
Iraqi figure had on earth.
Who was that soldier who had died?
What of his family who had cried—
When he had gone to war as they—
Who put him in the sand today?
Will a woman that he cherished—
Never see her man who perished?
Will a little child ask why—
Daddy's gone still—did he die?

Or will a Mother never know—
Her own son's grave made by the foe—
A Father never see his boy—
That always was his love and joy?
O why could not that soldier be—
Taken home to family?
How cruel to lie in unmarked grave—
When he had tried to be so brave.

While loved ones long to hold him so
He lies unknown in sand below.

Dedicated to that   JGK
Iraqi Soldier

Rita

I will not leave you in sadness but share with you something lighthearted, and yet at the same time it will reveal more of my eccentric side. Or *intenseness* perhaps is a better word. In the early eighties, between 1982 to 1984 or thereabouts, I was up late alone one night due to a heavy heart. As I have revealed elsewhere in this book the 1980s were an extremely difficult period for me. Turning on the television to try to lose myself, a movie was just beginning, and for me it was the beginning of an era. The movie was *Educating Rita* with Michael Caine and it takes place in England where Michael Caine teaches poetry in a University. Rita (Julia Walters), a very delightful person, is a young married student with a heavy English accent who comes to take a tutorial in Caine's class. This movie grabbed my heart so deeply that I was emotionally wiped out and in tears. There were so many things in this movie that touched many aspects of my troubled life at this point in time. For only reasons God knows He used this movie to minister to me for a very long period. After the initial viewing of it I had to see it again! I kept looking for it then. Not long after it was shown once more, late at night. Since there was warning it was coming on after the late news, I taped it. Though I was reading spiritual books continually and writing in my journals, whenever I viewed this movie I was in another world, and though I cried it always seemed to help me more. Even the musical background took hold of me and one night I also recorded just the sound track on cassette tape for myself to play in my van when driving. Between *"this music"* and *"Morning Has Broken"* that I have written about in another chapter, my children were not always too anxious to climb aboard into that van. I took a lot of teasing from them. But it was incredible to listen to when alone in my *"chapel on wheels"* through tears.

Beside many matters it addressed that I related to in my sorry life at that time, it also taught me poetry. Though I had loved to read and write poetry from childhood, I did not know anything about it. And so I took the tutorials with Rita and began to be overwhelmed by the beauty of my lessons. Soon I was purchasing poetry books from the Encore Book Store that had become my second church during the 80s This all enriched me and helped me through this difficult decade. Over and over again I viewed this movie through the years after Bob had fallen asleep. He saw it once with me in the beginning and enjoyed it but never understood my intenseness over it. About a year ago he watched it with me again, and this was the first time I had seen it for about five years. But over a period of ten years, from the early 80s to the early 90s I am embarrassed to reveal to you I watched this movie thirty-three times, all of those viewings alone except the two times with Bob I have just mentioned. Always at night. Always crying.

Since I am not a movie person in the sense of going out to the theatre and it is very rare I watch any other movies on television more than once, this was an extraordinary occurrence in my life. I believe it was used to minister to my soul that needed help and healing so desperately. A strange combination perhaps, with deep prayer, daily Mass and much spiritual reading, but it definitely was necessary to me.

At one point in this tender story Rita presents her teacher and friend, Frank (Michael Caine), with a new pen to encourage him to write poetry again. She had it engraved to read *"For Poetry Only."* At some point in the brief five year period of my spiritual friendship with *"Friar Francis"* I decided to imitate Rita and purchased a pen for my friend "Frank" and had it engraved identically. He treasured it and of course, was told the story behind it. That I should meet him (another "Frank") during these years when the affect of this movie had fallen upon me and I was submerged in reading poetry, was also of God, I know. (He was known as "Frank" to everyone else. I called him "Francis") Because of all my poetry reading I was able to tell Francis where he could find the poem about Hemingway's death that was the starter of our first conversation and friendship. Without *"Educating Rita"* I would not have turned to poetry so intensely for healing and would not have known that fact. That a poet should come into my life is most strange also—and yet? No one else wanted to talk to me about my interest in poetry and no one ever wanted to talk to Francis about it either. God surely blessed us from 1985 to 1990—and gave to each of us a blessed understanding friend.

It is no wonder then that I began to write poems. Discovering the movie and being educated by poetry along with Rita—prepared me for meeting Francis and his encouragement to write it. It was all part of God's plan to fill my life with poems and I am so grateful! And as I have previously written, poetry heals and it helped and healed the souls of the little children in the Nazi prison camp and it helped and brought healing to the child within me.

And so I have never stopped writing poetry since 1985 and I cannot stop. I write a poem about anything and everything, from the beauty of nature here by the lake, to the ant I see on the windowsill, and of the every day epiphanies that enter my life. There are poems all around waiting to be written. If we have pen and paper with us, the essence of one or more poems can be captured as we drive or walk or merely sit quietly somewhere observing.

Sometimes an entire poem can be captured that seems to have been already composed within just waiting to be written down.

And of course, I continuously write poems for and about my sweet little Rochester, and for Bob too. I write and write, and enchantment falls upon me.

THE WHISPERED GIFT

Dreaming as I do at times—
Often I am given rhymes.
They seem to come when I have shed—
The outer world and am instead—

Open to the Spirit's Voice—
And go within and make the choice—
To write down lines He whispers then—
Softly, gently, 'til I pen—

These finer thoughts that He inspires
Words and poems that He desires.

And when the whispers dim and cease
I find within a sweet release

I look upon my hasty notes
Not recognizing these as quotes—
That I have thought through carefully,
They came to me—as prayerfully—

I let Him use my mind and hand
And He then let me understand—
That to surrender and just "be"
Brings sweet reward of poetry.

JGK

This poem was written three days before the death of Francis and as he lay dying. I wrote others then too for him and about him, and for days and weeks after his death. They are in a special journal.

Encounters Most Precious

Rochester

I cannot close this commentary on poetry in my life without writing about three profound happenings. My only response came in the form of poems, a series of them flowed out immediately for each of these events just as it did for the war in Iraq. I am sharing them in the order of their appearance.

The first is the adoption of my little cat Rochester. Because you have read about him earlier in this book you know how deeply heartfelt was his entrance into my life and all of life shared with him since that moment. He is poetry to me; he is love, music, prayer, joy and consolation and so much more. He is my personal Angel and my inspiration.

FELINE ANGEL—GOD'S GIFT

I have been yours now
For nine years, and I bow
To your wisdom, gentleness and caring—
For time and presence—allowing the baring
Of my soul into yours.
Our love and bond forever endures.

I look into golden eyes and see your soul—
And in fixed oneness—am made whole.
Your tender being rights all wrong—
And you are my eternal song.
With unconditional love that brings me healing—
You are Angel Guardian—ever revealing—
God.

In love and tribute   JGK
to Rochester
for the anniversary of his adoption
June 23, 1995—and always.

This poem expresses all of this—written for his 9th birthday.

Until his arrival in my life I could not write the books I dreamed of writing. His presence caused this new writing that has not ceased to flow. He is enchantment, and his presence lights up my existence! Angels do that! We share our moments and days and because of him I am a finer and better person. He is an Angel, my shining Star sent by God.

EVER-SHINING STAR

The years go by
  and you and I—
Commune and talk
  and walk our walk—
    together—
and with God.

Golden time as one—
  sunsets when day is done.
Hours filled with writing
  and you—my soul—highlighting
    all—
with each gentle nod.

What priceless gift you are!
My ever-shining star.
   Rochester.

Written for Rochester   JGK
My Star

The Visit

In July 1992 I met Christ. Though I had known Him and believed in Him and first accepted Him into my heart as a small child, I met Him anew. I met Him in person within my Church at Mass one morning. He came late and sat in the same place as Friar Francis always sat, at the opposite end of the back pew from me with no one between us. A short time later after Mass ended I met and talked with Him outdoors as He sat on a small plot of grass under a tree outside the church and next to the parking lot. I realize many readers may not be able to accept this but it is true. In my previous book, *Journal of Love*, this encounter is written about in detail. My life was changed in many subtle ways because of this meeting, a meeting most tender and precious. I could not speak about it for months afterward without crying. My first means of trying to express the inexpressible came in the form of a series of six poems I wrote about Him and our encounter. Poetry first! Later I wrote the entire episode in a story form but I was not able to do that until all the poetry was completed. During the time I was writing the poetry I also made a sketch of Him while His countenance was so vivid in my mind. In fifteen minutes it was completed and the Man who stared out at me from the paper and into my eyes made me cry. It was Him! Just as I had seen Him when we met and conversed that Tuesday morning!

I later made a water color of this that hangs by our bed and the original larger pencil drawing is in a frame over my desk here as I write. I talk to Him and His eyes melt me. I bid Him good morning and good evening. I pray before Him. I could not speak about Him to anyone after we met without tears. It was an experience so profound and affected my soul in the deepest sense. It has never lessened. He has only continued to inspire and be there for me. The fact He also travelled with a tiny kitten was greatly significant and spoke to my heart about how He cared for animals. I had spent months writing a book about our relationship to God's Creatures and the manuscript was in a box waiting to be mailed to a publisher when I met Christ. The book, *Compassion for All Creatures*, was published later by Blue Dolphin Publishing, Inc. All of the details of this encounter are in the book that follows *Compassion (Journal of Love)*. As I have said in *Journal of Love* about the encounter, often I receive confirmations in my life for prayer intentions or unusual happenings that have been overwhelming. I have tried never to doubt in these areas—

and I do not need confirmations in order to believe, but a confirmation can be wonderful. Six years after I met Christ I discovered a recently written book titled *I am With You Always—True Stories of Encounters With Jesus* by G. Scott Sparrow. It was a true blessing to read and to learn that many others too have received a "Visit." None were like mine. Christ brought His kitten with Him for me alone and I have never been the same. I pray you will read the entire account in my previous book.

In signal moments, such as in this encounter with Him, it seems for me that the only complete and satisfying means of expressing the deepest heart thoughts and soul moving experiences is with poetry.

There is a poem I wrote the month before I met Christ and it reveals somewhat the state of the sadness of my soul at that period. The reason for this was revealed in a previous chapter.

Rx: Poetry

I live on the edge
Don't ask me why—
I won't try to hedge
And I'll tell you no lie.
But more times than not—
There's a tear in my eye,
(in fact—many times—
tears I just can't control)
And so I write rhymes
For they always console.

They get to the core—
Poems soothe what is wrong
Poetry opens the door
In my heart—puts a song.
And my soul lightens up
Before very long.

Dedicated to   JGK
the writing of rhymes

Following are two of the poems that seemed to almost write themselves depicting my encounter with Christ, July 28, 1992

A HOMELESS MAN?

While all had gone forward to *"receive"* Him
    in Communion
He appeared out of nowhere.
He sat in the last pew—to which I returned,
Head raised slightly in silent gaze—
In Communion also—with His Father.
Resting—waiting to be strengthened
    for the day ahead—
He seemed to be oblivious
    of communicants passing by
        leaving Church to go out
            into their world.
They too, appeared to be oblivious
    of Him—while momentarily
        in His Presence—
Yet their eyes took Him in
    as they moved quickly by
        His ragged form.
Long haired and bearded
    tattered and worn
We passed Christ by—
    and my heart was torn!
Was He meant only for my eyes
    and to all others was disguised?
Did no one else recognize
    our Silent Guest?

Written concerning the   JGK
appearance of Christ
in Church July 28, 1992

REVELATION

Christ appeared—quite unforeseen—
Setting heart and life askew—
Upsetting gently all routine,
And with His silent retinue—
Of love and awe, tears and conviction—
Entering in to ease my load—
I felt somehow His Benediction,
And my soul softly explode.

O Homeless Man I know Thou art—
Christ who lives within my heart.
Though disheveled, worn, unkempt—
I know the Christ of whom I've dreamt.
I can never ease Your strife—
And yet today you changed my life.

Written concerning the   JGK
appearance of Christ to me—
July 28, 1992

Amen

Angels

> *Angels work through syncronicity and if we remain open not closed,*
> *to all possibilities, we may receive their messages of insight, love, and hope*
> *through virtually any channel of earthly communication.*
> —Terry Lynn Taylor—Mary Beth Crain from "Angel Wiscom"
> 365 Meditations and Insights from the Heavens

I have believed in and been open to Angels since I was a child. Talking to my Guardian Angel brought me comfort, and writing about my Angel in my journals confirmed what I knew in my heart to be true. In my previous book, *Journal of Love*, I have written of numerous personal Angel experiences that brought such blessings and confirmations, yet there are others still to be shared and told. They continue to be recorded in my journals. Angels changed my life and have become part of my daily existence. In more recent years through prayer and meditation I receive written messages from my Angel and keep these in an enchanting journal with a glorious Angel on the cover, a gift from my loving friend Ruth. Angels are a part of my spiritual life and as I have written earlier, I believe also that Rochester is an Angel. He too has had Angel experiences of his own that I have witnessed and written about in my previous book.

My first inclination however in recent years is to first write a poem about my Angel encounter and this helps me to fully absorb within what occurred. Many Angel poems now exist in my journals and books.

The following poem was written after an angel experience shared again with Rochester, when my name was spoken aloud.

AN ANGEL SPOKE

An Angel spoke!
Yet I, in deep mediation
heard it invoke
my name—
Calling me forth from another realm
to mysteriously overwhelm
my soul.
And I, without hesitation
proclaim
it so.

JGK

One unusual encounter I have not shared before in my books happened in 1992. I will just include a portion of the poem. A dear friend had just died and I was grieving. He is a man I spoke of earlier named Ed who Rochester and I wrote get well cards and messages to, and now we were miles away and not able to attend his viewing or Mass that same evening.

THE VISIT OF MARCH 25TH

In my grief I sat alone—
Crying for someone I've known.
Through my tears I prayed his name
And as I did an angel came.

Yes, an angel swift and sure
Came to me so I'd endure—
Beneath my shoulder made a poke
Hard and strong—as if he spoke—
And told me to be calm—and cease—
My tears for Ed; he was at peace

Dedicated to my   J.G.K.
precious friend
Edward J. Wall, Jr.
Died March 21, 1992

I believe without a doubt an angel came to comfort me and in a sense the poke beneath my right shoulder was a loving reprimand to help me realize Ed was secure with God and the Angels. I was in my writing room at my desk and only Rochester was with me. Bob was elsewhere outdoors. The poke on my shoulder was so strong it startled me in my tears and I jumped up to look around. There is only one explanation and it was revealed to me instantly. No one visible was there but I knew my Angel surely was caring for me in my utter sadness, and shocked me to help clear my mind and to ease my aching heart. It is an knowledge I will ever hold dear. All the Angel experiences that have been given as gifts within our cottage Rochester was present with me to share.

Here within this chapter I am revealing about moments when an Angel revealed himself in a manner that left no doubt of true Angelic Presence, and those incidents were profound. But it is in the daily *"presence"* that is even more blessed, in the quietness and privacy of my little cottage and especially my writing room when I am given each day the *"knowing"* that cannot be shaken or questioned. Poems are written

about the "*unseen*" and "*unheard*" angels also who are here and share my
life and invisibly inspire and protect. Rochester often sees what I have
not, and poems were written about those spiritual occasions also and
included in my previous books. The simple poem that follows tells of the
"unseen" present, and presence.

WELCOME ANGELS

Angels, Angels—everywhere—
On the stair and in the air—
By my bed—'round desk and chair,
And I am blest that they are there.

Welcome, welcome, Angels dear—
When others jeer—you wipe my tear,
And banish fear and restore cheer—
And I am blest that you are here.

Dedicated to my   JGK
Angels

Angels too send or leave "*signs*" or "*gifts*" with wonder and great joy.
They can be right before us or waiting to be discovered in unlikely places.
My Angel Journal has entries concerning such enchantments recorded
in detail. If we are open and have a spirit of gratitude and love, the "signs"
will be discovered. I am always in awe and deeply appreciative that I
could be "*touched by an Angel*" in such directness and visibility. Following
is a poem written about the second feather in a series of three that was
sent to me, speaking instantly to me about a matter only I knew and that
was buried within. I sat down and this poem flowed out when I put pen
to paper. Peace came to my soul. The feather is with others that were sent
in a lovely tin box that I go to often.

THE SECOND FEATHER

I am the small white feather gliding to ground.
I land upright in the thick velvet grass
   to stand between green blades.
I am waiting to be found
   before daylight fades—
By one who will soon pass
   the one for whom I am intended.
Slender and delicate—a sign so splendid—
   the second feather to her in a week
     from an Angel—
       A feather to speak
         to her soul.

JGK

The poem that will close this short commentary on Angels tells of an utterance of my name in the silence of our living room here in our cottage. It was the day after my dear friend Francis' birthday and he had been in Heaven almost four years and I was thinking of him. Bob was outdoors waiting for me in our car as we had errands to attend to in nearby Sanford, Maine. Rochester was present and I had been hugging him good-bye as we watched the birds through the front sliding doors. I have always known in my spirit it was an angel of comfort and love. My name was said clearly and loudly enough to startle me. Again I turned to my right as with the other experience sensing it came from that direction. If one hears their name spoken most normally and distinctly there can be no doubt, for me, of Angelic presence when there is no visible human within distance. There have been other occasions also that an Angel has spoken my name within this cottage. Rochester was always with me.

THE PRESENCE

Through long glass doors I viewed my world.
A small red squirrel with tail unfurled—

Tunneled in the snow right there—
Outside my panes in winter air.
Birds at feeders took their fill—
I watched each tiny little bill—
That claimed the suet and the seed—
Such precious hungry ones, indeed.

Then suddenly my name was said
Audibly! and I was led—
To turn around—look to my right—
Yet *knew* there'd be no one in sight!
'Twas not my little cat that spoke—
Oh no, another did invoke—
And call out *"Jan"*—I heard my name!
And I *knew* then an Angel came!

I did not doubt—nor felt no fear—
When an Angel's voice God let me hear!

In gratitude and awe   J.G.K.
for the Angel's Presence—
the morning of
March 15, 1994

*"Dreams are spiritual messages that you are being lovingly cared for
by divine forces. They are like Angels, in that they bring forth both good
news and urgent warnings."*
— from "Wrestling with Your Angels" by Janet O. Hagberg

On September 12, 1997 I had a dream I remembered well after I
awoke. It was long and complicated and involved my daughter Jessica
and me. The dream is not important to share now but what happened
shortly before I was abruptly awakened is. In the dream we met a woman
singing a haunting melody. The words could not be explicitly heard but
the melody was completely and distinctly with me when I woke. I
immediately went in the living room to play it on the piano and then
wrote the notes down so I could forever have them. I played them singly

and heard the exact melody I had just heard in my dream. I added little chords to them and they were more beautiful.

Later in the afternoon after playing the *"dream refrain"* bestowed upon me in my dream, I effortlessly wrote down words that just flowed into my mind after hearing the melody again when I played it on the piano. Both music and words were received and completed within a couple of hours. I have never received music in a dream before but this was so clear, obviously a gift from the Angels, as are the words. Bob thought it was beautiful and he was able to play it for me in his relaxed way of playing *"by ear"* with lovely full chords, after he had heard me play it. We both were in awe that this lovely music was given, then completed by the words of poetry.

ANGELS' SONG

We're from the starry night
To keep your heart so bright.
We've brought this song to you
To say

anew—
We're always by your side
For we're your Angel guides—
You've seen through one disguise,
You're very

wise.
He's your Angel dressed in fur—
Who sings his song in purr.
And with you evermore
from

God.

When I finished writing this section about the Angels I went to one of my book shelves here in my writing room and took out Francis' green book of poems just to make a heavenly contact through poetry and his earthly gift to me. The book fell open to an envelope addressed to *"Trappistine Jan and Brother Bob Kolb."* It had been in there since 1989 as the post mark showed but it had been a very long time since I had looked into that particular envelope as I have many others from him. Inside was a lovely poem written to me and about me entitled "Reflection." It begins:

> On the last day of an Easter's advent
> I found Jan Kolb adoring God in pew
> Of church, in which she has so often spent
> Those moments of Solitude, known to few.

How amazing! It was a gift from Francis and most certainly, pointed out to me by an angel encouraging me to seek out and open Francis book after writing about poetry, a subject that consumed Francis in great love. How can anyone doubt the presence of Angels? They are everywhere and they are with you—and they are with me—and it fills me with awe and gratitude. I could have discovered another of his poems written about spiritual subjects, family, or nature, but instead I was shown a poem written in his handwriting about me and for me alone. That truly was of the Angels and I read it as for the first time.

One day later on a weekend in December and before I continued work on this book on Monday, the Clancys, (our extended family) Dennis, Patti, Sarah and Jenny, came from their cottage on the hill above us to present us with a birthday gift most extraordinary. Patti was cradling in her arms a large cement statue of an Angel Cherub sitting upon the back of a round shell font intended to hold water for the birds. The shell was fan-like with a concavity facing upwards like a basin. The Angel was

Rochester in company of Gabriella shortly after the statue was given to us

*Gabriella and Maraglo in
the garden with begonias
in the water font*

dangling her tiny feet into it waiting for me to fill it with water and was tenderly holding a bird on its nest in her arms. To me, birds too, are like Angels. It was a precious piece of creative art and I was so moved by this gift. In my heart it seemed it was a gift from the Angels after completing this chapter through our loving Clancys who are sensitive to the Angels.

It was our Clancys I wrote about in my previous book "*Journal of Love*" who appeared with a beautiful stuffed Unicorn image following my completion of writing a section on Unicorns. They had not know I had written about Unicorns. It was a synchronism of precious confirmation.

Sarah named the cherub Angel at my request and she is now known as "*Gabriella.*" We kept her indoors in our living room throughout the cold winter but just last week, in the final week of May as I completed this book and began to think of gardening after our black fly season here, we placed the statuary of Gabriella and Maraglo in my beach garden, one of my seven rock walled gardens. "Maraglo" is the name of a bird in a poem by E. B. White, a poem that is included in my previous book. It seemed the perfect name for Gabriella's bird, to make Maraglo seem more present in my life, a gentle visible poem. Sarah and Jenny approved of Gabriella's station.

Poems arrive. They hide in feelings
and images, in weeds and delivery vans,
daring us to notice and give them form
with our words. They take us to an
invisible world where light and dark,
inside and outside meet.

—Susan Goldsmith Wooldridge from *"Poemcrazy"*

POEM ALERT

My husband says when we go out—
There really shouldn't be such doubt—
That I am really there with him,
For soon my being becomes dim.
I sit and stare upon the roof—
And slowly drift away—like "poof!"
I'm in that place of alter state
Where poems form and I create!

In restaurant we come to dine—
Instead I'm fed line after line!
He says I sit there in the booth
With eyes glazed over and aloof!
I disappear into my shell—
And he knows well that's where I'll dwell!
He says I'm boring and in space—
But I know this is special grace!

How strange—when dull and introspective—
I'm receiving and receptive!
They ask if I'm in pain—or hurt—
He smiles—says "no"—it's a "poem alert"!

Dedicated to Bob
and written in a booth at
the Coo Coo's Nest

Reflect and Journal

☞ Perhaps you might consider reading some poetry from time to time—a favorite poet's work or you may want to discover a new one. There are inexpensive paperback books that include a collection of many poets between their covers.

☞ If you already enjoy poetry then let a favorite poem inspire you to explore it in writing in your journal, even rewrite it.

☞ Reflect quietly and often on the subjects written about in this chapter. Has anything deeply touched your heart or caused memories to surface? Write about it in your journal.

☞ Was there anyone or ones in your life, or situations that caused you to want to write or read poetry? Attempt to write a poem or poems about this, or write about it all in your journal.

☞ If you wish to truly enjoy and learn more about poetry and wish to begin to write poetry or begin anew—there is a delightful book that can cause all of this to happen for you. I reread my copy continuously—six times since I purchased it in 1997. It is one that I will continue to read. You will enjoy it!

The title is *Poemcrazy-Freeing Your Life With Words*, by Susan Goldsmith Wooldrige (Paperback, $13.00) Three Rivers Press New Your, New York

I am certain it can be ordered in any bookstore. Read it with journal and pen beside you. You will want to write poems, I promise.

CHAPTER NINETEEN

Journal Writing

*"In its very essence, journal therapy is a bridge into first our own humanity,
and then our own spirituality. The road stretches out before us,
and our ultimate task is the journey."*
—Kathleen Adams, M.A. from *"Journal to the Self"*

I BEGAN THIS BOOK by encouraging that you keep a journal and with only a few suggestions left you on your own. You may or may not have chosen to buy a journal and use it. Perhaps you decided to first read this book through as I also proposed and then hopefully had intentions of returning to it for some rereading and to use the *"Reflect and Journal"* thoughts that follow each chapter. I would like to further encourage you now to journal and make this always a part of your life. Entire books have been written on this subject alone and I am certain if I continued on this topic I too could do the same. Each book on journaling I have read has been wonderful and informative and different because each author's experience in journal keeping influences what is being written in each book. There are many out there that you can learn from. The basics, however, are to buy a journal that is appealing to you, both the cover and the pages within, and also the size. Some pages do not take ink well if you prefer to write in ink. Always look carefully at the paper. Also choose lined pages or unlined. This all influences whether or not you will continue and make your journal your constant companion. Some may prefer plain pages so that sketching or drawing can be more clearly done along with the writing, while others prefer lined because they like this order and only wish to write. (Although sketching can be done on lined pages too.) You learn as you go along in your journaling journey, but if it is your first journal or the first time in many years you decided to use one, then try carefully to please yourself in its selection and do not just hastily buy one. I guarantee you that what you choose will influence you as to whether or not you will faithfully use it. I have had so many, many journals yet on occasion I began one I thought was right for me at that time only to realize I had to stop using it at some point because it did not cause me to want to write in it. It may sound ridiculous but it is true. You are pouring yourself into your journal and it has to fit your mind and heart like a glove. If it is the wrong cover for some reason, the wrong paper, or it does not stay open well enough and you constantly have to fight it to lie back, then for a new journal keeper especially, it is enough to cause one to give up journaling. Even one who has kept a journal for a long time would get discouraged. It is such a personal book, so the day you decide to buy a journal and begin, allow sufficient time so you can make it a special occasion and take your time in deciding.

They can be purchased in book stores or stationery stores and some larger department type stores. If you make a mistake in selection the first time please do not give up. You would be giving up something essential to your well being. Better to just keep looking for the very kind you prefer. But even your preference will change as you continue to journal and you go through phases of becoming addicted to first one sort of journal, and cover and quality of page to another that might be totally opposite of the first. I know for I have been this way and have filled journals of every sort and size. Sometimes I get on a kick of a particular kind and use it for several years just buying as many different covers as possible though the maker, size and paper are the same. I recently went through this with a set of beautiful covers of various garden and mountain scenes all in the same series, and after completing and filling every journal in the series I began again, then filled many of a particular one with a cover filled with a glorious garden back and front of Spring flowers of every hue. The creamy white paper within was perfect for my favorite green ink pen and the predominant color on the covers is green. These journals were so lovely and also inexpensive hard covers, and they drew me to them one after another. At this time they are still my favorites, because I bought a fabric covered one for my present use and though I like it it does not call to me like my hardback series of nature scenes. I will complete it however. But sometimes you just cannot. I stress this so you will not think you are strange and give up. But even if you stop using a journal before you finish writing in it to the last page, always save the journal. It is part of your life. Never discard a journal!

I have been given exceptional journals through the years as gifts from my friend Ruth, of lovely covers with cats and Angels. I fill each one. One Angel journal from Ruth is the special one I write in regarding Angels in my life. A glorious Angel is on the hard cover and there are Angels throughout in soft pastel colors with names.

Some writers like to use loose leaf note books of every size, some preferring the small sizes and others larger. They often carry some blank pages with them then to capture thoughts while they are out in the world and then return the filled pages to their loose leaf books. This is good and works beautifully for many. Some who use this method never change and get totally addicted to it. The only drawback I see (and these are also suggested in various books on journaling) are that you can lose your pages that are carried with you. Also, if you have written something and later decide to destroy it it is much easier to do. I personally believe as do many other journal keepers, that the good and the bad should stay in a journal *permanently*, for you learn from both in rereading. You are less apt to tear out a page from a bound journal and so the whole continuity of your life is between the covers and this is good. The same thing could happen if you use a wire bound composition book. While these are nice and many attractive covers can be found especially at the beginning of a school year, you can be tempted to tear a page out if you are having a bad time or you have written something you felt should not have been written. If you are patient and do not destroy it, somewhere in the future you will learn the page or entry (perhaps several pages) truly belongs there. I will write later how the spiral notebooks can be used when another type of writing is shared.

However, only you can decide what type journal is for you. You learn as you try various journals and this is both fun and a time of discovery. Just keep writing through it all. Do not give up! Before long you will wonder how you ever existed without your journal keeping. You will also discover the size journal you prefer, from very small right on up to a large artist's sketch book that some journal keepers really like. In this, of course, you can sketch and glue in pictures or anything you wish, though you can still do these things in a medium sized journal with lined or unlined pages. Whatever keeps you writing and continually calls you to it, that is what is meant for you alone. You may find a journal and use the same kind forever! Some feel a plain colored cover is nice and each color they choose represents things to them or phases of their lives. Also many people name their diaries, one name for all, or individual names for each journal. You may remember that Anne Frank addressed her journal as "*Kitty*." This is the joy of it all, that a journal is personal and you as its keeper can make of it what you alone desire.

Please try not to censor yourself. Fill your journal with not only writing from your heart but with all sorts of odds and ends, a running list of books you read (I do this!), quotes (yes, always!) and anything that sparks your imagination like poems, (yes!) and even song lyrics that are meaningful. Unsent letters can also be written in your journal. If your heart is aching or you are in a rage, write to the individual who has wounded you and vent yourself on your journal pages. This brings a certain release and healing. There are no rules at all to journal keeping. None! So enjoy!

If your wish to take journal notes while away from home you can carry a simple note book of some sort and transfer the notes to your permanent journal later. In this method your journal is kept safely at home. This is my personal method and I have mentioned earlier I always have a stenopad with me in the car for poems that suddenly come, notes to myself and things I want to enter later in my journal. I am also a list maker. This has worked for me and I believe I also shared that these steno pads are extremely personal to me and I keep them all. Years ago I carried a very small journal, then a small note book. These worked too. But I would never carry my intimate journal out into the world. Again, it is each person's choice. I am only sharing from my heart things I have experienced and what I see as possible strengths and also obstacles. Journal keeping is amazing. I do hope that you will try it if you never have or have not journaled in a very long time. It is for your personal help and healing and your journal becomes your confidante.

There are many published journals and reading these can also inspire you. Many authors keep journals and these have been of interest to me. May Sarton is a writer who lived in New Hampshire then moved to

Maine, and her entries are so simple and yet profound. She speaks of the seasons, her beloved pets, her gardens, her old home, her fears. I cried at the death of Punch her parrot and enjoyed the writings about her precious animals and her writing habits. She inspires me to keep my own journals and to write books. In her journals is the raw material that later she transformed into her poetry and fiction. When she herself died several years ago in her eighties I cried also. I had just seen her interviewed shortly before on television and had been moved. Her writing fed her soul and the souls of others. Begin with perhaps her *"Journal of a Solitude"* which is well known and loved.

This was given to me in 1978 by my friend Ginny because May Sarton lived in New Hampshire and kept journals and Ginny felt I would discover she was a writer who would speak to me. She did and continues to do so. Her journal *"Recovering"* specifically helped me in the 1980s. All of her journals I have read numerous times. Her books and journals will continue to minister to me and to many others through the years.

Perhaps keep your journal by your bed at night too for once you begin using one you will want to record thoughts before sleep, or upon awakening, or if you have a dream. Even if only a few words are written following a dream and even in the dark, you will be able to write out the entire dream in the morning. Some people keep a separate journal for dreams. Still—you may prefer to keep your journal in an honored place or on your desk or altar in your writing space or room, and simply make notes in a bedside writing tablet concerning dreams, to be transferred later to your journal. It is your decision.

How Many Times

How many times I have come abruptly awake
Apparently for the sole purpose to take
    pen in hand—
        to try to understand
            a passing thought or dream—
That would float through my unconsciousness
    in a stream
        of mystery and confusion.

And I, trying to sort through reality and illusion—
Would be left a tiny strand
    on which to clutch—
With the hope I might understand
    that strand—that fleeting touch
        upon me, that came unfurled
           from an unknown world.

JGK

Journals for Those Who Grieve

It is also caring to give a journal as a gift to someone who is grieving and who has lost a loved one be it a human or an animal companion. Even if they have never written in a journal before they may turn to one now if one is presented to them. Since you cannot know their choice of design or colors simply pray and you will be guided, or ask his or her color preferences for a gift you have in mind, or if the person is attracted to floral patterns or plainness. Perhaps it will lighten the person's spirit to know you are trying to please them and they can anticipate a surprise. Nothing can ever replace their loss but if the gift is accompanied with a written note from you to say its purpose then when the person is alone they may quietly discover its intent and beauty. I have known this to be true numerous time after giving a journal as a gift to one who is in deep sorrow. I too, have been helped in this way.

My friend Bertha keeps journals for each of her dear cat companions who have died. She had deep sorrow when three of her dear ones from the same litter, Manny, Moses and Jackie, died in the same year when they were thirteen years old, followed by April, her precious twenty-year-old cat who died this year, three years later. Bertha is consoled by writing and it has been my solace to have presented her with journals at the time of their deaths and on the anniversaries of their deaths. I was at a loss as to how else to help her aside from prayer. She fills every journal and this has been her strength in her sadness and she now has these journals to aid her in healing, and she in turn helps others in this way. Journal keeping in regard to the death of animal companions is discussed more fully in my book *Compassion for All Creatures,* and I believe you would find the thoughts consoling and helpful.

My daughter Laurel presented the mother of a friend with a journal and the response was overwhelming. This friend had driven at a time when he was in an emotional state that sent him speeding up a main route in our area in Pennsylvania. The ride ended in a fiery crash and the young man's death. The mother in an inconsolable state found a journal Laurel left on her doorstep with a note. She sat up all night writing and filled the journal and then called Laurel to tell her how it had saved her sanity. She bought another journal and continued to write and God helped her in this tragedy through her writing and gradually restored her peace. Your own personal journals are the journals that will bring you healing and joy, where you can bare your soul, journals for you alone.

Journals for Your Family

In 1985 before my retreat and before I began writing my books, I began a group of seven journals. These were to get me writing more (along with my own personal journal) as well as to eventually be gifts to my six children and to a young girl to whom I was a sponsor at the time of her confirmation and who is my daughter Janna's best friend. It was Eileen and Janna when they were smaller who used to knock on the window of my closet as I created tapes.

I intended writing thoughts, memories and encouragements in each like a love letter to each child. Lovely journals bought in an oriental store with silk floral designed covers were ones I chose, all different in color. On one trip to New Hampshire I began all seven journals and it was a great deal of work, love work yes, but work. I tried my best to write in these journals along with my own but when I began writing books I could no longer keep up on these journals. It made me sad but I had dreamed and waited for years to be able to be a writer of books when my children were grown, and this had to come first. And so these journals are safe secure and incomplete. Perhaps one day I can complete them. I mention them because perhaps those of you with smaller families might want to undertake such journal keeping. But first—write in your own personal journal always!

Mother's Journals / Father's Journals

There are now journals being sold that are filled with suggestions and blank spaces in which to write in your responses. These are meant to give to your children and came along at least ten years after I had begun the seven journals for my family. I have filled out a *"Mother's Journal"* and then Bob made five more copies of it for me so all six of our children would have one. He also made several additional copies for some of my close friends since it included my entire history.

I have given these *"Mother's Journals"* to each of my daughters and to close friends so they too can fill them out for their children. Just last year a *"Father's Journal"* was also in the stores so I got one for my son and several of my sons-in-law. Bob, at this point, is not inclined to do one for his days are filled with creativity and not enough hours.

Again, these are wonderful but are asides to your own personal journal. They are not the personal journal I continually write about in the pages of this book meant for your eyes alone. They are *"gift journals"*— totally different that others may read. They can *never* replace personal journal keeping!

Photographic Journals (?)

In recent reading I have learned that photo albums and scrap books can be a form of journal keeping but I never considered mine as such. But I will make mention of these for you might want to put more writing into these type books if you enjoy recording life's events in this way, and then they would be more journal-like. But they do not replace your journal! NEVER!

When we were first married I began a scrap book (manilla pages) and put everything into it (photos, keepsakes etc.) of the first two years of our marriage. It also included items and photos Bob sent me while he was overseas in Japan and other places those six months. I wrote mini entries next to all the things of further explanation or if there was a story connected to it. For instance there was a photo taken of Bob receiving the telegram I sent telling him of the birth of his first child, our daughter

June. Next to it I wrote personal jottings about the event. But I never considered this a journal. And there was a church Bulletin from a church in Bremerton, Washington from the first Mother's Day I ever spent in church as a new Mother. Bob and baby June were with me, and I wrote about it near the program.

Also I kept photo albums for our six children. Each had their own album and as they grew each began to own a number of albums then. Many! The pages I chose were gray or tan (not black like most photo albums are) and I wrote details about the pictures and little asides that made them more meaningful. I did not simply put each photo in with name and date only. To learn now these can be a form of journal is very good because I spent hours on these creating heirlooms to one day give my children. I lost momentum on this very large endeavor (because it takes a great deal of time to do for six children) when I became involved in my tape ministry for eight years. There were only so many hours in a day.

While scrapbooks and photo albums are a precious form of record keeping when accompanied by notes, I definitely do not think of it as the journal keeping that I have written about throughout this book and earlier in this chapter. While it is lovely to do it does not fulfill the same needs as regular journal keeping in a journal. I am talking about writing that will *heal* you and that is *soul-writing*. I am certain by now you too know the difference. Since scrapbooks and photo-albums are usually shown to family and others, then for me I cannot quite regard those as a form of journal keeping in the sense I have been sharing with you about throughout this book. Your journal is private and for you alone so that you can explore your life and all it contains. *That* is the kind of journal keeping I am encouraging, *that* is the journal writing to make time for in your life. *That* is the journal keeping that will keep you writing everyday and it will change your life. It will!

Anne Frank

"The unbosomings of an ugly duckling," will be the title of all this nonsense.

—Anne Frank

This young girl must be mentioned in this chapter for she has shown us through her brief life ended too soon, courage, endurance, and that writing truly can minister to and sustain the human soul in all circumstances. The quotation above is humorously and lovingly directed at her journal as she contemplates the possibility that one day perhaps it could be published. She had heard that diaries would be collected after the war and decided to rewrite her own diary so that it too could be published. While copying it she added some things and the fresh copy was made on thin sheets of tracing paper. She often doubted the point of doing all this and on April 14, 1944 she wrote:

> *Everything here is so mixed up, nothing's connected any more, and sometimes I very much doubt whether in the future anyone will be interested in all my task.*

She then closed with the words of quotation that begin this section. She also fantasized about writing a romance of the *"Secret Annex"* (March 29, 1944) and a week later she wrote, *"Will I ever become a journalist or a writer? I hope so, oh I hope so very much, for I can recapture everything when I write, my thoughts, my ideas and my fantasies"* (April 5, 1944).

Then on May 11, 1944 she confided in her diary: *"You've known for a long time that my greatest wish is to become a journalist someday and later on a famous writer."* She confides in her diary further then and she hopes to publish a book, *Let Achterhuis* (The Secret Annex). This she intends to do after the war and she writes, *". . . whether I shall succeed or not, I cannot say, but my diary will be a great help."*

Two months later on July 21, 1944, Anne was happy and optimistic. News of the war seemed hopeful and eleven days later, she made one last entry in her diary. It is written that on August 4 between ten o'clock and half past ten in the morning, the German Police stormed the Secret

Annex. They had been betrayed. Tuesday, August 1, 1944 was the last entry she made in her diary. Margot, Anne's sister died in the concentration camp Bergen-Belsen and Anne died there a few days later in March 1945. The camp was liberated by British soldiers a few weeks later in April.

Anne has left her legacy to all in her diary. Anne's sister Margot, who was three years older also kept a diary but it was lost when they were taken to the concentration camp.

During the period Anne and her family were in hiding (July 1942 to August 1944) in the Secret Annex, Anne was sustained by writing in the diary given to her by her parents on her thirteenth birthday June 12, 1942. Later when this became filled and pages and photos were added to it, she was given exercise and accounting books by her protectors Niep and Bep so that she could continue to keep her diary. The original hardcover diary had been a red and white checkered book, her best friend whom she named *"Kitty."* Anne and Margo wrote letters to each other also while in the Annex. Anne confides in her diary about this exchange—*"Because I can say what I mean much better on paper"* (March 20, 1944). Writing helped both these young girls.

Anne enjoyed writing so much that she also wrote stories and began writing a book titled *Stories and Events from the Secret Annex,* and memories from her school days, as well as fairy tales. She wrote other imaginary tales too which she called *"Made Up Stories."*

It is revealed that the one thing you notice immediately about the story book is its neatness. Anne wrote with her fountain pen in fine script page after page, hardly ever making a mistake or crossing out and the chapters were divided as if in a real book. Several of the stories she wrote down were told to her by her father when she was little about a girl named Paula. Anne *"loathed"* Algebra, Geometry and figures of any sort just as I had, but loved all other subjects. Like myself, Anne had a beloved cat Moortje that had to remain behind when they fled their home. Anne wrote: *No one knows how often I think of her; whenever I think of her I get tears in my eyes"* (July 12, 1942). Along with all else, she had to leave her dear cat.

How can it not be understood that writing is essential for the survival of the soul? The examples given by this young girl should be lessons and teachings enough for the ages to us all, if no one else ever again mentioned the subject of writing. Again the verse from scripture comes to mind, "*And a little child shall lead them.*"

How can one read about Anne Frank and not realize the importance and strength and beauty in writing. Look at other young teenagers you know between thirteen and fifteen years. Could they endure being locked in an attic for two years? Would they have something as incredibly valuable as Anne's writing to help and sustain them to live out this time? Would they turn to writing? We cannot answer but we pray it would be so. That she loved to write at such an early age before she had to be hidden away was her great asset. Does it not speak to hearts reading both this and her diaries to consider encouraging the joy of writing to young ones you know? Some never want to pick up a pen unless it is necessary for school. Anne's legacy to all is *writing* for it is life sustaining! She never wrote about hatred anywhere in her diary but said she believed in the goodness of people. I believe through her writing great insights were given to her. I have talked elsewhere about what we are given when we put pen to paper. Enough cannot be written about this young girl and yet I have personally known three people to say she and her diary never existed nor did the holocaust. With words like these we can understand why there is such hatred in this world, but it did not exist for Anne.

Anne wrote to her diary on May 11, 1944, "*You've known for a long time that my greatest wish is to become . . . a famous writer.*"

After her death Anne Frank's wish was fulfilled, for people throughout the world have read her diary. She became a symbol for the millions of Jews who perished in the Second World War.

Her diary was translated into fifty-five languages and more than 20 million copies have been sold. Films too have been made and many schools and streets all over the world have been named after this young girl. She has become a symbol of good ness and courage. Can we not follow in her example of writing? If she cannot convince you of the importance of writing and journal keeping then I am not certain that I can. But oh, I am trying here for the sake of your souls, for writing will transform you. It will!

If you have never read *The Diary of Anne Frank*, you may be moved to do so now. You may learn much more about Anne than I have shared here from a book that also contains many photos of her diary pages, her family, the hiding place and all else pertaining to Anne's life. It is a true keepsake that I am thankful to own, along with several copies of her diary I have had for years that I only recently discovered.

Anne Frank: Beyond the Diary
A Photographic Remembrance
Ruud van der Rob and Rian Verhoeven
for the Anne Frank House
Introduction by Anna Quindlen
Puffin Books, 1995, Published by Penguin Books

There is also a paperback book of her stories available I have just discovered.

Writing Instruments

Your choice of pen or pencil is important because it has to be an implement you enjoy. If you prefer a pen make sure it is not a cheap one that will asphyxiate you as you write with its odor or make blotches of ink. There are so many inexpensive pens that are marvelous and you just have to experiment. Your writing implement influences you as to whether or not you become a serious journal keeper just as does the choice of the journal you select. If you find a pen you love buy a box of them and some come in various colors. This is fun to have a variety of colors, or you may use one color ink with one particular journal and then switch to another color when you begin a new journal. Also when you switch journals, as you complete one you may want to try unlined pages if you have been writing on lined pages and vice versa. All these things add to the joy of writing and help to hold your interest. Pray before you begin a new journal and you will be led to choose one and the writing implements. Honor the practice of journal keeping and you will be blessed and shown the way. Before you begin a new journal it is nice to say a prayer or write a little greeting to it in the front and thank it for its help and anything else that might come to mind. And again, perhaps you may wish to give it a name as did Anne Frank.

But the pen you use is important. Perhaps you already have a special pen or you may want to buy one. Most writers that write daily have favorite pens. Cross pens are marvelous and I used one for years. Also Waterman pens. And of course there was my Blessed Mother Blue Parker pen I have written about in Chapter Fourteen. I even wrote this poem about it shortly after meeting my friend *"Friar"* Francis and my return to writing poetry. It was one of the first poems I wrote then.

ODE TO MY PEN

How faithful you stand
As I take you in hand
You write on command
You meet my demand.

You know what I need
Incredible speed—
Free flowing ink
On call in a wink!

Ah, yes I salute you
With me forever
I guard you as life
Loan you out? Never!

Now others I know
Would not go to this end
But God called me to write
And my pen is my friend.

This was my loving tribute to the pen who had been my friend.

I sadly disposed of the pen in direct opposition of Stanza three as I wrote earlier, when I heard it was made by Gillette who tests on animals. It was not easy to do, perhaps even wrong, for it had served me so well, but animals' lives were far more important to me.

The green ink pens I have used for the last ten years as I have stated earlier are Sanford Uni-ball Onyx pens, fine point. Though the casing is black with green end, the ink is a wonderful shade of green and the point excellent so that the pen glides smoothly over the paper. I also use another green ink pen whose barrel is bright green, Pentel Rolling Writer. This is a medium point and also writes wonderfully. As to writing swiftly and smoothly they so far out-write the Parker ball point pen of the poem that it is difficult to explain the joy of writing with them. They never drag. I write very fast and these green ink pens made by these companies mentioned are a dream for any writer. The ink is fluid-like fountain pen ink.

Pencils are also wonderful. I have written all of my books with number 2 pencils on loose leaf paper. Many people use pencils for journal writing. You must find the lead that is perfect for you, hard or soft. I also use colored pencils for drawing in my journals and it is a nice treat to buy a box of these. Many journal keepers use highlighter pens, the transparent variety to emphasize things of importance. These too come in various colors. This is not something I do but I can understand how it can be helpful.

Begin to Write

"Talking to paper is talking to the divine. Paper is infinitely patient. It will wait decades for you to put together the first faint traces of your own code, a code you might have understood as a small child but which you are now gathering on a new level of understanding."

—Burghild Nina Holzer
from "A Walk Between Heaven and Earth"

It is very nice to begin with a meditation before writing in your journal and to quiet yourself. If you are going to spend a longer time writing you could light a candle and set a mood. Some people like to play their favorite music and make a cup of coffee or tea. Other times may not allow for extended leisure in writing accompanied by candles or tea. It is very important that you date every journal entry no matter where or when you write. Another author and journal keeper suggests you wrap your journal in a lovely soft scarf or piece of material and keep it in your quiet corner, place, or room and perhaps on an altar if you have made one in the area where you pray and write. I thought that was a lovely idea and

I am looking for a significant scarf for my Angel Journal. The author also suggests that the unwrapping of your journal could become a ritual and could include carefully folding the scarf or draping it over a cushion adding to the beauty of the setting. These last two thoughts are from a very loving and inspiring book entitled *Find a Quiet Corner—A Guide to Self-Peace* by Nancy O'Hara

There are so many things to write about journal keeping but I have already interspersed thoughts on it throughout this book, and so perhaps I have said enough. To say more would be risky for me for journals mean very much to me and this truly could expand into a book as I have suggested earlier. To write in a journal is a joy and it is also like having your own therapist in times that are difficult. I could not survive without writing in my journal if that is any indication as to its strength and importance in my life. It also makes me feel closer to God and my Angels. I keep a separate journal for my Angels because I felt it necessary.

Try to write in a free flowing way so that what you are feeling within flows out, and also things that are deeply buried inside you will come forth on the page. All these writings will help you and heal you. Please, open your mind and heart and attempt to be a journal keeper and you will be on a new plane and feel that you have a sanctuary to return to again and again.

One thing I would *advise* strongly (for there are no rules) is to guard your journal's privacy. Never let anyone read your journal for you will then find yourself censoring your entries or writing as if for an audience. If you wish to share an entry from your journal with a close friend for reasons only you would know, copy the entry out onto another paper and even then be cautious as to what you share. These are writings from your heart for the edification and healing and solace of your soul—so use discretion. I have used two entries in two of my books but never have shared any others.

There are many books on journal keeping but there are two that seem to have so many basics in them especially for those just beginning. I love reading from them often for they put sparkle in my already present enthusiasm for the journal. Perhaps through what I have written here and in reading elsewhere throughout my book, you will be interested in making journaling a practice in your life. May you always be a journal keeper.

The books I have just made mention of are:

Journal to the Self—Twenty-two Paths to Personal Growth
by Kathleen Adams, M.A., a Time Warner Book
and
A Walk Between Heaven and Earth:
A Personal Journal on Writing and the Creative Process
by Burghild Nina Holzer, Bell Tower, division of Crown Publishers

On one of my periods in Pennsylvania in 1994 my daughter June and I went to the Jenkintown Barnes and Noble store to browse, shop and to sit and sip some unusual coffee. While there she lovingly instructed me to select two books as a Mother's Day gift from herself and Rob. The two books I have just listed for you were the ones I chose, one newly published that year and one in 1990, and both have been reread many times and will continue to be so. Each is unique and different. I could not recommend one over the other. Both will take you places you have never been and inspire you to write. I would not want to be without either one. The first is more practical and considers everything possible in connection to journal keeping (Journal To The Self) and the other is more mystical to me. (A Walk Between Heaven and Earth) On a day when inspiration is needed to write, either of these would give this to you.

> "A man would do well to carry
> a pencil in his pocket and write
> down the thoughts of the moment.
> Those that come unsought are
> commonly the most valuable
> and should be secured—because
> they seldom return." . . . BACON

WRITING THERAPY

My writing is a deepening need
And pen slips o'er the page with speed.
And oft when I look back to read—
I see God meant my soul to feed!

But when my hand goes on a spree—
It is no certain guarantee—
That it brings inward harmony,
Sometimes it stirs up dark debris!

And then I must stop to inspect—
And interject; pause and reflect—
And disconnect with all neglect—
In retrospect—pray and correct!

And now my pen glides on with ease—
My thoughts are cleansed and I am pleased—
For I have dealt with all disease
Entrapped in those soliloquies!

If I'm to live—then I must write!
It brings delight—and new insight!
It lessens fright—makes my soul bright—
If every night—I can "moonlight."

In silent times—then things external
Are blotted out—and the Eternal—
Touches me—and with my journal,
I write and live—in hours nocturnal!

Dedicated to   JGK
Writing

Reflect and Journal

☞ Write a memory from your childhood or a series of memories and begin with *"I remember."*

☞ Write about several things in life that sustain you emotionally and spiritually.

☞ Record a quotation that moves you and write about why it moves you so.

☞ Write about why you selected the particular journal that you are beginning and create a prayer to record in it to bless your journal writing.

☞ Describe the room or place in which you are writing in your journal using all five senses.

☞ Perhaps choose a name for your journal and record it inside just as Anne Frank did. Perhaps even draw a design around the chosen name using your colored pencils.

Anne Frank would be seventy years old this year (June 12, 1929) and was not yet sixteen when she died.

CHAPTER TWENTY

The Daddy
in the Dell

Jesus loves the little children
All the children of the world—
Red and yellow, black and white
They are precious in his sight—
Jesus loves the little children of the world.

(unknown, A Sunday School Hymn)

SHORTLY AFTER COMPLETING the chapter you have just finished reading, Bob and I were sitting in church this past Sunday on the first
Sunday in Advent. Behind us in the next pew was a young father with his
little boy, who was about three to four years old. We did not meet them
until we turned around during Mass to extend the greeting of peace. By
the time I saw them I wanted to hug them but I refrained. My hope was
to talk to them after the service so we merely greeted them as we did all
the other people around us.

From the time of the arrival of this father and son there was constant
low conversation that eventually grew louder on the child's part with the
father still whispering, though more emphatically. The little boy wanted
to sing, and sing he did. We had to admire his spirit. He had songs to sing,
songs in his heart, and he was in church and heard the others singing and
he wanted his songs to be sung too. The songs were obviously taught to

him by his Daddy or Mommy. Why should his songs be silenced when all around him others were singing their songs? He wanted to share his too! It touched my soul. He tried to sing the songs he knew while the congregation sang their hymns. It was frustrating to him. And so in the interims between hymns and during Mass this little child sweetly sang the songs he loved, not in a fresh or loud way but very gently and it all made my eyes grow misty.

When I was a little girl I sat silently with my parents in our little Methodist Church and even if I had felt inclined (and I would not have!) I would never have spoken or sung out in the service unless it was the proper time to speak or sing. The possibility of me spontaneously singing out alone could perhaps ridiculously be compared to my performing solo in the present on a Broadway stage. It could never happen! Not even in my dreams! Even if I had the voice of an Angel— which I do not!

Years later I too would have tried to keep my child or children from singing their own songs in church during the silent periods. It was not proper for children, or anyone, to speak during the service unless it was part of the service. All parents tried to keep their little children amused and silent. I am speaking now of when we raised our children in the Methodist Church. I have noticed through the years how filled with childrens' voices and cries the Catholic Mass is even though silence is desired there also. Perhaps too I was extremely sensitive to this entire matter because one morning in the middle of a minister's sermon in the Methodist Church a terrible moment occurred. We allowed one of our younger teenage daughters to sit with a friend two rows ahead of our family's pew and right under the minister's pulpit. The young girls whispered to each other as many people occasionally did. Only this time the minister stopped dead in his sermon, covered the microphone with his hand, and leaned over the pulpit. In a strong whisper heard by most everyone in the unexpected silence he said sharply to the two girls, and with emphasis on each word—*"Shut Up!"* We all nearly died of embarrassment. We also felt it was extremely wrong.

The minister was also our close friend so it was bewildering and hurtful that he singled these young girls out. Perhaps he had a turmoil of another sort within himself and took it out on the two girls. It has been memorable.

With a moment like this in our past, it is really not so amazing then that I felt such love and confirmation for this free spirited little child wanting to sing, and for his unnerved but loving father. As I listened to this little boy repeat two lines again and again I grew more emotional within. *"Daddy I want to sing for you. Daddy, I want to sing for the people."* It was like a little chant when his Daddy tried to quiet him. Then the boy would begin to sing again, dear little nursery rhymes of which he knew every word. The only song he sang differently through the changing of one word, moved us so much. He sang *"The Daddy in the Dell"* instead of *"The Farmer in the Dell"*. It was so tender. These songs and the interchange between the Daddy and his son were a sermon that vied for attention in competition with Fr. Edmund's. But Fr. Edmund did not seem to mind or be distracted because he has the precious quality of being *"child-like"* and spontaneous himself. Right in the middle of his sermon while the little boy was singing, Fr. Edmund had stopped the sermon to greet an old friend he spotted in the back of the church. Not once, but twice! After his initial greeting of welcome to him he thought of something else he wanted to say to him and said it. I listen to Fr. Edmund because he *is* child-like and free and yet he expresses things of God so beautifully. Did not our Lord say we must become as little children to enter the kingdom of Heaven? (*Matthew 18:3* KJV)

Perhaps this little boy sensed that Fr. Edmund would not mind his singing, for Father is always lighthearted and gives special attention to children. He also enjoys telling stories about his little wired hair terrier Asta who shares his life and the Rectory. This means so much to me. I have never heard of other pastors in our experience who speak of any animals in their sermons. He is not ashamed to show his tenderness and love for Asta.

We each have a song to sing in our hearts and yet so often we are silenced too, and our song dies and we become afraid to sing. Perhaps this is why I wrote so much ever since I was a young child. In the silence forced upon me I could still express myself in writing. I felt I had a voice.

Though all my family has always sung out their songs and each member has a fine voice I sing in a whisper at church and not at all at home. Bob often teases me and repeats the old familiar joke—*"Sing over by the window and I'll help you out."*

Burghild Nina Holzer writes in her book on journal keeping, "*A Walk Between Heaven and Earth*" encouraging words to my soul. She states:

Maybe my throat wants to tell me of all the songs held back. Held back in fear, or in doubt, or in anger, all the songs that the heart already knows but that I have not voiced. Perhaps I need to walk in that place, down my throat to the vocal cords. And maybe I need to write in my journal about the huge clump that sits there, blocking the air, blocking the sound, blocking the blood flow, causing pain.

I identify with her deep feelings and words as if she is writing about myself. She continues by writing that perhaps there is a big boulder she needs to discover sitting in her throat. Perhaps huge masses of words are compacted into stone. She considers that they could be words too frightening to face, words that have been pushed back or perhaps words too beautiful and tender to bring forth and admit. She closes her reflection by saying "*So many words waiting to be born, all held back.*" Perhaps too, one day my songs will be born.

As a young Mother I did sing gently soft lullabies to my babies in the quiet sacred moments spent together. I always sing inside myself now though and I love music! My Rochester too is silent, but oh I know he too sings within himself. We sing duets all day long in our glorious silence while I write at my desk.

Perhaps one day soon I will be free enough to sing joyfully aloud as well, maybe here in my writing room to Rochester, even if it is only one note. The little boy at church has given me something to think about and of course, he caused me now to write about him. Always the need to write is there, to capture precious moments like I have just described. Because I have changed and am being healed and have become more child-like, I loved the songs of that little child spontaneously sung in church. Yet years ago out of fear I would have tried to prevent my own children of such spontaneity. And Bob's merest "*look*" at one of our children in church would have silenced any song being sung aloud in the silence. But Bob too was so moved by this little boy. We have been touched by God and are thankful for our child-like spirits. I realize there is a time for everything, like being respectful in church—and we are, but oh, this little boy was not disrespectful! He wanted to sing for the people and he sang so sweetly. I believe Jesus loved his songs with all His heart just as He loves this little boy.

I wanted to thank that little boy and his Daddy and hug them after Mass. They brought me a tiny bit closer to the moment when I too can sing what is in my heart like that little child. But when we turned around at the end of Mass to speak to the father and son they were gone. The father probably felt some embarrassment and slipped out during the final hymn, something no one is encouraged to do at St. Anthony's. Fr. Edmund asks each week that all remain to the end which is correct. But in this Daddy's heart perhaps he was nervous to speak with others, though he loved his little son so. I look forward to one Sunday telling this *"Daddy in the Dell"* and his little boy the joy they gave me and how they loosened the bindings on my vocal chords as I timidly wait until one day I too will break out in song. It is written in scripture *"And a little child shall lead them"* (Isaiah 11:6 KJV).

And I am glad I have written it all down for you (and for myself in my journal) for now it can go on to perhaps help free other timid voices. There is no end to what writing can accomplish, the healing it can bring. And too, even a poem was given to me later in the quiet about this little boy.

Because you have read this true account perhaps it will touch you who too need your voices liberated and released and in so doing perhaps you will record it in a journal or write about it one day in a book. Perhaps then it will go on to speak to others who need to sing and have been silenced. And so this chain of love continues. That is the power of the written word.

> The "Daddy in the Dell"
> Attempted to quiet his little child—
> While we sat there and smiled—
> For O he sang so very well!

> Dear little boy—
> With overflowing heart of song—
> You are where you belong!
> Sing out in joy!

We need your song!
>Let your sweet heart take wing—
>Your baby voice joyfully sing—
You do no wrong!

It is we—
>Who need to follow you—
>And sing our songs so true,
Then we will be free!

JGK

I do not believe Jesus would have silenced this little child—for Jesus loves the little children, all the children of the world.

Reflect and Journal

✏ Think about some of the songs that have blessed you through the years and in your journal write about one or two of them and why they are meaningful.

✏ Would you like to try to sing them too? Well maybe one?

✏ If you sang, try to express in your journal what it meant to you and how it felt.

CHAPTER TWENTY-ONE

Stars

"Silently one by one, in the infinite meadows of heaven,
blossomed the lovely stars, the forget-me-nots of the angels!"
—Longfellow

EACH WINTER FOR THE PAST SIX YEARS I have experienced the enchantment of being surrounded by stars. These are stars cut from yellow
poster board to symbolize the sparkling and glowing stars we have been
overwhelmed by in reality. For years we have stood here in front of our
cottage by the lake in silence with heads back to gaze at the heavens
above. Never, until being in New Hampshire had we experienced such
night skies. It is other-worldly to be alone together in the utter darkness
of the woods with the limitless expanse of black above us filled with
millions of dancing stars. On one of these occasions of sharing the star-
filled night skies with Bob I came indoors and penned this poem that just
seemed to flow out of me.

STAR OWNERS

Returning from Sanford, Maine
On dark country road devoid of cars—
Our headlights guiding us on the lane
And the heaven above packed tight with stars—
We felt alone here on this planet—

250

And driving into our State of Granite
And through our woods so black and still—
Saw the lake at last—just down our hill.

And there—under majesty of velvet dome
We stood silently outside our home—
Heads back—gazing into God's vast spaces—
While millions of stars shone on our faces.

It seemed we owned the world and night—
We two together in starlight.

JGK

With these stars of reality then present to us it gives me great joy to create stars out of poster board. And my cut out stars are in a dancing pose as I seem to see the dancing ones on high!

The project of creating stars is not original with me but I am grateful to have been touched by the light of these stars and the desire to share them. The tradition has been passed onto me by my close friend Ginny Leopold, a Presbyterian Pastor, whom I have written about lovingly in my two previous books and mentioned earlier within this one. It is interesting too that some years ago she gave me a framed print of the quotation by Longfellow that begins this chapter. The beautiful words by him are surrounded by dark blue symbolizing the night sky. Stars and pale blue forget-me-nots also surround the quotation.

Ginny had been a fourth grade school teacher for sixteen years and was my daughter Barbara's favorite teacher of all time. Barb had been the only one of our six children to be taught by Ginny and it has remained a highlight in Barb's life.

During the late 1970s and into the 1980s Ginny and I spent much time together and also wrote an endless chain of letters to each other while enduring a painful period in our lives. For a number of years Janna (who was a third grader when Ginny and I met) carried our letters back and forth to each other daily. We were deep spiritual friends then and remain so still. At the end of this extreme *"dark night of the soul"* for each of us Ginny left teaching and entered Princeton University to study for the ministry and her work as a pastor is her life now. I went away on the retreat to *"Higher Ground"* which was then our summer cottage but now in the past several years has become Bob's and my permanent home. It is interesting that during that period of our *"dark nights"* we wrote extensively to each other because we were in need of healing, and a star

My friend Ginny Leopold (on left) and myself (on right) in Pennsylvania

entered our lives then also. I write about this in my book *Higher Ground*—the book I wrote following the retreat I made. I wrote this book in order to help myself as I have written about previously, and also to help others with similar problems. I reread it from time to time if I realize I am in need to review what pushed me to make that retreat in September of 1986.

In it I write that for approximately five years I had a stuffed blue and white cotton print Christmas ornament hanging from my dashboard. Embroidered in its middle is the word "HOPE." It was a prayer reminder—not that I needed one—to persevere in prayer for the difficult persons and situations in my life. I write in my book how I had the dream I could change THEM and that was my HOPE. I reveal how tenseness and restlessness would always be in my spirit as I relentlessly prayed, even feeling guilty if I found myself relaxing. Throughout most of my drives in my car I would cry—never ceasing my prayer while the HOPE ornament danced before me and I remained tearful and uptight. Things only grew worse. But I always had HOPE and tried to see the good in the person or situation and I thought I could CHANGE THEM—so that the good was *evident* and not always not *unseen or unfelt.*

I relate how after my Retreat my husband and I saw a bumper sticker that made us break into laughter. It read *"Since I've given up HOPE, I'm feeling much better."*

Because I had been changed I knew the real meaning behind this funny quote. I had known the heartache and pain of continuously and intensely trying to change someone or something, of pinning my HOPE on their being changed. It was only after my own inner change that I could laugh at the bumper sticker and myself. My friend Ginny who has been a part of my spiritual journey had the same HOPE ornament dangling from her dashboard for we had bought these ornaments in a Christian bookstore one day while together. Depressed and upset over our individual lives and our severe problems she had even personally installed mine in my Plymouth Volare as an act of her love and encouragement. About a year later noticing hers was gone, I learned she had ripped it from her car in a fit of anger and despair. I understood! I had hated mine too! But now I am reconciled with it, as I was at the time I wrote *Higher Ground*, for it holds new meaning. For some time I let it remain in my car to remind me of the bumper sticker, so I would laugh instead of cry as before. Now that HOPE ornament is in my writing room reminding me of essential things for my spiritual well-being. It has only been recently that I realized this too is a star! How could I have not realized? It is a six pointed star however, not five and the points are flattened. I had never seen it as a star before only as an ornament. My heart was filled with light when I realized this too had been a star all along also to guide my way. It was just more modernistic. Before I complete this book I plan to stitch each flattened point until they are pointed as they should be. It is as if there has been a concealed secret within it and I have only recently been shown it and permitted to discover it. This is my "*star*" as it has always been, but soon it shall appear as the concealed star that has been within it all these eighteen years when I eventually sit down with my needle and thread and reveal it.

Perhaps it is a veiled message to us all, that we must look for *hidden stars* to light the way for us and lighten our lives. There is a lovely quotation that has meaning for me:

"*Reach for the moon. Even if you miss you will be amongst the stars*" (Unknown).

What a precious place to be!

The 1980s had been a period of extreme sadness and pain for me despite my spiritual joy of being so close to Jesus. My son-in-law Bill once said to me: "Some people have a bad day, but you had a bad decade," and we laughed together over this impromptu remark. And how wonderful it is to be able to have again joy and laughter!

It was through much prayer and much writing that healing came to me and this is usually how it is in my life, prayer and writing. Through extensive writing in a new journal I bought for that retreat in September of 1986 I began to write my book *Higher Ground* in Fall of 1987. The writing brought healing to others and to many in the world I will never know and even to some close to me I do know. And very especially to myself.

Star Envoys

And now stars too bring healing, and also joy and mystery and direction and yes, enchantment, to all the receivers of these yellow poster board symbols of the real stars on high. Each star must be cut by hand and originally this was not too time consuming for I began by cutting approximately thirty so that I could give one to each friend in my morning Mass group and still have a couple extra.

This group is known as "The Muffins," and they have been written about in my previous books and a previous chapter in this one, and are still my precious close friends though I now live in New Hampshire. And they still receive stars!

Because the stars struck a responsive spiritual note in each receiver I had requests for more so that they could give stars to other family members and friends. I, too, wanted my own family members to each have a star, so with Bob's help we cut out ninety-one stars that first year. He never helped me cut again, but is very supportive and cheerful when watching me do it in the years that followed. And he has bought me endless sheets of yellow poster board and our supply for the coming year is already bought and hidden under the living room sofa to keep it flat and out of the way. The Angels must approve of this heavenly project for in the past each poster board sheet was close to $2.00, but this past summer we discovered piles of it in a store we enjoy shopping in for unusual gifts.

Each sheet was only three cents (!!!) a piece and much larger than the conventional size sold in other stores where I always purchased it. We bought a huge pile and it is a wonder our sofa is not raised up closer to the stars from what lies now beneath it hidden. The next time we returned to the store two weeks later all evidence of the yellow poster board was gone and we have never seen it since. Yes, it was help from the Angels, of course.

When I had finally finished sending out all the stars this past year it was the month of June! I had so many to do it took me months longer but no one seemed to mind. The late comers who received them still had six months to learn from the star they each received. Also, I could not work on stars each day for I was intently working on my previous book, *Journal of Love.* Star-making was for the in-between times of other things in my life that also required attention. This year too, almost 400 stars were cut and sent out and the mailing list continues to grow. Soon I will have to ask the Angels and Elves and Fairies of Higher Ground to help me work with greater speed or perhaps they can help me in cutting!

I have failed to mention the most important thing—and that is the writing involved. Yes, *the enchantment of writing* combined with the enchantment of stars! Writing is the delightful part while cutting is the work. If only I had a magic star cookie cutter that could stamp right through heavy poster board! I keep reminding Bob to invent one for he has invented so many other wondrous things. But it would have to create the same image of my playful dancing star and not a traditional straight and even five pointed star. My stars are enchanting, you see.

But the writing is the joy! As explained in the letter sent or given to each recipient of a star, first I ask the Holy Spirit in prayer for *"star words"* and then I sit and list them all as they are *"given"* to me. A one time sitting in prayer is never enough. I return to prayer many time in order to obtain enough words. I have always requested uplifting and positive words and also magical and enchanting words. I then print a word on each golden star in my green ink and they are ready. If a person picks a star personally, with closed eyes they reach into a little colorful bag I have and select one. If they want others for a friend or relative they select those in the same way. Since moving to New Hampshire almost all the stars are now mailed out. I select a star for each person in the way I have just described, with closed eyes and from the little bag. I then slip each star into a small envelope and its secrecy is sealed in and enclosed with a star letter exactly like I will include in this chapter. If the person has requested more than one star or many, then many thick envelopes are mailed out because each recipient also needs a star letter of explanation. Though the letter was typed by Bob and I constantly updated it and he made the copies of it on our copier, I still write personal letters on almost every star letter that goes out. I write my handwritten letters on the back of the typed one to add added encouragement or to explain stars further to new recipients, or to add anything unusual that might be nice for each person receiving. Naturally all these written letters take much time but the *enchantment of writing* I hope conveys to each person my love, and that they will receive many blessings from the star that is with my letter. Friends and family look forward to their new stars each year and often remind me it is time. Also most people save their stars from year to year for each star becomes very personal to its owner after such a long period. I keep mine on my desk to see daily and Bob keeps his in sight also in his office. Each one has great significance attached to it as well as memories. I have recorded many personal things about each of my stars that happened in the life of each particular star and my own while intertwined for a year's time. I suggest journal keeping in the star letter but I know not everyone tries that or does it. Yet I can only say it adds so much more to the life of your star in your own life and is helpful and insightful in the future when rereading while you still have the star, and even after it is not your current star. You will become attached to each star in a unique way, I feel. I surely do as does Bob and others who have shared this with me.

When I first began creating stars I took my little star-filled bag over to our daughter June's home in Jenkintown one morning after sharing the stars with my "*Muffin*" friends following Mass. June with closed eyes picked stars for herself and husband Rob and for several of her older children. We felt maybe the younger children might not grasp the full meaning that the stars were not merely stars but were meant to become a part of their lives. Suddenly before we could stop him, baby Teddy reached into the bag of stars and his tiny hand came out clutching a star. It was so sweet and happened in a split second. When the star was read we were in awe. In his little chubby hand was the star of "*Innocence.*"

While this was one of the first indicators of how the Holy Spirit truly is present in the selection there have been so many more sharings and stories about stars received.

Just last year I decided Rochester should have a star also and was ashamed I had never done this earlier. We sat together and with closed eyes I picked out a star for him. His star was *"Guide."* If ever there has been a *"guide"* in my life it has been my beloved Rochester. We simply cannot doubt the stars are inspired and go to the intended recipients.

Star Samplings

Perhaps a sampling of some star words will cause you to consider more deeply the joy and inspiration of being a *"star-owner"* and *"star-creator."* I know if you could hear the many blessings shared with me through these past years or I could write in detail about my own, you would realize the deepness of each star's inspiration if the recipient takes it seriously and applies all the concepts written about in the *"star letter."*

These words were given to me in prayer this past year while creating stars, only a few of the nearly 400 that were sent out.

simplify	legacy	acceptance
inward	steppingstones	quietude
colors	rocks	journal
transformation	Angels	humaneness
solitude	wilderness	manifest
magical	symbols	sparkle
embrace	seek	channel

My own star words have had great meaning for me as have Bob's. Several have been bright stars that led the way for joys that manifested in the months of the same year I received each of the significant stars.

My first star when I began creating them myself was *"Enchantment."* If ever there is an enchanting word to me it is *"Enchantment."* It fills me with spiritual joy just hearing it, and also child-like joy that brings forth images of fairies and gnomes and all other-worldly enchanting life. To my writing room I have given the mystical name of *"Enchantments,"* and to receive this as my star word was pure joy. And it was a beautiful and magical year! I have also received *"Harmony"* and this proved to be inspiring but not to the degree of *"Enchantment"* and others. But that is me. Another receiving the *"Harmony"* might be overwhelmed with that word and that year. I treasured that star, but all things in our lives are not equal. We frequently get more joy from one joy over another, one star over another.

My star *"Messenger"* was especially significant in that I was experiencing a deeper knowledge spiritually and a relationship with Angels. And they, of course, are God's *Messengers*. And the very year I was blessed to sign a contract for the publication of my book *Compassion for All Creatures* with Blue Dolphin Publishing, Inc. In writing this book for and about God's Creatures and their rights, I felt I was a *"Messenger"* for the animal kingdom. And so this star was amazingly a messenger of joy and spirituality to me all year and to a dream come true, the eventual publication of my book. This publication occurred the following year when my star word was *"Animals"*! Imagine! These are just some amazing examples of how the stars have held great spiritual meaning in my own life and also actual events rose up and were blessings. There are so many other details of my stars I could share but I believe I have expressed sufficiently, and hopefully have shown you their significance.

Further Touches

All other joys about the stars are written about in the star letter. Maybe you will be touched by knowing of the stars and as a reader would like to dispense stars to others as I do. I am certain this could happen. Perhaps there will be many readers who might like to begin a *"Star Ministry"* of their own. I know you will be blessed and in turn bless so many others.

It is wonderful to read the stories that are shared with me throughout each year about the stars received. Friends and even strangers write to me about their stars and tell me unusual happenings in their lives as a result of receiving a star and becoming aware. It is all very beautiful. I try to answer each one. Again—*the enchantment of writing* enters in, in these spiritual and inspiring exchanges. They enjoy confiding their star words to me.

My friend Ginny does not dispense her stars through letters as I do. Since she is a Pastor she gives out her stars on the first Sunday of each year following the church service. They are in baskets and each parishioner selects one. Originally she placed stars in the pews but the basket permits more privacy. Her ministry too of stars has grown so that she need helpers to cut the stars.

My friend Ruth Murray that I have written about in a previous chapter was completely taken by the stars she and her husband received. Enchantment took its hold upon her! As a result she sent me long lists containing names of friends she hoped I would have time to create stars for and mail them out. Each person also had other persons connected to them and one had an entire prayer group who wanted stars. And so this past year my star making increased immensely but it was so meaningful to me that the stars meant so much to my friend Ruth, and that she in turn wanted her family and friends to be blessed. And oh they were!! I received wonderful letters from many of them. It was a part of Ruth's legacy to them, for dear Ruth died recently and is with our Lord. And I will do my best to fulfill her wishes by continuing to send stars to all her family and friends each year, for they all love Ruth so dearly. It is a deep sadness to me never to receive her long, sweet letters anymore, but I know making and sending stars to her loved ones will be one of many ways her presence will remain close to me. She was a shining star in the lives of all who knew her.

If any of you feel led to begin a star ministry you may freely use my star letter I created that will follow, or perhaps with some little changes in order to personalize it. Or you may just use it as a guide to create a totally new one. I know you will be blessed and many others will be also through you and your "star work." And if you have never experienced it before perhaps you will come to know *"the enchantment of writing."*

Star Letter

Here now is my star letter that is continually updated but only in reference to the number of stars sent out, for I have stated everything else in it as clearly as possible. May one day in some way you be the recipient of one—and too, a star!

A Presbyterian Pastor and close friend of mine—for many years has cut out stars for her parishioners. She then asks the Holy Spirit to give her a word to be written on each star. As the New Year begins she has them draw a star from a basket filled with such stars. Since these were all conceived in prayer—even the original idea of it all—she asks that they believe then that the word they receive is meant for them. They are to keep this star and word throughout the entire year and by doing so they will find out how this word will work in their lives many times over and in various ways. By the end of each year each word has come to have great meaning to each parishioner.

Some years ago I decided to follow her example—for I have been the recipient of several of her stars in past years, and the words I received have been important in my life. I have prayed for words from the Holy Spirit just *as she has and Bob helped me cut out ninety-one stars to go with each word received that first year. Now almost 400 Stars are being cut and sent out and it is my ministry now with Bob encouraging and copying these letters for me as his part. Since you cannot be right here to* pick a star out of the little gift bag for yourself—I have prayed and reached in and asked the Holy Spirit to select one for you and slipped it into the envelope without looking at it.

Your word may seem strange to you—even ridiculous. Or you may realize at once it was meant for you alone—or that it has potential for you. Whatever—be patient.

You are to spiritualize this word into your life and carry it with you or keep it in a book or close by you referring to it daily. It may be something (the word) that you will give to others throughout the year—or that others may give to you. It may vary from day to day. It will turn up unexpectedly at times—or you may deliberately use it. There are endless possibilities—but it is for your spiritual growth and with the potential to touch others. Sometimes it may be of the heart and soul and other times is quite literal. It helps to record in a journal or notebook each time the word has had meaning to you throughout the year so you may have a permanent record. It is also helpful to look it up in a thesaurus for this will give you different aspects of your word to be aware of that you may encounter. Do not just look at the obvious meaning—though that too—but seek different and deeper dimensions of your Star too. If you include it in your daily prayers and be mindful of it daily you will learn from it and be blessed. Bob and I keep our Stars on our desks, past and present. He has laminated ours. Each one of mine has been significant on my spiritual journey. But any word (Star) you get when thought about deeply can be applied to many areas of your life.

Though the original thought of using a star is to represent a heavenly touch on your word—the star can also symbolize a "*star fish*" and remind you to be a "*star thrower*" as you go through the year. (re: the story of "*The Star Thrower*" by Loren Eiseley)

Enjoy your star and make it your companion. —God bless You.

P.S. You may share your word and tell others—or just tell a close friend—or you may wish to keep it a secret. It is your choice.

Inspirations

Stars are mystical and inspiring. I have a gold one hanging on a gold cord in my window here in front of my desk, and I have other white stars that glow in the dark scattered around the wooden frames of my two windows. When I finish my work here at my desk in the winter months about 8 PM (when darkness comes as early as 3:45 to 4 PM in the early winter months) I enjoy turning the lights out to have a word of prayer and thanksgiving for all I have been able to accomplish in my writing throughout the day. It is then these luminous stars around my windows glow in the dark and make me smile and feel like a child. But when I go downstairs and step outside it is then my joy is full to see the night skies covered with millions of magical sparkling stars above me—and above our precious home and woods and lake. I feel connected to God and to the Angels, to my loved ones in Heaven and all is well.

A poem that has ministered to me through the years since the death of my parents and other loved ones is the very moving poem by Anne Morrow Lindbergh that begins:

ELEGY UNDER THE STARS

I here; you there—
But under those eyes, space is all—where.

I alive; you dead—
But under those eyes, all—time is spread.

There is more as she goes on to say how we are all joined under *"those eyes."* It can be read in its entirety in her book *The Unicorn and Other Poems.*

Stars write too. They know the enchantment of writing all across the night skies their message of God's love.

CELESTIAL GIFTS

Tall pointed firs and pines reaching into the dark—
Seem to sweep and tickle the vast illuminated arc—
Scattering stardust everywhere—
On boughs and rocks and in our hair.

Can it be Angels in these night hours—
Who gather stars for their own flowers
And too—shower down on us their grace
Upon every searching, uplifted face?

Standing on the wooded shore covered in moonglow
Our spirits are quickened—and we know.
Moonglow, Angel grace and stardust fall—
And we are the blest recipients of them all.

Dedicated   J.G.K.
to the Angels

STAR LEGACY

You, who have called
The Stars
And determined their number,
You also call each one
Of your people by name.
Your know us from afar,
God both far and near.
You are the
Light of our eyes

Huub Oster Huis

There are many reasons why I should get involved in the love work of creating stars. I am sure you will detect reasons throughout this book beside the fact that stars are so mystical and utterly enchanting and spiritual to many beside myself. But it is also interesting that approximately six years go I discovered a small collection of my Mother's belongings in a closet on the third floor in our home in Jenkintown, Pennsylvania. After my parents' sudden deaths twenty and twenty-one years ago, these belongings must have been tucked away as were many other items that were theirs. I do not ever remember this particular collection of papers, envelopes and photos in an old blue dishpan however. It was a major discovery to me and most moving.

Among these personal things I found a piece of torn paper all creased and folded unevenly. It looked like trash. But unfolding it carefully I found within a treasure. I read what I had discovered through tears.

I never saw my Mother engaged in writing and I have only several tiny thank you notes from her. And her handwriting was a scribble that I could never understand without effort. Yet here before me in this hasty writing I knew—was a poem. She had written a poem about me—and also about my tiny first baby. There was no date, but it had to be written while my daughter June was an infant. As I have shared with you earlier, we two lived in my parents' home then while Bob was in the Navy and serving six months on a destroyer tender overseas in Japan's waters. And it had to have been written within the very first year of our marriage, which makes it especially meaningful. As I too have written earlier, my

Mother apologized repeatedly after I married for her silence to me through the years, and I accepted this the first time she said it. I believe this poem was a love gift from the depths of her heart for me—and for my tiny baby. Perhaps it helped her in her healing to write and express herself through poetry in the year that I married. Perhaps she did not feel the need to give it to me. The poem could have been written as a gift for God who brought healing to her and to us.

In all the years that followed until her death my Mother never gave me this tender poem that I would have loved receiving with all my heart. I had never known she ever wrote a poem! Yet here it was scribbled on a torn scrap of paper. I cried too just contemplating that I might never have discovered it at all, and yet I cried also because I *had* discovered it. To see the title and the poem was like receiving a touch from heaven. I would like to share it as I near the close of this chapter. Stars have always held meaning for me. Perhaps the Angels now were revealing why through the first *"lost"* then *"found"* poem. What if I had never discovered it? I am so grateful I did. It was like a letter sent from *"beyond the stars"* and delivered by the Angels. I have always been intrigued with the name everyone knew my Mother by (her first and last, not her middle maiden name.) It consisted of two colors. I believed that day that from *"somewhere over the rainbow"* my very colorful (and she was!) Mother had left me a gift more priceless than the pot of gold. My love for her too reaches to beyond the stars and she knows this.

My Mother as she looked during the period when she wrote this poem (1955–56)

JANICE ELIZABETH

My lucky star—this little girl
　　So peaceful in her bed,
With big blue eyes and curly hair
　　And dimpled cheeks so red.

She grasped my little finger
　　With her tiny slender hand
And held it tight in greeting
Long . . . that I would understand.

Her names are Janice and Elizabeth
    And echo in my heart
Of golden promise,
    That we'll never be apart.

And so I think in years to come
    That she will always be—
As on the day that she arrived
    My lucky star to me.

And now my Daughter's tiny tot
    My little June Leslie who—
Just like her Mother long ago
    Now holds my finger too.

—Mother
Written by Violet McKay Gray

It is not unusual then that I should see my Rochester as a *Star* in my life for he has lightened my heart and soul all these past years and travelled a healing path with me. He has brightened my existence with the light and height and depth of his love.

MY STAR

I gaze up at the heavens
     and see the brilliant, shimmering stars
          in the night sky—
And in wonder feel that I
     am one
          with all creation.
And yet this inward elation
     cannot compare
          to what I feel
When I gaze upon the radiant star
     who shares my nights and days—
          shining his love in tender ways
              everywhere we are !
He is my Angel of Light
     my one true star—
          more beauteous
              than all the stars of night.

For Rochester   JGK
with inexpressible love
on his birthday
May 30, 1998 (from my *Journal of Love*)

After the discovery of my Mother's poem written for me, I responded with a poem in my awe at finding it and in my joy.

FROM AFAR

In a faded pale blue dishpan
Found in a closet used for storage—
I came upon old photos of the clan
Of McKay; and I began to forage
Amongst them all in pleasure.
Birth certificates, wedding announcements and more—

And then—a startling treasure
Surfaced to make my spirit soar.
And as I read—I cried—
For a poem written by my Mother
That would have died
In this old dishpan—'til I could discover
It, (and maybe I never would have!)
Became a healing salve
From another realm; a balm for my soul.
And I reread it—and claimed
It, for it belonged to me—
Buried in my parents' papers
This poem she never let me see
In her lifetime. Now I am doing one of my capers—
A pleasurable one—of writing *this* poem,
To say *hers* found its home
In my heart—
Swift as a dart—
As it spoke of her tiny child
Her only one—and that this infant would always be her "lucky star."

And the sweetness of it left me beguiled
This love poem—from *"afar."*

Dedicated to	J.G.K.
Violet Matilda (McKay) Gray	July 31, 1994
(Entered Heaven September 26, 1978)	New Hampshire

Journal Legacy

Several years before discovering my Mother's *"Star Legacy"* in the old blue dishpan, I found a large box stored in the closet of that same room. It too was something I had never known about or seen before. It contained writings, and a journal that had belonged to my Mother's brother Elmer. He and my Dad had died close together one year before my Mother. With so much sadness that year and following, this carton had been probably removed from my Uncle's home after his death and taken to my Mother's home along with many other belongings. Bob and I had helped her move these personal things, but I knew nothing about this carton and its contents back in 1977. Nor did I know of it in 1978 when my Mother died and we moved many things from her home to our home after giving away as much as possible to our children and to a few of her friends.

Discovering this carton was such a joy. This man, my Uncle, was a dear, quiet, sensitive man and extremely intelligent. He held a high

My Uncle Elmer

Aunt
Elizabeth

Grandmother and myself

Grandmother with her dog, Pat

position in the firm of N. W. Ayer in Philadelphia and he was a great reader of books. He had contributed financially to our three youngest children's college education because he loved me and believed so in education. He is also the man who paid my tuition in the Philadelphia Museum School of Art for two years while I was still in high school. I could write a book just about this fine man and of all his generosity to others. It extended far beyond family. People came to my Mother and to us after his death telling of operations he had paid for to help those in illness, financial support given for college attendance and much more. He left his great library of books to Bob and me and we had the joy of spending hours and days going through them and dividing them. We gave several hundred handsome hardbacks to two college libraries is his name, and kept the ones we felt he would want us to have, his huge collection of paperback classics. We enjoy them here in our cottage to this day.

My Uncle lived with my Aunt Elizabeth, his and my Mother's sister. Neither had married and they had made a home together, at first sharing it with my Grandmother until her death when I was eight years old. My middle name was given to me to honor my grandmother and aunt.

Now before me on this day of discovery was this dear man's journal. This has touched me and influenced me greatly, that in his quiet, steady love for his sister Elizabeth, he had kept a journal of her last weeks of illness and all the events surrounding her death and the funeral arrangements. In the handwriting I knew so well he left a legacy of love about someone that had been a "*star*" in his life. In all the years I knew them I had never seen my aunt and uncle argue or heard of any disputes, yet there were major family rifts from time to time, but not in their home. They were simple old-fashioned people and respected each other. And now this journal too was a legacy of respect and love for his sister who had shared an unusual life with him. I admire my Uncle even more deeply since finding this journal for it takes love, time, patience and deep incentive to keep a journal. The fact that he did gave me new insights about him and heightened my love. He shall always be a "*star*" in my life. Perhaps he had kept other journals also.

Too, he and my aunt and Grandmother owned a sweet wire-haired terrier dog named Pat that was a part of my childhood and teen years, and

I have always remembered their extreme love for this dog. After my Grandmother's death Pat remained always with my aunt and uncle until his death many years later. Their caring for Pat's needs and their unabashed delight in this sweet dog revealed deeper areas of my uncle's and aunt's sensitive natures to me and it has all been a permanent memory and gift of love to me. My uncle's love of Pat, of family, of books and that he kept a journal makes me happy to this day. I feel connected to him in prayer, through writing, reading and in gazing at a star filled sky. Perhaps my aunt also read and kept journals but these facts were never revealed to me. How often I think about these loving people and their sweet dog.

One other tender aside I shall share before closing this chapter. On the day of my uncle's funeral and church service in our Methodist Church, the casket had just been closed shortly before the Minister was to speak. Suddenly a woman appeared next to my Mother who was sitting on the aisle and I next to my Mother. The woman whispered to my Mother through tears that she had worked with my Uncle for many years and that she admired his character and nature and his abilities so very much. My Mother took her by the hand and led her to the casket asking permission that the lid be raised again so that my uncle's dear friend might say good-bye to him. She had not seen him in a very long time. It was such a tender moment.

Shortly after the funeral my Mother received a beautiful letter from this woman sharing more about her association with my Uncle. She also revealed to my Mother she had been in love with him but never told him. This touched us so much. I wonder how the knowing of her love would have changed his life? She closed by saying that she was writing with a beautiful fountain pen that my Uncle had given to her when she left the firm and how she treasured it. Learning my Uncle chose an implement of writing as a very special gift to a friend was so moving to me. That he expressed his feelings through the gift of a pen allowed me to realize further his love for the written word in letters—and in the books he had treasured. There is nothing quite like the written word and my Uncle knew and expressed this in life. I have tried to follow his example in the years since his death by giving a pen to those I feel have shown an interest in writing but that need encouragement.

ODE TO AN UNCLE

A shy and quiet man was he—
Yet gently but deliberately,
He spent his time in continual giving—
All the while that he was living.
He'd pay attention to a need,
And for that one would intercede.

He'd observe and would discern
Who needed help—and in concern—
He would be there—he would arise,
So others then might realize,
A hope—a dream—perhaps a cure—
But asked that he remain obscure.

But when he died so many came—
To his family—lovingly said his name,
Revealing then what he had done—
They told their stories one by one.

When I was young with talent to draw—
He took an interest—this he saw!
In generosity from his heart—
He paid tuition to school of art!

Great nieces and nephews he would enjoy
Giving books—perhaps a toy
He'd personally wrap each tiny gift
His very presence gave a lift.

But after death—generous participation—
In providing funds for their education!
He died alone—we shall ever remember—
His precious life—and the sixth of November.

Dedicated to our Uncle Elmer Russell McKay on the anniversary
of his death, Nov. 6, 1991 (died November 6, 1977)

Reflect and Journal

✏ Write in your journal or in a poem how stars have touched your life in the past.

✏ Perhaps think about creating a star ministry to bless others.

✏ Let stars speak to your soul often by taking time to be outside under the vast dome of the night sky to stand in awe beneath the stars.

✏ Write about these star encounters in some way—in your journal, or in a poem, or in a letter to another.

CHAPTER TWENTY-TWO

Your Path of Lovely Smooth Rocks and Stones

"If you make the effort, beings seen and unseen will help.
There are angels cheering for us when we lift up our pens,
because they know we want to do it. In this torrential moment
we have decided to change the energy of the world.
We are going to write down what we think. Right or wrong doesn't matter.
We are standing up and saying who we are."
—Natalie Goldberg from "Wild Mind"

WHEN YOU BEGAN TO READ THIS BOOK I invited you along my personal path of lovely smooth rocks and stones to lead you to a safe place of healing and delight. By travelling this path I prayed you would discover *"the enchantment of writing,"* and also long to find your own path so that your personal writing might begin.

In each chapter I have tried to write deeply from my heart in order that you too might be inspired to write deeply from yours. Hopefully you were motivated to try some of the suggestions following each chapter that I prayed would lead you to begin your personal journey and journal. If you decided to read the book through first and then go back to reread and pick up your pen, I know if you once begin you will be rewarded and want to continue. For those who did begin while reading this book I am so thankful. Never again let a day pass without writing something from your heart in your journal or otherwise. If you commit to this you will soon find yourself desiring more and more time to be alone to write. It is inevitable. But you must take the first step, no, even better, you must jump with both feet onto that path of writing.

Natalie Goldberg has written wonderful words for you in the quotation that opens this chapter. Read them often. I have attempted to say similar things throughout this book. Treat her words as a loving command and obey them. Natalie has further words of encouragement.

> *Writing is elemental. Once you have tasted its essential life, you cannot turn from it without some deep denial and depression. It would be like turning from water. Water is in your blood. You can't go without it.*

And I repeat. Writing is essential to everyone! You cannot go without it and live a full life. Only until you begin to write, if you have not already, will you understand the truth of these statements. Part of you does not live and remains dormant until you release it through writing. Gradually you will be amazed at what comes forth. At times you feel that someone else is guiding your pen if you only allow yourself to begin and then to faithfully write "*something*" each day. Write!—and find parts of yourself you never even knew existed! They are buried within you waiting to be released through your pen. Perhaps at times memories deep and as if asleep will surface also, and some may be painful and have been suppressed. But they are better brought forth than left within. Now they are outside of you, and though you may have tears, you can write and write and work through what was released from you, and in time the writing will heal you. It is true! It is the story of my life!

Soon too, you will learn to trust your writing voice. Respecting yourself will lead you to be able to find your voice and it is a very sacred experience. Many things are written about finding your authentic voice but it can be explained very simply by saying that if we write the way that we speak, then we have found our voice. Do not try to write like others. You are an unique being and have precious things to write and explore that no one else has, and the way that you write naturally is your voice.

Everyone has their own writing voice and each is incomparable. When you write, write honestly and from your heart and then your writing voice emerges. My youngest daughter Janna told me recently that when she was reading my *Compassion for All Creatures* it was just as if I was talking to her. It made her giggle as she expressed this because my writing voice was so exactly like my speaking voice. She did not realize how much this helped me because no one had ever discussed it with me before. When we write from our hearts openly then our voice is there. Janna confirmed this for me. God put our voice there within us and we should honor it and listen to it. The more we write and use it we realize this. It is natural and not artificial. We will trust our voice then and appreciate it and never abuse it. We should write what is in our heart always. It does not matter if it is popular or not, we must listen and write the truth. Unexpected things happen so be prepared. Many matters cannot be explained that come forth on paper. I have written about this elsewhere in this book in various ways.

Before we write we should quiet ourselves and pray and go deeply within. Our voice has a double quality for there is the outer voice and the inner. The inner is the one that gives us messages. We must quiet ourselves to hear this voice—or at times it also surfaces unexpectedly. This is our spiritual dimension and is most sacred, for we alone have things to write that no one else has and we must listen. Our outer voice is the way we write down what we hear from within. Our inner voice helps us to write and we have to listen to its messages and this will help to intensify our writing. When we keep a notebook with us when we are out in the world, and even within our home (I have written about carrying a steno pad around with me), we then can jot down instantly anything our inner voice tells us. If we do not it is lost! God chose us to write the things only we can write. Messages slip easily away from us if not claimed immediately in writing.

> *A thoughtful person cannot risk being without a notebook. Its presence encourages capturing on paper that which might otherwise be lost forever.* —JGK

First lines of poetry also come and they can be moving and precious. These should be captured in your notebook too awaiting for later when the rest of the poem will flow from it. Poetry comes when we are walking, driving, even sleeping.

Yesterday I awoke with a poem within me, and I grabbed my notebook and pen by my bed and wrote down so quickly sixteen short lines that poured out. I took my pad with me on the drive to church and the last four lines were given to me then. The poem follows. I think God is speaking to me about singing! It is the second poem in several months that emerged quickly out of me on this subject. The other appears in chapter 19. Since I have not yet acted on the first poem personally (though it is about the little boy in church) perhaps He is speaking to me again, for this poem was already written within me as I slept! I was compelled to write it at once before I did anything else. I could even see the line structure in my mind's eye, not just the words. (I am thinking right now I had better begin to sing!)

SING!

Just as dear birds
    on wing—
We have our songs
    to sing—
All have melodious notes
    to fling—
Into the sky.

If we do not release
    them—
Our songs will cease
    then—
Soon they will die.

Lift up your heart
    and voice—
Make then the glorious
    choice—
To let your notes
    be.

To set your songs
free!

JGK

Within us is another world! To discover it you need to write! It is true! Let the words flow out from you for then you are writing to heal. You need words to write to yourself about all that is within you. Without a pen in hand, journal, and time apart and prayer, mysteries will stay deep within you unplumbed. Can you risk not knowing these mysteries? Are you not even curious?

Words written can take us away from the hurt and pain even when we may discover it within. The more we write the more we become healed. We can find such treasures within! We can write our stories and help to heal ourselves. Let the words flow out and write and write and you will discover magic, healing, and imagery.

In 1986 when I needed healing and came on my Retreat, it was writing and prayer that God used to initiate my healing, and the presence of my sweet little kitten Rochester. Without his angelic entrance into my life I would never have gone on the Retreat and received healing, and my life would have been so very different. I knew I wanted to write books but I could not somehow begin. Later Bob would sit and write a paragraph about some incident in my life to get me started when I was in a period of intense discouragement and despair then. He would push me until I continued on with the story even though I felt drained and limp with nothing to offer the page. I was still in progress in my healing, just beginning really, and though I wrote all the time I could not begin to write my books. Eventually I did, of course, and I have always been thankful Bob did this. I felt inadequate and did not think I could write anything that anyone would want to read. Though I had some distance to go in my healing, my writing took off and I have been writing my books ever since, as well as all that I ever wrote before (journals, letters, poetry, etc.).

Later in that same year of 1986 an incredible book came into my life. I recommend it so highly to you if you are serious about writing and even if you are not, for you cannot read it without wanting to write. Certainly it had this affect on me and I continue to reread it thirteen years later, and the author's other books on writing as well. This book will get your pen moving and bring you joy and healing for that is what writing gives you as its gift.

The book is:

Writing Down the Bones by Natalie Goldberg
published in 1986 by Shambhala Publications, Inc.
Boston, MA 02116

It can be found in most any bookstore and will help you in your journey of writing. Until you buy a copy you can follow Natalie's instructions and "*practice writing*" by purchasing a simple spiral notebook (I mentioned previously in the chapter on "*Journal keeping*" that I would suggest a use for this type notebook). These note books are the ones used by school children and about 8x10 inches with all sorts of designs on like the Muppets, Garfield, Disney Characters and Star Wars. There is a big selection of them in September in stores when school starts. They cost a little more than the plain spirals, not much, and it is fun to have the designed covers. One series I purchased was very unlike the others and quite mystical, all in subdued blue and white colors with pictures of unicorns, swans and other creatures and scenes.

The pen Natalie suggests to use for these notebooks is a Shaeffer fountain pen. Other implements at the time she wrote this slowed your hand down such as pencils, felt tip pens or ballpoints. The fountain pen is a fast writing pen and I bought several. At the time they were $2.98 but now are sure to be more. All colored ink cartridges can be bought and this adds to the inspiration of writing. You feel the connection to the paper with this fountain pen. My new roller ball pens are fast also and do not drag, but I have loved the fountain pen only for these notebooks because I began using it before discovering my green pens. I have filled dozens of the books. I used a variety of ink colors at first but then used only green from 1989 on. I have shared earlier about this in my use of green pens for my vegetarianism.

Once you get a notebook and the right pen, begin to write. Keep your hand moving. At first you may only be able to write ten minutes without stopping but the more you do it you will be able to write several hours. (without stopping) These writings will be your uncensored first thoughts, and emotions will also surface as you write, for things are coming forth from you you never dreamed were there. Sometimes I cry when I write but I write right through this for truth is found in this way. Write about anything at first. Simply write even if you repeat yourself. Later give yourself little assignments, like write ten minutes about the dinner you ate last night or the tree in your front yard.

What I have shared are the essentials, and from this type writing you can better write then in a regular way your creative stories, poems and all other writing. It frees your inner being and is good to do more than once a day for as long a period each time you can allow. Better still it would be very wise to buy and read the book for if you are serious about your writing it will be an essential tool for frequent rereading. And *"practice writing"* is fun to do, and the book so inspiring to read. There is very much more to be learned from this book than the tiny essentials I have shared. Having the book will continually motivate you for it is a joyful book that makes you *want* to keep your pen moving. I am still rereading Natalie's book after thirteen years!

Julia Cameron too has written a remarkable book I own and appreciate. The paperback version was published in 1992 and it is the one I use.

> *The Artists Way: A Spiritual Path to Higher Creativity*
> Jeremy P Tarcher, Inc.

Julia Cameron's pivotal tools in creative recovery are: "*The morning pages*" and "*The artist date.*" I will speak only about the *morning pages.* These are three pages of long hand writing, strictly stream of consciousness writing (as is the writing suggested by Natalie) These are meant to be done first thing in the morning where as Natalie's instructions are for any time of day or night and any amount of writing, Julia states the morning pages are the primary tool in your creative recovery. Just keep your hand moving across the page. Writing the censor's thoughts is permissible, or not write them. Never miss doing your morning pages, three pages of whatever crosses your mind. Anyone who faithfully writes Julia's "*morning pages*" and the "*writing practice*" taught by Natalie, *will* write! These will free you, I promise! I do both. I began with Natalie's method and found it liberating. After reading Julia's book some seven years later and after two of my books had been published, I took on *"morning pages"* as well. To differentiate I still use the spiral note books with design covers on as suggested by Natalie for the *"writing practice,"* and then use the hardback marbelized copy books (these come in many wonderful colors not only in black and white and are sold in the school supplies section) for my *"morning pages."* Actually it should be a larger book for these but this is all I can fill along with the spontaneous *"writing practice,"* for I am also writing my own books and poetry, letters etc. But these two wonderful methods of keeping the pen moving have helped me, and one or the other or both can help you limber up and discover things within and be freed to write your stories and all creative writing. I consider them absolutely necessary for a writer. No matter how often you refer to them or reread these two books in entirety you are inspired and livened and glad you are a writer. Natalie's book got my pen moving back in 1986 and I am grateful. Perhaps either or both of these books combined with mine will liberate you to be inspired to write your own books. I sincerely recommend them. Both authors have written other books since these and it would be excellent to treat yourself to these too as you progress in your daily writing.

Writing creates a need to take the time to be with yourself, to let words just flow out of you. Do not edit them. Writing leads you to discover the joys of being alone even though you can go to restaurants and other places where people and activity are to write too. Many writers do this and stay for hours at the same table. But there are always the times you *need to be alone* to write and writing brings such fulfillment in these times and all times. For myself I prefer to write alone with Rochester's presence with me only, in my lovely writing room. It took me many years to at last have *"a room of my own"* for this deep need for my soul. I cherish being here day after day into evening as I have told you previously.

Writing is essential and should be done every day for it is a life-long process in order to find out all that is within you. Do you not want to find the unknown and discover all things hidden? The more you write the more will emerge from within you and your healing process will be in progress. Writing is like a bridge to another world. You will be amazed at all that will cross that bridge and emerge from the interior of your being through your pen and onto the page. Knowing all these things, can you go on without writing in your life if it is barely existent there now? Can you risk not having this spiritual practice in your life?

As I wrote in the introduction, memories and happenings surface and are freed to live again to be reviewed anew and enjoyed, or to bring healing, even if at first they come in the form of sadness or pain. You will write through this sadness or pain and it will no longer be in you. Ignore the *"critic"* that may also appear at your shoulder telling you you are wasting your time and your writing is of no worth. If you cannot ignore it, then write about the *"critic"* and make fun of it, or write a terrible poem about it and refuse to listen to its disparaging words. It is like the devil trying to stop you from healing through the writing you have decided to embrace. Everyone comes up against this. Ridicule its attempts to stop you! Write on!

The more we write the more emerges for us to discover. Even as I wrote the last paragraph memories surfaced of other writing I had done in the seventies that I have not spoken about in this book. Apparently it became buried but wants to be expressed here right now! I have not thought of it in years and would have included it in an earlier chapter of that era in my life if it had risen up and shown itself. This is an example of what I have mentioned throughout. The more we write the more is revealed to us from within us. Often too they are things we never knew before! In this case it was a spiritual discipline that I just have not thought about in years because so many lovely events and many traumatic events of the eighties overlayed it. I had done it to help myself become stronger interiorly.

In the seventies a group in our Methodist Church, Bob and myself included, became part of a program that was inspired by John Wesley's life and devotional practice, Wesley being the founder of the Methodist Church. We made a commitment to rise early at 5 AM for reading, prayer and writing. We were to first read scripture, then pray, and from these write down what we felt the Lord was teaching us. This was difficult to do; to set the alarm and rise this early, get yourself alert, and then proceed. Shortly after beginning this program I realized it would work better for me if I could awake at 4 AM, and so set the alarm an hour earlier. With six children I had early morning responsibilities, and I needed to separate this hour of reading, prayer and writing from the first activities of morning when the house was suddenly alive. And so I communed with God and wrote from 4 AM to 5 AM and then went back to sleep for one and a half hours. This worked for me and it was precious,

Holy time. The program eventually ended because it was difficult for most, but I eliminated the reading portion so I did not have to turn on a light, and merely sat up in bed so as not to disturb Bob. I prayed and wrote in the dark, keeping a tiny flashlight available when needed. In the darkness (rather that getting up and going to a well lighted room) I felt connected to God much more and was truly inspired to write. Much from within myself poured out. This was kept in a separate notebook from my regular journal. It all helped me to be more aware of what can be captured on paper and created a unique closeness with the Lord. As I write about it now I feel He wanted it to be included here in case it can help you in any way. Any form of writing is spiritual medicine. Perhaps these early morning hours of prayer and writing that continued for a year and a half or so, were my spiritual medicine in storage within my being to help me through the 1980s, spiritual back-up medicine in the form of the written word and prayers. I remember well now that journal, a book of comfort referred to often in a decade of intenseness and sorrow. Yet I had needed to write in the seventies too. My under-current of helplessness and sadness, caused by an on-going situation written about in a previous chapter yet combined with precious joys as well, ever flowed throughout *every* decade, though I felt so blessed to have a loving husband and children and a very active and rewarding life shared with them!

When we write and record our stories it is amazing how much healing can come from such a simple act. And too, in sharing our writing we are then able to help others to heal. We become empowered through the writing, and others through the reading, and they in turn want to write and receive and give healing. However, we never have to share our writing unless we absolutely feel comfortable doing so. There is a time for everything. Out of our souls and hearts our life stories rise and it is all very sacred, and to capture it all through writing helps us to come out of the darkness into the light. Each day of our lives is filled with marvelous extraordinary moments, and too moments most ordinary, and by writing down what we experience we are given joy and healing. We become more attentive to everyday moments when we keep pen and paper ready and available. I remember well the morning a baby deer swam across our lake after *"ice-out"* and up onto our property. It gave me such joy, and I not only wrote about it in my journal but it is now also in my previous book, *Journal of Love*. Moments are waiting to be discovered and are filled with beauty and secrets that only our own individual hearts and souls register in their own unique ways. If we do not write them they will not forever be remembered. Written words are so much more powerful, permanent, surer and stronger. They live on! Sometimes, most times, there is such a strength in putting a thought on paper! You can let it be, and also observe it from all angles in Spirit when it is written down. Perhaps come back later to sojourn with it a bit and experience it then in a deeper way. You may want to add to it slightly and give it more detail. It may have been sent to you for a reason that you may not understand in the present but will be shown at a later time. But you have written it down and claimed it as your own!

For all who hope to write and record your life you must allow time to do this and you will be healed and filled with new feelings you never before experienced. Each person who has a goal in life or interest or vocation, trains in some way to achieve this. You must allow time to write; to write your sacred moments, dreams, goals, and you must write to discover all that is submerged and buried within your being. It is an on-going mystical journey down that stone path. To achieve this, aim to write every day and treat your writing as if it is sacred and essential to life. It is! Attempt to write at least an hour a day. Though that sounds overwhelming it is not. You will be surprised once you begin. The hour disappears too quickly and you long to retrieve it. Eventually do it for as long as you are able. It is sacred, remember that. It is not a past time or hobby, it is soul work, sacred and holy!

Because your writing *is* sacred you should make a special place for your writing and I have written about my special place in previous chapters. If you establish a corner or area or room of your own you further place sacredness upon your writing. Perhaps reread those earlier chapters to further inspire you in creating your own writing room or sacred space. Begin to collect little symbols or treasures to keep in your writing place or room that have or give meaning to your writing and reinforce your writing life. Perhaps in your sacred place you will create an altar or shrine to further inspire your writing life as I have. Many do this who write.

There are so many other ideas and lovely secrets I could speak of but I have told you so many. Perhaps you are anxious to begin on your own path very seriously now and will create incentives for yourself. If I write much further in this chapter it will become a book of its own. It is such an exciting subject for me to be sharing with you. It is what I have been called to do!

This chapter cannot end however without once again mentioning the sacred because I cannot over emphasize enough the power of prayer and meditation and contemplation. The spiritual life of writers is so important. Choose the way you prefer to commune with God and then make this a part of your writing life and ritual. I personally begin each day in my writing room in my prayer chair there in prayer of various forms (any one of the three just mentioned) and close each evening there in this way also, thanking God for His help before I leave my writing room. I pray inwardly throughout each day. You will receive guidance at this time too from Him and unseen realms and your Angels as you write or while in prayer and meditation.

Angels are such a significant part of my prayer and writing life, my entire life really, and I know without a doubt they are present. I greet them, invite and welcome them always. Often in difficult times I kneel down before the altar on my desk and the picture of my Christ and pray again. In lovely weather I too pray outdoors in my prayer chair by the lake before beginning to write and also return there at night. There is a unique closeness with Christ and my Angels there and all of nature. But no matter what the time of year, prayer begins and ends my periods of writing each day—and covers it in between.

The writing life is so beautiful to me that often I have to be reminded by Bob to end my writing for the day and come downstairs. Having dinner between 9 and 10 PM is happening more and more. Rochester often gives his gentle reminder too when he comes from his favorite places on the bed next to my desk and on my desk or in the open screened in window, and lies right down on what I am writing or sits upon it and gazes into my eyes. It is precious. That he is my faithful companion all day, day after day, gives him the right (in my heart) to say *"enough is enough."* He is my joy and inspiration and to have his never ending presence is a gift from God that I am eternally ever aware of and grateful for day and night. I spend my life with this little Angel who communicates with me and lets me experience life in another realm. Without him this book and my others would not have been written. I pray you too have felt his loving presence throughout this book as you read, for his gentle paws have touched the penciled pages as I have written. His golden eyes are gazing at me now and he is requesting that I come to the end of this book and say good-bye. We pray you will think of us as friends and return often to meet with us in the pages of this book. We will always be waiting there, and too, you will be in our prayers. We pray you have come to experience in your soul the *"enchantment of writing"* and that you will find *"spiritual healing and delight through the written word."*

Your Angels are with you.

Our cottage in our woods during a winter snow storm—
where this was book was written.
"Higher Ground," Lake Balch, N.H.
The upper front windows are where my desk is and where I write.

Afterword

"Once we get away from the idea that the purpose in reading and writing is to exchange information then we may discover the enchantment power of letters and books . . . we may have an entirely different appreciation for all the paraphernalia of books and writing—libraries, bookstores, pens, computers, paper, illustration . We might become magicians of the page, learning both how to enchant others and to be enchanted through the image of words."
—Thomas Moore from *The Re-Enchantment of Everyday Life*

MUCH HAS BEEN WRITTEN IN THIS BOOK to hopefully inspire you to daily write, but I would like to leave you with some last words of encouragement for I know in your heart you are longing to write.

Meditation

Always allow time for meditation before writing, at least ten minutes, but twenty or so if possible. At the end of your writing day again take time for meditation, this being in thanksgiving for all you have been given to write. When you meditate in the morning you will feel assured and so peaceful and centered and will face your day in a wonderful way. You will be able to unwind and relax when you close your day or period of writing with meditation.

In meditation one is often given insights and images and direction in life. You quiet your soul and feel a serenity. It all reflects in your writing and aids you in your writing. Guidance too is given. When we go into the silence our lives become changed. Many people like to meditate to a mantra or quiet music or to prayer. Others require nothing but silence. Silence is my strength and way. The more you meditate the more deeply you will go within. You will find you will want to stay in this meditative state for a longer period of time. There is no set time.

In my past I have had two extraordinary experiences that stand out in my memory, actually with some humor involved. One I have written about in my book *Higher Ground*.

One afternoon I went into a deep meditative state while in my prayer chair. During this time an unusual thing happened right in front of me but I did not know about it until I returned to the cottage and to family members. They asked if I had enjoyed seeing the seaplane. I had no idea what they were talking about but learned a seaplane had landed in the lake in the area in front of my prayer chair and after a few moments had taken off again. This is an example of how the deepness of meditation can be experienced.

Another day in my life while here in New Hampshire some years ago before we lived here, I went up to our neighbor's cottage on the hill to pray and meditate. Our neighbors Dennis and Patti, are like our family and we are always here for each other. At this time they were in their other home in Massachusetts. It was in the eighties. I had concerns and needed time apart and Bob had decided to build bookshelves, a very noisy project. I went into deep meditation in their cottage and then returned to our own cottage thinking a short time had passed. Peace had descended on me and I felt quite wonderful. When I returned I found Bob had built and completed two nine shelved bookcases on either side of a closet door connected by a shelf in the center over the door. The shelves had even been neatly stacked and filled totally with rows of books. I had been gone hours.

These were exceptions but I can only encourage you to practice daily meditation before and after your periods of writing.

There are many aspects of meditation. I am only writing about the essential. Only you can determine how long you wish to do it. Meditation can help you in so many ways. I am only touching the surface. Before I begin I always center on my sketch of Christ, and Rochester is constantly my companion. No one meditates more deeply than Rochester.

Spiritual Communion

This is a spiritual practice I also do daily also in the morning. When I cannot go to Mass I make Spiritual Communions. There are formal prayers and prayer books for this but my way has become most simple. In my own words I pray to Jesus and with my sketch of Christ before me I spiritually receive *"in image"* the Host followed by the wine; Body and Blood of Christ. This is essential to me before I begin my day of writing. I pray spontaneously from my heart before and after *"receiving."* It is also comforting.

Bob has received Communion in this way *only* since 1984 when, following a successful lung operation and to begin life anew together in gratefulness, he began to attend St. Anthony's Catholic Church with me here in New Hampshire whenever we were here. We have lived here permanently these last four years, and he has attended every Sunday unless we have been snowed in. We are one in our spirituality now, but that does not mean he is Catholic, for he is not. Nor is he permitted to receive Communion in the Catholic Church, a great sadness to us and to many. But he makes spiritual communions every day as I do, and we know they are as real as if we had *"received the Elements."* We are filled with Christ.

Journal

During periods of meditation my journal is always with me just as is Rochester, and also during my Spiritual Communions. At these times when insights are given it is necessary to write them down immediately afterwards, so they do not escape. Perhaps they were given to me to use in my writing that very day. Everything must be written down or in time it is lost.

Angels

Ask your Guardian Angel to be with you before you begin meditating or receiving a Spiritual Communion. Your Angel is always with you but still it is for your own benefit to do this, to purposefully imagine your Angel present as you awake, begin meditating and then writing. This too is comforting for it makes you aware then of the Holy presence who never leaves you. Pray first and if you have not already done so, give your Angel a name so you can better communicate. Or, you can in meditation ask the name of your Angel and perhaps it will be given to you in your spirit. This is how I learned my Angel's name as did several others I know. My Angel's name is "*Vincent.*" Rochester's Angel is "*Rosee.*" This too was given to me in prayer. All the letters are from Rochester's name. When it was given I actually saw the name printed out behind my closed eye lids in this spelling, which is an unusual way to spell it.

Lastly I would suggest one more very important point.

Think of Yourself as a Writer.

You are! Now it is time to begin to write everyday if you have not as yet done so.

I pray these five suggestions will guide you and help you along your path of writing. To me they are totally necessary.

An Angel Visualization

In addition to the five points I have suggested to you I would like to give you an "*Angel Visualization.*" This can be done any time of day or night and as frequently as you wish. Only you can know when it is most needed and most convenient to do. Enough time should be allowed for it to be done in relaxation to acquire its benefits. You may simply sit in your desk chair to do this, or light candles to create atmosphere, or use incense, or anything that will enhance it. For myself I simply sit in any one of my prayer chairs (in writing room or by the lake) and say a brief prayer and then I begin. Never begin unless your journal is with you so that when the visualization is completed you can immediately write down things you learned or saw, or were given. Ask that each visualization be used to help you on your path of writing. After you complete reading this meditation and chapter it may be helpful to record the meditation on cassette tape so that you can relax and be guided. Embellish it in any way you wish.

Meditation

Quiet yourself in meditation with eyes closed. Imagine that you are in a beautiful wooded area by a lake. At once you are aware of a lovely path of smooth rocks and stones leading into a denser portion of the woods. You begin to walk this path and slowly follow it, all the while noticing the various trees and flowers and singing birds and bustling wildlife within the lower green plants. It is a place of coolness and utter greenness and your heart is now light within. Now after travelling this long lovely path of rocks and stones (and take as long as you wish on the path) you are arriving in a clearing. Delightful birds and animals of every kind surround this green dell and luscious plant life and trees are vibrant with intense colors. In the center of this area is a large rock and a beautiful Angel awaits you. Only you can see her delicate features and she is dressed in a violet gown. She is welcoming you and instructing you to notice everything within your surroundings as she guides you to the rock to rest. She whispers her name and asks you to carry it in your heart forever. Because you are a writer she is showing you many things that can enhance your writing life and telling you secrets that will bless your work. In this magical area, this "fairy ring" where other lovely angels and fairies are silently present and mingling with the wildlife that surrounds you, your "Angel in violet" is showing you the spiritual aspects of writing, and revealing to you that writing is as important to your life as the spiritual, for writing is spiritual. It is as important as the need for water, for it is life giving. Your Angel continues to speak lovingly to you and then is placing a blessing upon your forehead. She tells you it is time to leave this wooded glen and the "fairy ring" and to go back to your world following the path of smooth rocks and stones. She reveals to you you have gained great insights while there with her but in order to fully realize this you must begin to write as soon as you are safely home. It is through writing you will also discover her name she whispered to you. And too, it is only through writing that you will obtain all the wisdom within you. She requests you write yourself a letter that contains all that you have just been told and shown. Do not reread it. Put it into an envelope, address it to yourself and seal and stamp it. She requests you place it upon your altar for one day and then mail it. When the letter arrives in the mail you are to sit quietly in your place of meditation and read it. Think of it as a letter from the "Angel in violet" who inspired all of the knowledge you have written within the letter. By now you will know her name. Again place the letter on your altar and each day from then on follow the advice that is written in the letter. When you feel you need more love, help and inspiration and instruction, again in meditation go down the path of smooth rocks and stones to the wooded glen and the Angel will be waiting for you.

After each visit with her follow her instructions of writing a letter to yourself and mailing it. After a period of time when you have several letters find a container for them that speaks to your soul and store all of your Angel letters, present and future, within the container and keep it on or near by your altar. Any time you need inspiration between these meditations of travelling the path of smooth rocks and stones, you may prayerfully draw out one of the Angel letters. You will be amazed at the spiritual knowledge for your writing that will be within these letters. It cannot be written or explained here. You must experience it for yourself.

If you wish you can also listen to meditational music of your own choice if you decide not to record the meditation for yourself. Or you can use both methods alternating at each meditation. The most enchanting haunting mystical music I can recommend for this or any meditation is "The Fairy Ring" by Mike Rowland. May God Bless You.

This meditation is from my heart to yours but you may feel free to change it and adapt it in anyway to your own spirituality. Because I live in the woods this inspiration was given to me. It is very real for me when used, for I begin and end it in a wooded area by a lake in reality. If you prefer a masculine angel or presence, envision then one whom will best touch your soul, a spiritual entity that will minister to you in the wooded glen and give you precious insights. In time, these will be treasured moments when you, in meditation, go to this mystical place. Meditations have a way of taking on a life of their own too, and often images and entities appear that will surprise you. You will soon become more peaceful and calm of spirit and feel closer to God. If you have a precious animal companion as I have my Rochester, invite your companion to go with you each time in Spirit. Envision your companion by your side and meeting the angel. It is comforting.

The Fairy Ring

"*The Fairy Ring*" by Mike Rowland is music I have written about in my previous books. It was a cassette given to me in 1989 by my friend Ruth Depman brought back to me from Acadia National Park, one that has ministered to me and to Rochester ever since. Each night I play it before sleep and in meditation and it has brought tears and unimaginable healing. Rochester too has shown how it is essential to him. I have written about this in *Compassion For All Creatures*. It is mystical, exquisitely haunting, deeply moving and spiritually needed for my inner being. You too may want to own this music tape. It cannot be played while driving a car. My son George relayed this to me as warning, for you are drawn into a deeper state of being and relaxation while listening and it is not safe. It is meant for times alone and while in meditation. It is not background music.

THE FAIRY RING

Tonight I cannot sleep—
I have feelings that run deep.
They are causing tears inside—
On the outside too—I've cried.
There is sadness; yes, unrest—
(But for the others smiles and jest.)
Too many things swirl 'round and 'round—
And as usual I have found—
That in order to belie it,

I need the solace and the quiet.
And so I've come apart to find—
Mystical music to flood my mind—
And wash my soul just like a balm,
Bringing order and sweet calm.
I close my eyes now to receive—
I believe—and I achieve—
A gentle peace and silent healing.
I can sleep; my soul is kneeling.

A Prelude to "The Fairy Ring"

Each night too, before playing *"The Fairy Ring"* I recite this lovely prayer aloud for Bob, Rochester and myself in addition to our own individual silent prayers. It is a new prayer Bob wrote for me several years ago adapted from an old one we recited as children, and far more comforting. I included it in a previous book and would like to again share it with readers. Writing, *always writing*, to express the heart's thoughts, to soothe mind and soul.

As I lay down to sleep this night,
Please keep me safe 'til morning light.
Grant me sleep and needed rest
And fill my dreams with happiness.
For Lord, I know that with you near,
There's nothing that I have to fear.
Please guide me where you want to lead,
And be with those I love and need.

RAK, Jr. from *Compassion For All Creatures*

Escrito en Espanol

In Peru I have a dear friend Pedro Rodriguiz and our only means of communication is in Spanish. In past years I have been able to write letters in Spanish to him by using a Spanish/English dictionary and teaching myself. Any remnants of Spanish from my high school days are slim. When he called me from Peru unexpectedly on Mother's Day to surprise me I was caught unaware and only able to say brief greetings to him. He speaks only Spanish. Our conversation was very humorous but filled with "*amor*"—our only mutual understandable word, it seems. (Bob was teasing me about my end of it because of the repetition of the one word.) Had I had time to prepare I could have written out my greeting to him in Spanish and read it to him, and he would have had more than one understandable word from me. Even in Spanish, "*writing it down*" has been my only means of conveying my deep thoughts. As a result he has many letters from me through the years as I do from him that we can reread, but we have no memorable conversations to recall except the fun of surprise and talking a mile a minute to each other with no understanding. But still the love and laughter and friendship is always present. Again, "*through writing*" comes love and deep communication that far outweighs the spoken word. Letters can be saved and reread and yet even the smallest significant phrase is often lost in the spoken word on the phone.

Through spending time in Spanish dictionaries I learned the lovely word "*Querencia.*" It is a word that is beautiful to me and refers to the "*most loved Place.*" It is "*the place to which one returns for healing of the spirit.*" For myself and so many others, this is necessary. My personal "*Querencia*" (and Bob's and Rochester's) is our own "*Higher Ground*" here in the woods on Lake Balch. For twenty two years we returned to it again and again to be healed of matters written about within this book, until at last now we live here permanently. It shall forever be our "*Querencia.*" More recently I was totally surprised to see this word mentioned also in a fine book on writing titled *Journey Notes—Writing for Recovery and Spiritual Growth* by Richard Solly and Roseann Floyd. The authors suggest you often sit quietly and revisit all the places on earth you love (your *Querencias*) and to learn which place gives you the greatest feeling of peace. Or you can create imaginary places. As I have suggested in an earlier chapter, these authors too mention visiting a painting you like, one of a place that is meaningful to you or a place of fantasy. All of these visits in meditation can be written down later to give you further inspiration in future writing.

But that is not enough, for it is in finding your own personal "*Querencia*" on this earth that you will be able to free yourselves within through the creative process of writing.

Often writing for me (and for others) can create altered states of consciousness, and without trying, mystical and unusual things come forth in my writing, and in turn influence my life. It is through *writing* and in prayer I have been able to record messages from my Angels. It is by *writing* that my little cat Rochester and I have been able to communicate. It was through *writing* that fifty-two messages were given to me by the Holy Spirit. But unless we take our pen in hand every day we will never discover these other dimensions or bring forth all that is within our beings.

I pray that this book has touched your soul and that you will write from this day forth. Such hidden treasures within are waiting to be discovered by putting pen to paper. Now that you have read all that I have written in this book you are accountable to all that is within you waiting to come forth in writing. A pen is a connection to guidance and insights. When you write you are praying. You are meditating. You are creating. To write will bring healing. From this very moment may you realize that the "*gift of writing*" is yours. May it bless you now and forevermore.

Thank you and God Bless You.

Jesus My Saviour

Robert A. Kol

1) Jesus my Saviour is Lord of my life now. His will, not
2) Now I feel joy in the commonplace moment, praise fills my
3) His might is greater than all of the oceans, greater than
4) Without your love Lord my life would be empty, easily
5) Give me the strength Lord to follow Your teachings, help me to

my will, shall over me reign. He is my comfort my constant co
soul without reason or cause. Life has new meaning it now has
even the fury of storms. He is the Master of all of cr
filled by the forces of sin. My need is constant, just living d
see through life's folly and greed. Then your goals for me will be my ol

panion, glory and honor to His Holy Name.
purpose. He is my Master I'll live by His laws.
ation. Ruler of nature in all of its forms.
pletes me. My heart is open oh dear Lord come in.
jectives. You are the Saviour - the Lord God in - deed.

Janice Kolb along with her husband Bob are the parents of six grown children and have eighteen grandchildren. Their life has revolved around raising a loving family with religious values. In addition to raising their family, Janice developed a letter writing and audio tape ministry that gives encouragement and spiritual support to those who need it all over the United States.

Other inspirational works published by Janice Kolb include: *Journal of Love, Compassion for All Creatures, Higher Ground, The Pine Cone Journal,* and *Silent Violence.* In a cooperative effort, Janice wrote the book, *Whispered Notes,* with her husband Bob.

Any correspondence to the author of this book may be addressed to
    Box #5
    East Wakefield, NH 03830
    jangk@theglobe.com

Also by Janice Kolb

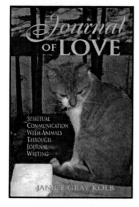

Journal of Love
Spiritual Communication with Animals Through Journal Writing

ISBN: 1-57733-046-3, 180 pp., 30 illus., $14.95

"Animal whisperer" Janice Kolb shares her heart-lifting journey of discovery as she learns to communicate with her beloved feline companion, Rochester—first by using her intuition and then by writing a journal of their "conversations."

"Once again the delightful and insightful Jan Kolb has provided all of us who truly love animals with another warm and wonderful book about how we may enter into deeper communication with our beloved pets. Journal of Love is destined to become a classic in the field of transpecies communication."
—Brad Steiger and Sherry Hansen Steiger, authors of *Animal Miracles*

Compassion for All Creatures
An Inspirational Guide for Healing the Ostrich Syndrome

ISBN: 1-57733-008-0, 264 pp., 47 illus., $12.95

A very personal book of experiences, confessions, and deep thoughts praising all God's creatures through photos, poems and meditations.

Higher Ground

ISBN: 1-57733-071-4, 176 pp., 16 illus., $14.95

The experiences and thoughts of a woman on retreat in the woods of New Hampshire. She deals with personal fears and family problems and shares her faith as an effective tool in problem solving and achieving inner peace.

Beneath the Stars & Trees ... there is a place
A Woodland Retreat

ISBN: 1-57733-106-0, 372 pp., 47 illus., 6x9, $19.95

Beneath the Stars & Trees will help you withdraw from life's distractions and retreat to a place where you can see clearly the multitude of complex factors that make up your life. Share in thoughts and experiences which can open your mind to a world of peace and new possibilities for your life.

"Join Janice Kolb in a sometimes quirky, always perky, jaunt through lake-in-the-woods living, full of shapeshifting and kitty-cat angels, touching journal entries and frolicking poems, prayer chairs and little gnome tea parties—plus a spiritual encounter with a moose you're sure to remember forever."
                                    —Michael Burnham, writer/journalist

"Jan's Woodland Retreat is a place teeming with animal and human life, and yet peaceful and serene. It is a perfect place to meditate, reflect, and renew your spirit. Beneath the stars and trees, there truly is a special place, and Jan's book will transport you there, as often as you wish."
        —Mark Sardella, columnist, *The Wakefield Daily Item*

Beside the Still Waters
Creative Meditations from the Woods

ISBN: 1-57733-122-2, 276 pp., 11 illus., 6x9, $16.95

Beside the Still Waters is a personal view of prayer. Jan suggests a variety of ways to be in constant contact with God. These meditations can transform your prayer life into a source of personal fulfillment, power and strength. Many of these prayers may be familiar; others may be new to you. Being open to all that you read, you may discover new pathways to God and loving consolation. Though written from a Christian perspective, these prayers can be adapted to other traditions.

In Corridors of Eternal Time
A Passage Through Grief: A Journal

ISBN: 1-57733-135-4, 272 pp., 38 illus., 6x9,
paperback, $16.95

As readers of Jan Kolb's previous books
know well, the author has had a deeply
loving and sacred relationship with her cat,
Rochester. He spent his entire life with her
as companion, encourager, precious friend,
and Angel. With his sudden illness and
death, Jan's life was plunged into grief, and
she began this book immediately to honor
Rochester and help herself and others experiencing grief.

The book is a passage through grief, written in journal form. It is
for human grief also, as there is no difference in grief—we all experience it when we lose someone we love. It explores dreams, visions,
walking, memory loss, depression, the consolation of cremation,
examples of ways humans have grieved for humans, journal writing,
ways to help ourselves, and through it all, the passage through days
and nights of mourning the physical absence of a beloved companion.

Many do not anticipate that our loved ones' spirits never leave us,
even though they have gone to Heaven and await us there. Many do
not want to have a continual presence of a loved one who has passed,
but many do. For those who are open to this prayerfully, it truly
happens, as Jan attests in her experience of the blessing and comfort of
Rochester's continuing spiritual presence. This book can bring comfort
to those who love deeply and desire this incredible bond.

*"In Corridors of Eternal Time is a remarkable book, not just because
the author takes us through the various stages of her grief at the death of her
pet, but because, after death, her pet cat repeatedly and in continuously new
ways let her know that he is still conscious and still cares for her the same as
when he was alive. We are left wondering if there are similar ways in which
our own deceased pets may also be attempting to communicate with us."*

—Christopher Comins